## LOVE FOR K...

I asked some (mildly) insta-famous ex-boyfriends to endorse my book, which they respectfully declined (actually they failed to respond at all), but much like how I felt at the end of those relationships . . . their loss!

All jokes aside, my friends and family are the opinions I value most. I once had a publisher not only decline my book, but point out my lack of a social media following by saying, "no one cares who you are to read what you have to say." So! I'm recording the opinions and thoughts of those I value as a reminder to myself to keep showing up.

**–JJ**

I never expected to cry reading a book called *Kinda Funny*. Somehow, JJ had me not only **crying from laughter**, but crying from connecting with shared truths that she uses humorously and surgically to heal places in me I didn't realize were hurt. The publisher who once said, "no one cares who you are," was a liar. I care. Others will care too. **JJ's stories and experiences are expertly crafted in simplicity, and her humor and humanity reach the heart,** she reached my heart. I can't wait till everyone else gets to experience what laughter from the deepest part of the soul feels like. **World, meet JJ Barrows. This is how she do it.**

### –MONTELL JORDAN
Husband, Father, Author, Grammy Nominated Recording Artist, and working on being JJ's pastor

If you ever find yourself wondering who JJ is when she is off stage, you will find much of who she is woven into the pages of this book. You cannot find a more humble, genuine, big-hearted, and talented woman. She is able to **embrace both the joyful *and* the heartbreaking parts**

**of life** in the most beautiful way. JJ is authentically and unequivocally herself, 100% of the time, and that is so rare in our world. **She is able to connect to so many people by sharing her laughter and tears,** and I absolutely can't wait for you to read this book and connect to more of who you are through her stories.

**–JOSH NEWTON**

Number One Fan and Husband

JJ's exemplary knack for **lighthearted, pointed and meaningful storytelling** is like a Trojan Horse, often finding its way right into the heart of our human experience.

**–LAKI KARAVIAS**

Filmmaker & Family Media Producer

**JJ Barrows is honest and bold.** Her relatable stories made me laugh out loud, cry, and self-reflect. JJ is an artist through and through and it all comes out in her writing. She observes and experiences the world in an authentic way that feel good on the brain. JJ's stories are a blend of serious and witty while offering hope."

**–LISA PIDGE**

Founder/Producer of The Laugh Cellar

My friend JJ is everything you think she is: **raw, funny, honest, relatable,** cool, and someone you definitely want to hang with. Think of this book as a series of coffee/beer/whiskey dates with the girl who's going to give it to you straight. Wrestle along with JJ through some important themes. Laugh along with 90's church culture nostalgia, quirks of human nature, weird medical terminology and be challenged at the same time to see some things from a different perspective. You'll feel like JJ's BFF by the end. Or at least like you have some really good dirt on her. Either way, just read it. And buy your own copy, don't borrow one. I'm serious, authors work hard, we need to get paid.

**–KATE MERRICK**

Author of *And Still She Laughs* and *Here, Now*

**As someone who was a witness to some of JJ's stories, you won't be disappointed.** I have sat and exchanged dreams with JJ and cried with JJ. We were roommates bonded by our hope and exhaustion. It's been years since I've shared a roof with JJ, but it's beautiful to see her dreams come true. **JJ's talents explode on the page and now others get to receive the gift of "Jennie Joy."** And thank you, JJ, for getting me to care about football... even if it only lasted three years.

### –LIZ VICE
Filmmaker, Singer/Songwriter, and Former Football Fan

I love JJ's writing style. JJ has a way of pulling you into her life with wit and humor while also being real about her struggles. **She breathes hope, joy and possibility.** Thank you, JJ.

### –LISA GILBERT
Comedian, Proud Triplet Mom

It's kinda funny that after raising JJ, she now influences me to cultivate areas of my life through her writing, art, comedy, and storytelling. With her authenticity & humor, she challenges me (& others) to be a person of love and truth in everyday experiences. I hope to be more like JJ as I grow old. As long as I am living, my baby she'll be!

### –LYDIA BARROWS
JJ's Proud Momma/Marmie, Nana, and rooting for Montell Jordan to be her pastor!

# KINDA FUNNY

## STORIES BY A FULL-TIME COMEDIAN (WITH FOUR PART-TIME JOBS)

## JJ BARROWS

**PUNCHLINE**
PUBLISHERS

First paperback edition February 2024
Cover and interior design by Erik M. Peterson
Cover photos copyright © 2024 by Josh Newton
ISBN 978-1-955051-30-9 (hardback)
ISBN 978-1-955051-35-4 (paperback)
ISBN 978-1-955051-32-3 (eBook)
Published by Punchline Publishers
www.punchlineagency.com
www.jjbarrows.com
@jjbarrows @jjbarrowsart

*My first book was dedicated to the good women in my life.*
*This one is dedicated to a couple of good fellows . . .*


Josh Newton
*My husband, my friend, my everything bagel.*
*I like us a lot and I love you more.*
*Thank you for being you, you're my favorite.*


Bob Barrows
*My dad, my friend, my road trip buddy.*
*You are such a good dad.*
*I just wanted you to always have that in writing.*

# TABLE OF CONTENTS

## That's Life (and Other Spiritual Stuff)

# INTRODUCTION

**AHHH,** the good old-fashioned introduction. Gotta love it, especially in today's age where social media platforms tend to dictate one's ability to sell a book (at least to publishers who've stopped taking risks on "unknowns," as I've so eloquently been called throughout each of my book publishing experiences). But wait, perhaps I should tell you a little more about who I am in case you haven't read my other book—yet. First, you should know it's okay if you haven't. Second, you should go read it. Third, I'm just kidding. Well, kinda.

How should one introduce oneself? Let's see, I'm a self-published author and I'm incredibly proud of this because despite what Pinterest seems to suggest, DIY is not that easy! I'm also a stand-up comedian, although I don't know how much longer that will be true as the comedic journey is long and hard and I continually question how much grit I have... more on that later. And I'm an artist through and through, obsessed with color— I like slapping it on canvases, being covered in it, being surrounded by it, and wearing it— I paint a lot! I paint pretty things and sad things and I mostly enjoy just sitting in my little office/studio, surrounded by paint bottles, staring at a blank canvas wondering what it's going to become. More than all of that and most of all, I am a storyteller. That is the best word I can think of to describe myself. Quite simply, I use words, comedy, and art as ways to tell my stories.

And while I'm on the topic of me, there's "more" to me. I run but I'm not a runner (okay, I walk fast, that's about it). I surf but I'm not a surfer. I do yoga but I'm not a yoga-er (or yogi I guess is the more appropriate term). I like and do a lot of things that don't define me but make me feel better when I do them. I don't do these things enough to be labeled by them, but it doesn't mean I shouldn't do them at all. You don't have to be a professional anything to do something you love; you just do it. (Nike did not sponsor that sentence).

So, there you have it… Author, comedian, artist—those are the facets, the avenues, the descriptors I use simply to tell my stories. I always have and always will believe in the power of stories through the written word or the spoken word, or through the more abstract colors on a canvas or notes on an instrument. Oh, I also used to play guitar, and skateboard. But I decided I can't do everything *and* get good at everything. Time is fleeting, so I let go of guitar and skateboarding. I just decided that this morning when I looked at my guitar propped in the corner and my skateboard hiding in my closet. Closet skateboarder. There's a story title in the making I could use one day. Okay, I made a note.

I won't lie to you: my first book was kinda sad, hints of hope and whispers of happiness, but nonetheless sad. I wrote a lot about my parents' divorce because it's what I was processing at the time. Actually, I never would have thought I'd find myself where I am now, mostly happy… it's hard to write when you're happy—what do you write about that people will relate to? I used to hate happy people. I thought they didn't get life. Maybe some of them don't, but maybe some of them do. Maybe some happy people have been through the struggle and have learned how to make peace with it. Maybe it's not "happily ever after," maybe it's just "peace for now."

So, is this book happier? Well, kinda. It's still a mix, like life. Some stories are kinda funny, some are kinda deep, some are kinda spiritual. This book is my journey and I'm bringing you with me.

When I started writing this book I was stepping into a few new things: a marriage, a comedy/public speaking career, and a waiting period (until book number one could be published and sold). People often tell their success stories after they've gone through the hard stuff so they can say, "See? I did it and you can, too!" Me? I'm writing this in the middle of my story, not knowing how successful it will be, not knowing if I can do it because my grit level is low and I'm not even sure what 'it' is. Perhaps I'm hoping to figure 'it' out along the way.

Sure, these are my stories, but in a way, they're all of our stories. All of us as humans— wondering who we are, what we're doing. And even if we figure 'it' out, then we wonder what happens next? What happens when the newness wears off and the hype winds down and we're left with the reality of the mundaneness of life? If we slow down long enough, we just might find depth and beauty in surprising places, not instead of the mundane, but *because* of the mundane. So, this is all of that, a journey uncertain of its end, but mostly determined to not give up, set on keeping its eyes focused on the present moment instead of the unclear end. This isn't a "from beginning to end" story of my life with all the details in between. This is a collection of stories, mere snippets, journal entries, and tales of confusing dating games along the way. My stories are meant to be read individually—no need to read the earlier chapter unless there's an obvious labeling: "Part 1, 2, 3." That said you certainly can read these stories all the way through, and, you know, make it all the way to the end (every author's hope).

If you're looking for a book strictly about comedy and what it's like to be a stand-up comedian, I'll be honest, this isn't it. This is a wide assortment of stories in which comedy is discovered along the way, but certainly not the point of the book. I'm more comfortable being called "kinda funny" than I am being called "a professional comedian." Part of that has to do with my own insecurities (I'll dive into *that* later), the other part of that has to do with the numerous other jobs I've also had to do while doing comedy. I've been a barista, a babysitter, a caterer, a tour guide, a wedding videographer, and a personal assistant all while traveling the country in pursuit of a comedy career. Thankfully, I no longer manage four part-time jobs at the same time, but I do still keep a few in my back pocket that I can whip out should the world shut down and live events no longer be a source of income. Oh wait, that did happen! (More on *that* later, too.) All of this to say...

Thanks for taking the time to journey with me. Thanks for taking the risk to find out if this book was worth what you paid for it (or for some of you, doing your mom a favor by reading it— shout-out to all the moms who bought my first book for their daughters!). That's what life is, trying things to see if they work, and having people around you to celebrate with—whether to celebrate the accomplishment or celebrate the survival of something hard, either way, you tried. Yay!

And with that, away we go...

# CHILDHOOD, SINGLE LIFE (AND GETTIN' HITCHED)

# 1

# GERiATRiC MiLLENNiAL

**IT'S JULY OF 2019** and I am thirty-five years old. From here on out, if I were to get pregnant it would be considered a geriatric pregnancy. *Geriatric.* I'm confused as to how life went by so fast, yet it took so long for me to meet someone I would even consider having a child with (more on him in another chapter). Being in my mid-thirties, I feel like I'm supposed to have everything all figured out and be at least a few years into my career, but in reality, I feel like I'm still in college trying to decide on a major. I've changed jobs every year for the last ten years! *And* I still don't know what I want to do, nor do I even feel responsible enough to pay my rent on time, let alone raise a human being. How can I be thrown into a category with people in an age bracket that qualifies them for bedpans, assisted living facilities, and discounted coffee at McDonalds!?

Right now, I'm sitting at a cafe where a woman has left her date sitting alone at their table so she could take her juice to a different table and set it up for what appears to be the perfect social media picture. I watch her circle the table as she snaps photos with her phone, alternating between kneeling and standing to get just the right angle *on her juice cup*. Her date scrolls through his phone, unfazed by her absence and her actions. She returns to the table, sits down, and dedicates herself to finding the perfect filter for her 'juicy' photo. The two sit, staring at their phones. I waited five minutes before writing that sentence. No, really. I timed it. Five minutes is a long time to be sitting at a table with someone and not talking to them—at all. Try doing it without a phone to distract you—it will feel like forever.

I grew up in the '90s, which was to me the last really good decade. Technology was advancing but not overtaking things. We still went to the video store to rent movies, *physical video tapes* we had to insert into a machine in order to watch a movie in our home. For television, there was no binging entire seasons, we waited all week for the next episode of our favorite TV show to air. As for music, if we simply couldn't wait for our new favorite album to be sold in stores, we posted ourselves by the radio and waited for the song to play so we could record it onto a cassette tape. You had to be ready to hit the record button as soon as the first notes played, or you'd end up with only half a great song. Mix tapes were still a thing that eventually morphed into mix CDs, but nonetheless you could still hand someone a curated, tangible soundtrack to your life.

T.G.I.F was a series of tv shows on Friday nights that included *Step by Step* and *Family Matters*, and Saturday morning cartoons turned into watching *Saved by The Bell* as we got older. We played outside after school, sometimes until dark, before we were all called in for dinner. We built forts and treehouses, and we didn't think much about hurrying to grow up. At least I didn't. I don't think kids rushing to grow up began until technology really took over. When my family first got the internet, we had to download it onto our computer with a CD. Even then, it was only on *that computer* in our house, nobody was walking around with the internet in their hand. We still had telephones with land lines (no one had a cell phone in my family, not even my parents), and you couldn't be on the phone and use the internet at the same time. If someone picked up the phone while you were on the internet, AOL (America Online) would kindly say "goodbye" and then kick you off the internet. Your life was compartmentalized into when you used technology and when you didn't. Of course, now you can be online shopping while scrolling Instagram and simultaneously watching every episode of Selling Sunset before you even realize you've wasted a day or two... so I've been told.

I loved the '90s. I don't know how aware I was that I loved them while I was in them and that makes me kinda sad. It's one of those 'you never know what a good thing you have until it's gone' kind of situations, but I remain hopelessly devoted to the revival of '90s nostalgia.

For one thing, in the '90s I was obsessed with puff paint. I gooped it (and gooped is the only appropriate word even if it's not a "real word") on everything I owned. All of my allowance went to pogs, slammers, and absolutely anything Lisa Frank, the biggest art movement of the late 1900s, in my opinion. My school supplies looked like someone had vomited neon rainbows all over it, perhaps the true inspiration for that one Snapchat filter. And then there was my seemingly incurable obsession with my own personal trinity... the Hanson brothers.

My younger sister, Betsy, and I quickly caught Hanson fever upon the release of "MMMBop" in 1997. Back then there was no Spotify nor iTunes, there was VH1 and MTV— music video channels that would release new music into the world through the television. Watching music videos would allow us to see the faces behind the voices we could only hear on the radio. As preacher's kids, we were of course not allowed to watch either of the music video channels, but we had friends whose parents didn't mind, and we'd frequent their houses to finally get our glimpses of the Hanson Brothers. I was thirteen years old when I first saw Taylor Hanson, the middle brother, who quickly became the love of my life. Like plenty of other young girls in the '90s, we were transfixed, almost foaming at the mouth at the sight of these three long-haired blondes, fresh out of Tulsa, Oklahoma, squeaking out their teenybopper sound in their prepubescent voices. For as much as we understood the concept, we were in love.

Our friend Jessica had managed to record Hanson's music video onto a VHS tape while it played on MTV. We'd go over to her house and watch the recording on repeat. ON REPEAT. One song, one video. ON REPEAT. ALL. DAY. Her mother actually had to tell us to take a break, "get up and go outside for a while," she'd say. Every time Jessica's older brother would walk through the living room, he would make fun of the blue-eyed blondes. "They look like girls," he'd laugh, and steam would fume from our ears.

"YOU'RE JUST JEALOUS," we'd scream. "THEY DON'T LOOK LIKE GIRLS, YOU'RE JUST UGLY!" We were *not* mean kids, and we were certainly not the type to name-call given our own insecurities as awkward middle schoolers, but the Hanson brothers? Off limits. We would absolutely defend Hanson from any name-callers. To the death. I have yet to see any generation post-90s match the wrath of a Hanson-obsessed teeny bopper when someone calls Taylor Hanson a girl. Hell hath no fury...

Previous to Hanson, Betsy and I each had our own bedroom. Once Hanson entered the scene, we decided to move into the same room so we could cover the walls in Hanson posters. Cover. The. Walls. Not one square inch of wall was left showing. It's safe to say it was a shrine. On top of driving everyone else in our house nuts with our crying over the Hansons and attempts to figure out how we could meet and marry them, we had a "ritual" of singing to their posters. I guess you would call it a ritual. In retrospect, that ritual alone possibly could have qualified us for a psychiatric evaluation.

LeAnn Rimes had just come out with the song, "How Do I Live Without You?" and I'm not sure why this song became our theme song, perhaps because it's truly how we felt, but every time it came on the radio, one of us would scream to the other "THE SONG'S ON!" And we would sprint up to our room, blast the song on full volume and belt it out as we sang to our Hanson posters, "HOW DO I LIVE WITHOUT YOOOOOU? I WANT TO KNOW! HOW DO I BREATHE WITHOUT YOOOU!?" And we may have been caressing their cheeks, their poster cheeks, as we sang.

Yeah, it was bad. Oddly enough, it was also fairly typical behavior amongst Hanson fans. I'm pretty sure parents were trying to form recovery groups. Girls would fight over who was a bigger fan. We knew there was absolutely no way anyone was a bigger fan than us, but that is what every girl thought about herself. It was a legit fever. A seemingly incurable fever that gave us a sense of purpose… to figure out how to get to Tulsa, Oklahoma, find the Hanson brothers, and introduce ourselves as their future wives.

One year Betsy mailed a cake mix box and party decorations to Zac Hanson, the youngest brother in the group, for his birthday. She figured he'd be too busy out on the road, and she wanted to make sure he was properly celebrated. I'm pretty sure he never got the package because he never sent a Thank You card. In an attempt to win tickets to see Hanson in concert, we kept a phone number to the local radio station taped to the telephone for an entire week. On the last day of the competition, when we couldn't get through to the station and only got the busy signal, we were inconsolable. Our parents felt helpless as they held their tween daughters crying over unrequited love. We even bought clothes that looked exactly like theirs. Though we got mad at people for making fun of Hanson for looking like girls, they did have some really cute clothes that we often found in the Delia's catalog—another win for the '90s—Delia's.

Though our obsession with Hanson may have estranged us for a while from anyone who wasn't a fan, it brought Betsy and I closer together. We had something to bond over, to share a room over, to lose our ever-loving minds over. Like all good and trendy things, the obsession eventually faded. My Hanson fever wore off first. Betsy started to notice when I didn't go sing to the posters as frequently.

"JENNIE, THE SONG WAS ON! WHERE WERE YOU? YOU MISSED IT!"

"Oh, sorry, I didn't hear it," I'd say sheepishly, even though I had. I remember when Third Eye Blind came out with "Semi-Charmed Life," I instantly loved it and made the mistake of saying so in front of Betsy.

"This is my new favorite song! Doo doo doo doo doo doo doo," I blurted out.

Betsy looked at me like I was a traitor. "How can you say that?" she asked with disappointment and what looked like mild heartbreak.

Then, eventually Betsy's fever died too. We gradually went back to our own bedrooms and expanded our musical horizons to include The Spice Girls and Mariah Carey. N'SYNC and Backstreet Boys never caught our attention as much because we had already been wooed, already been in love, already felt the heartache of loving a boyband that didn't love us back. We enjoyed the songs of N'SYNC and Backstreet Boys well enough, but we weren't in love with those bands—they were "posers" (remember that word? It was an even meaner way to call someone a copycat). The best boyband had already come along, who did these guys think they were? I know, I know, thems is fightin' words for '90s kids. Whichever boyband you were obsessed with—that was the best one, right?

I often wonder how I got here... thirty-five years old. How time seems to go by so fast and yet so slow. When you're young and in lust or in love, it almost feels as if time has stopped, like you'll never get old enough to live out your daydreams of marrying your childhood crush. Then you actually get older and wonder where all that time actually went.

The older I get, the more I understand mid-life crisis. I know I'm not mid-life yet, but I'm certainly on my way there. Time ain't going backwards if you know what I mean. The older I get, the more I think about it. Time. How do I want to use it? How have I used it? How much time did I actually waste not being myself because I was so afraid of what other people thought? At thirty-five, I can honestly say I have wasted a lot of time worrying about what other people think. Worrying about people who aren't actually worried about me. Why is that one of the harder lessons to learn in life? People just aren't that concerned with you... live your life.

In an attempt to make up for lost time, I find myself making odd purchases—or at least odd for my age. I think this is where many people's mid-life crises manifest themselves, they are trying to bring back what they lost, be it youth or time or just a nostalgia for what was. They buy sports cars or dye their hair or sleep with someone younger. It lasts for however long it takes them to realize they can't actually reverse time, nor can they bring back what was—be it their youth or their natural hair color without the streaks of age and dashes of stress. Everyone's mid-life crisis looks different, perhaps even when it happens. I'm sure I'll go through it eventually. I'm not there yet so I'm not sure how it all works, but I do know I'm going through something right now, some kind of a grieving, so to speak, for time wasted and wrinkles gained.

I'm sure the wrinkles thing sounds shallow, but shallow as it is, it's my truth. It bothers me to see age happening, to feel my body not quite working as well or as quickly as it used to. This is where anyone older than me usually scoffs, and believe me, I know I've got plenty of time. I'm technically not even "old," and the older I get the younger "old" seems, but I'm just calling it as I go so as not to continue to let it rob me—to see age for what it is, acknowledge it's happening, and move on.

So, I guess for me this is my pre-mid-life crisis, an attempt not necessarily to feel younger again, rather an attempt to get back the time I wasted on what I thought everyone else was thinking. I didn't buy a new car or dye my hair or sleep with someone younger. Instead, I dipped back into all my '90s nostalgia and puff-painted sweatshirts while listening to Lisa Loeb and Alanis Morissette (God help the 21-year-old who, at the mention of Alanis Morissette, asked me: "*Who's that?*")

As for those "odd purchases"... I've gone on eBay and Poshmark intending to purchase every Lisa Frank item I could find, only to find out '90s Lisa Frank is now considered vintage and people are charging $120 FOR A TRAPPER KEEPER!!! Yea, remember those!? I thought it'd be fun to have one again, memories, you know, without the awkward middle school encounters of being made fun of in the hallway. Well, apparently there are a lot of '90s kids who want to enjoy their youth without the awkward encounters because they are buying up old school supplies like hotcakes. Our junk is now considered vintage. When I was younger, vintage stuff was from the '70s and any decade before that. I didn't realize that as time went on, other decades would eventually also get categorized as vintage. How is that possible!?!

So, while I was able to practice enough self-control *not* to buy a $120 Lisa Frank Trapper Keeper that was probably $5 in the '90s, I may have spent $15 on a single folder… and maybe I spent $45 on a used t-shirt… made (and first worn) 20 years ago. I also bought some stickers and a lunchbox. If only I had known all my '90s memorabilia would be vintage one day, I could have avoided working in the service industry all together.

All this to say: Hoard up, kids! Your junk might be worth something someday. I'm kidding, that's not the point of all this. I don't necessarily have a point to this or an answer for what to do about the passing of time—I think we all approach it differently, some people get new cars, some people get old stickers. Whatever it may be, I think it's okay that the passing of time may initially freak us out. It's jarring the day you wake up and realize you're only getting older. I don't want to sound depressing; I don't think getting old is bad, I'm just in that transitional phase of figuring out what it looks like for me. I think change of any sort is an adjustment. It just is what it is. All these thoughts and feelings are natural and normal and very separate from the deeper life questions about how I am going to pay rent or the mortgage or help people in need. It's okay that our heads are just a mix of it all, the deep and the shallow.

I hear the older you get, the more fun you have because you stop caring so much about what other people think of you. And to be honest, I'm really excited about that. I used to be jealous of younger people, but then I remembered what a prison it was to feel so trapped by the opinions of others, especially now with social media, talk about wasting time. I'm fortunate I grew up when I did, just before screens hijacked our ability to engage humanity in person. In some ways I've become jealous of older people, living in the freedom of their age, not even worried about the opinions of others. Sometimes I think it's older people who are the only ones really living.

But mostly I'm just trying to let go of the jealousy thing all together, the judgements of different generations, and just be right where I am—an '80s baby shaped in the '90s, currently trying to survive the '20s, oscillating between loving social media and hating it, wanting to act my age and wear grown-up clothes, but finding comfort and nostalgia in my new (but old) neon Lisa Frank t-shirt. I'm confused, curious and happy. And I think that's okay, feeling a little different from day to day and taking each day as it comes. No resolve necessary, just the ability to adjust and be kind to myself in the process.

It's kinda funny to look back now and realize the song, "MMMBop," was actually about the passing of time—in an mmmbop, it's gone (that's a boyband way of saying "in an instant"). I was thirteen yesterday and in an mmmbop, I'm age-appropriate for a geriatric pregnancy.

Mmmbop, dop ba du wop.

# 2

# DA BEARS AND EATING DISORDERS

**A FEW MORNINGS AGO,** I made a mug cake for breakfast. A mug cake is when you put the ingredients of a cake into a mug and zap it in the microwave until it "bakes" and it gives you the tiniest, laziest cake ever made. It's genius, as well as delicious. It's almost too easy, like dangerously easy, like I could make mug cake for breakfast every day for the rest of my life and be totally content that I never got married or had kids. The combination of peanut butter and chocolate will make up for any great loss in life ... except for weight loss.

Speaking of, I used to be vegan. Technically I was anorexic, but I had convinced myself I was just being vegan, and I told people I was vegan, mainly because it sounded healthier than saying I was anorexic. When I did eat, I avoided all meat, dairy, gluten, soy, wheat, and anything else made by man or God. What started out as a health journey after college turned into a self-generated "bad foods" list that kept getting longer and longer, and a "good foods" list that kept getting shorter and shorter. It got to the point where I ate about three nuts a day, sometimes wrapped in lettuce. On particularly crazy days I would squirt a little mustard in the wrap. Best. Vegan. Wraps. Ever. (Or so I told myself). I could have marketed my wraps, but I was too tired and too cold to do anything. As a vegan I napped a lot, so I might have appeared aloof, and in some ways, I was because I'm not sure my brain was getting enough fuel. I was also very passionate about certain topics, mostly involving food. My lack of calories led me to exhibit some "aggressive" behaviors over certain things, like say, strawberries, particularly when I planned to go a little crazy and have *two* strawberries, instead of just *one*, for a meal.

For example, I remember one time excitedly going into the fridge for my double portion of strawberries, only to discover that my mother (who had purchased the strawberries, thereby technically making her the owner of the strawberries) apparently had the audacity to eat the last of them.

"WHO ATE THE MOTHER-FREAKING STRAWBERRIES!?" I yelled. (I wanted it to be known I meant business, but even for as passionate as I could get about those strawberries, I could never bring myself to drop the actual F-bomb in my mother's house.)

My mother was sitting calmly at the table doing some sort of paperwork and without even looking up she responded, "Your freaking mother."

I slammed the refrigerator door and walked at a mildly fast pace up to my bedroom to cry. I would have run but I was too tired.

I went to rehab in Chicago in February of 2007. I'll never forget it because the Chicago Bears were in the Super Bowl that year. First time since 1986. Once we had boarded the airplane, the pilot came over the intercom and said something to the effect of...

"Good evening, ladies and gentlemen, on behalf of [whatever-whatever] airlines we'd like to thank you for flying with us this evening to the home of this year's Super Bowl contenders, DA BEARS!" And in unison, as if it was some sort of flash mob or IMPROV Everywhere skit, everyone on the plane pumped their fists in the air and yelled "DA BEARS!"

A flight attendant came over the intercom and encouraged their behavior by repeating over and over again, "DA BEARS, DA BEARS, DA BEARS, DA BEARS, DA BEARS!"

And everyone responded in unison, "DA BEARS, DA BEARS, DA BEARS, DA BEARS, DA BEARS!"

I had flashbacks of early '90s SNL skits with Michael Jordan wearing a hula skirt as Chris Farley was having a sausage-induced heart-attack. It was then I realized I was going somewhere special; I was going to the land of HURRICANE DITKA. Hurricane Ditka was the nickname of former Chicago Bears coach, Mike Ditka, who had been the last coach to have led the Bears to Super Bowl victory in 1986, and therefore was still loved and admired by Bears' fans. Prior to the plane ride, I only had a few SNL references to know who Mike Ditka was, but in 2007 on my way to rehab, I learned more than I ever thought I would about Hurricane Ditka and DAAAA BEARS!

The SNL fangirl in me was excited beyond belief. But the exhausted vegan in me, still unable to fully admit I had an eating disorder, was a little terrified to be going to a place known for their hot dogs, deep-dish pizzas, and polish sausages. *Perhaps I can introduce them to my vegan wraps*, I thought to myself. But then I thought about Mike Ditka and the fact that my vegan wraps were roughly the size of his pinky finger (if even), and I couldn't foresee my delicious three-nut (mustard optional) lettuce wraps going over so well as part of a meal plan in "make that an extra-cheese, extra-large-deep-dish-pizza with a side of polish sausage, please" Chicago.

What I considered an entire meal was basically a salad garnish to a Chicagoan, or really to anybody, had I been completely honest with myself. Nonetheless, it was kinda funny when I thought of Mike Ditka eating one of my "vegan wraps." For the first time in a long time, I laughed.

I will never forget that plane ride. People were singing, cheering, and chanting. It felt like we were on board the Polar Express on our way to see Santa Claus as played by Mike Ditka. No one started out knowing anybody but bonding over the same excitement (in this case, the Bears) made everyone family. I mostly just observed from my seat, terrified and amazed. I was terrified of the foods that lay ahead of me and I was amazed by how passionate everyone seemed about something other than strawberries.

Truth be told, I boarded that plane not wanting to live much longer. I was tired of living each day terrified. Terrified of what the day held, terrified of what I would or wouldn't eat, terrified of my own self and my own actions. I was exhausted, and in my exhaustion, I felt stuck. I didn't know how to get myself out of the patterns I had set. I was functioning in survival mode, and survival alone didn't seem like much of a reason to keep going. Hearing old SNL references to DA BEARS on that plane triggered memories of a time I had forgotten, a time when I was happy and hopeful and less bogged down by the expectations of the world.

I arrived in Chicago the day before the Super Bowl. By the time the plane landed, I was curious enough to want to see this game that had so strongly united this large group of strangers—so strongly that they were all hugging and high-fiving by the end of flight. To have something to look forward to other than a second strawberry or an extra nut in my wrap was a feeling I had forgotten I liked. It had been years since I had been excited about something other than food. Something as simple as a football game gave me the tiniest inkling of desire.

"I desire to see this game," I told myself, which in bigger terms could be translated into "I desire to live one more day." So, it caught me off guard when I stepped off the plane feeling hopeful about going to the land of Hurricane Ditka to recover from Hurricane ED. (In rehab most of us learned to name our eating disorder and most of us chose to name it ED. I know it's not that original, but we were all just really tired).

The Bears lost the Super Bowl and I remember being bummed, but when I realized I actually cared about something other than food, I felt the slightest bit of excitement over the fact that I wasn't numb anymore, but in fact, bummed! I entered rehab the day after the Super Bowl and began my long and slow process of seeking recovery, of discovering that I wasn't just a tired vegan with misplaced passions, I was sick, and I had been sick for a fairly long time.

I say this to say sometimes it's not always the fire on the mountain or the lightning bolt experiences that wake us up or instantly cure us of our "diseases." Sometimes it's not the church service or the community service that gets us to step outside of ourselves to see that people need help, and to see that we ourselves are a part of that people group in need of help. Sometimes God works in the quietest, simplest, and even funniest of ways, like through SNL skits from the '90s, through an airplane ride of happy, hopeful strangers, and through the Chicago Bears getting a chance to reclaim their Super Bowl title, to take us on a journey of healing, instead of an instant cure-all snap of the fingers. Sometimes it's the little things, as little as thinking *I want to see that game*, which lead us to the next little thing and the next little thing, and all those little things add up over time to become a very big thing called LIFE.

I am where I am now because I boarded that plane to Chicago in 2007. The Chicago Bears played a surprising and odd role in my recovery, one I did not see coming. They gave me something to look forward to at a time when I was hopeless, and the thought of Mike Ditka eating one of my "vegan wraps" brought laughter to me at a time when nothing seemed funny. As I remembered the SNL skits of the '90s, I recalled a time when I used to enjoy life, and it was then that I began the journey of searching for that girl who got lost somewhere along the way.

I can't sit here on this side of the story and say I am cured, but I can say I am better than I was. I am fully enjoying life, and I still hope to one day share a burger with Mike Ditka (on a gluten-free bun, we gotta meet in the middle), perhaps with a vegan wrap as garnish.

I also still hope for a Chicago Bears Super Bowl victory one day. After all, a girl who chooses to live is a girl who can dream.

# 3

# WAIT!
# ME TOO!

**IN THE SUMMER OF 2017,** at thirty-three years old, I had been single for what Hollywood would call *an eternity*. In reality, it had been four years (six if you aren't including that one weird on-again-off-again situation), but if I were an active member of Tinseltown where life-long marriages last approximately seven years, my four-to-six-year stint of single-hood would have been dubbed *eternally long*, perhaps even *eternally hopeless*.

In that four-to-six-year time span, I went on dates, here and there—five total, to be exact and only one of those made it to a second date, which never went past that since I wouldn't sleep with the guy *after meeting him twice*. What a prude, I know. There was only one guy I went out with who I *wanted* the time to extend beyond the first date storyline, but I was a little too eager for him to want the same thing and I completely botched our first (and last) breakfast date. I figured this out while processing the whole date (and my inability to be myself) on the way home with the help of my Uber driver.

I had Ubered to the date because my car broke down on the morning I was supposed to meet up with the guy who I couldn't believe asked me out, if for no other reason than he was extremely good looking *and* well-employed—a type who hadn't previously expressed interest in *me*, a part-time barista who was trying to grow her first dreadlock. We'll call him Greg, and *sure* it was just breakfast, which seemed a little odd for a date, but less pressure with no possibility for an awkward "your place or mine?" scenario after. *Neither! It's breakfast, not bedtime.*

"Of course!" I yelled as I tried to start the car that morning, asking God to pleeeeaseeee give me a jump because this date was of utmost importance! I had met Greg a year prior. He was a customer in the coffee shop where I worked, and I swooned every time he came in. I swooned for nearly a year, and then one day I ran into him at the grocery store, without the milk-stained apron and my distaste for humanity due to lack of tips, and for reasons unbeknownst to me (as I was still flaunting my nub of a dreadlock), he asked me out. So clearly, utmost importance! *Where are you, God!? It's me JJ, I need this!* I thought as I turned my key for the tenth time, to no success. But I think He was too busy helping France make it illegal to pay for sex to zap my car into action. I later found out the law actually did pass on April 6th, 2016, the same day as my breakfast date, and I remember thinking, *oh, that's where you were, God. Fair enough.*

I was incredibly late to the breakfast date, in part because my car wouldn't start and I had to wait for an Uber, but also in part because the location was twenty-five minutes away in La Jolla and I didn't want to be difficult by asking Greg if we could meet somewhere closer to me. God forbid I have the nerve to ask for convenience—or at least compromise.

I also didn't tell Greg ahead of time that my car broke down, a legitimate excuse for being late, because I was embarrassed that I was even driving a car that broke down so easily, or more accurately, still trying to drive the 1984 Volkswagen Vanagon that I used to live in. In retrospect, had I had any amount of self-confidence, I would have told myself that if he didn't think the van was cool then *he* was lame and probably not someone I wanted to date anyway. It's something you tell yourself when someone doesn't like you back—"their loss"—even though deep down you can't help but feel like they're probably right and not losing out on much. I was already struggling with how I saw myself, a thirty-two-year-old starving artist, which, as a recovering anorexic, was not something I was proud to call myself. But, when you paint things in exchange for groceries and are still trying to figure out how to pay rent, you pick the title back up, very carefully explaining to people: "I'm starving because I'm poor, not because of my mental disorder."

Looking back, I can see this mindset is where it all went wrong. The core issue wasn't that my van wouldn't start... it was the way I saw myself. Greg was always dressed like he had somewhere important to be, so when I got up that morning, I scoured my closet for something, *anything* that would evoke the word "class." No easy feat at that phase in my life, living by the beach and making art. Everything was either cut off or covered in paint. I borrowed a cardigan from my roommate, a blatant signal to people that I was not acting like myself. When I started to tell this story to my friends later on, all they could say was—*"You wore a cardigan!?"*

I had also caked my face in makeup, which is still not something I do on a normal basis, but something I thought Greg might like, a more 'put together' woman. I'm not an advocate for going all-natural, I just don't enjoy how makeup feels on my face; like wearing jeans that are too tight, make-up is reserved for special occasions. I didn't consider that not only did I usually *not* wear makeup (including every time Greg saw me at the coffee shop *and* when he asked me out) but seeing as how it was also a breakfast date, it was morning, which is no time for heavy makeup, unless you are, in fact, a news anchor.

For some reason, I also felt the need to carry a handbag, which I borrowed from another roommate, perhaps because I had always assumed Greg's type to be more feminine, and a handbag definitely felt more feminine than my usual backpack. Normally, I carried a backpack around—to the beach (full of sunscreen and a wetsuit), or to work (to carry my lunch in), so I wasn't actually sure what to carry in the handbag. I figured most girls probably carried makeup, but I was wearing enough makeup for three people, so I didn't think I needed to bring more. Since I was going to eat breakfast, I didn't need to pack a lunch, and seeing as how I was dressed like a politician's wife on casual Friday, a wetsuit also seemed unnecessary.

I didn't want it to look like I was carrying an empty handbag, what an amateur of a woman, so I filled three glass water bottles and wrapped them in paper towels so they wouldn't clink when I walked, like an alcoholic trying to hide her problem. This alone is comical to me—the fact that at the time I saw this act as normal, not at all as borderline insane, or at the very least, desperate.

When my van wouldn't start, I called an Uber, texted Greg I'd be running late, and waited on the curb, caked in makeup with a handbag full of glass water bottles… at *eight in the morning*. After re-telling this story to a friend, she nicknamed me the "IHOP whore," laughing while asking, "Who else would wear that much makeup to breakfast!?" She had a point, but in an attempt to defend myself, I suggested a news anchor.

When I arrived at the date, completely flustered, Greg was waiting *out front*, meaning he *saw me* pull up in the Uber so I had to explain why I didn't have a car, or at least why my car wouldn't start. My plan had been to meet him *in* the restaurant where my mode of transportation wouldn't even come up. I'm not sure what I would have done when the date was over if he had offered to walk me to my car, but I think somewhere deep down, I knew the date wouldn't go well enough for me to be escorted out, at least not by him.

"Uber, huh?" he asked as I got out of the car cradling my handbag full of glass water bottles.

"Yea, it was the craziest thing, my car wouldn't start this morning," I blurted out. *Oh God, shut up!* Five seconds into the date and I'm already telling myself to shut up. *This is going to go swimmingly.*

"Oh no," he said, "you should have told me. I could have picked you up, or we could have met closer to your place, so you didn't have to pay for an Uber all the way out here!"

I would have been struck by his kindness, but I was too caught up in how desperate I must have seemed, and then on top of it, distracted by my own shame for being too insecure to share about my car troubles. I can say with certainty that I have since learned to love myself, though I am still prone to wading in a pool of self-doubt, I have realized it's a shallow pool and I can stand up and get out without anyone's permission. At the time though, I was drowning face down in a shame-filled kiddy pool of my own doing. I don't know why I felt so much shame, perhaps because I had already decided I wasn't good enough for Greg. I served him coffee and could barely grow a single dread, which *should* be the easiest of hair styles, but come to find out dreads are incredibly high maintenance, more so than highlights and blowouts, so don't be fooled by the hippies. I digress.

I honestly can't remember how I responded, I think I kind of blacked out, I remember managing to get out a "naaaah," not that different from the way an old redneck or a hip-hop artist would say it. Kinda funny how they make similar sound effects yet tend to think of themselves as so different from each other.

"Naaaah, I couldn't have had you do that," I said as we walked, wondering to myself *why not?*

We sat down at a table overlooking the ocean, and, internally, I tried to remind myself that I was safe, that I had nothing to prove, and that I already mattered, followed by a *yeah right*. The waitress came over and asked if she could get us anything to drink, Greg motioned to me to order first.

"I'll have a coffee and a water," I said, motioning back to Greg that it was his turn.

"Coffee for me," he said. The waitress asked if he would like water as well. "No thanks, I brought my own," he replied, and he pulled a glass water bottle out of his backpack.

I started to panic. Do I stop the order and say, *WAIT, ME TOO*, in an effort to show him how similar we are, bringing our own water in glass bottles so as not to waste water *or* plastic!? Never mind that I had *three* water bottles for a completely different reason! Or would that look desperate, obvious that I wanted to be like him? Surely, I didn't *all of a sudden* remember I had three water bottles in my bag. I thought about it too long and the waitress walked away. I said nothing and smiled awkwardly.

We made small talk, some of which involved me sharing about my therapist, which I know is a first date no-no, but I couldn't help myself—she's like a best friend you pay for, and I often find myself saying things like, "You just gotta meet her!"

"She sounds great," Greg said, sounding kind with the slightest bit of pity in his voice. The waitress brought my water and set our coffees down on the table. I usually always drink my coffee black, certainly if it's my first cup, only every now and then opting for an afternoon splash of cream, but *never* under any circumstances do I put sugar in my coffee. I didn't even realize I was doing it, scooping well-rounded spoonfuls of sugar straight into my coffee, until Greg actually said "Wow!" And I didn't stop there, I loaded the cup with cream. Not wanting to come across as though I had blacked out, unaware of what I was doing, I said, "I like a little sweet treat in the morning."

*What was I saying!? I like a little sweet treat in the morning?* Who was this cardigan-wearing, sugar-addicted carnival creature?

"I can tell," Greg said as I passed him the cream. "No thanks, I like it black."

My eyes grew wide because again I wanted to say, *WAIT, ME TOO!* But it was too late, I had already created my sweet treat concoction, and there was no going back. I took a sip, and it was horrible, so naturally, I said, "Ahhh, delicious."

When the waitress returned to take our orders, I wanted to impress Greg that I was not the typical girl who didn't eat much on dates. Sure, maybe I wouldn't eat much prior to rehab, but that was different. Now, I'm a woman who eats big meals and meat and grunts like Tim the Tool Man Taylor.

Except none of that was really true, minus the woman part, but the big meals, meats, and grunting? Definitely not true. In rehab, I learned moderation and the importance of snacks and smaller meals throughout the day, and I keep that practice to this day. Not only do I eat small meals frequently, but I've also never been much of a meat-eater; even before the eating disorder, I was just never prone to meat.

One time during a therapy session, the counselor asked me why I was vegan. I had been vegan for almost two years at that point, which had more to do with the fact that it was easier to be secretly anorexic by claiming to be vegan. Plus "animal rights" sounded a lot better than "mental disorder," especially on a date. I'm not vegan anymore, if for no other reason than the strictness of it disrupts my recovery, but I do prefer eating plants. I'm not an activist about it, I'm just a little iron deficient due to a preference for roasted cauliflower over grilled chicken.

That said, while on my date with Greg, I really wanted the oatmeal on the menu, but oatmeal seemed like a lame thing to order on a date. As the waitress stood there, hovering her pencil above the notepad she was ready to write our order on, I felt pressure to order something *good*. Good to whom? I don't know, but the insecurity of my own history with food and wanting to impress this guy with the fact that I wasn't a typical Southern California girl who only ate almonds and tree bark (even though I kind of was), I ordered like I was a college kid fresh off a night of drinking, ready for some Waffle House.

"I'll have the breakfast basket," (a pancakes, eggs, and sausage combo) "and could I also get a side of bacon?" I added.

"You got it, girl," the waitress said with a tone that said she was impressed. I sat up a little taller. "And you?" She turned to Greg.

"Well, I'm going to feel a little lame after that," he said, "but I'll just have the oatmeal."

*I could have died.* I felt like I did die, like someone had shot me in the stomach, or at the very least, shot the IHOP whore who kept trying to show up on my date. *WAIT! ME TOO!* I wanted to shout and retract my order. We seemed to be so similar, and yet I couldn't tell him that because I was too busy trying to be who I thought a guy wanted me to be… a cardigan-wearing, handbag-carrying, meat-eating woman who donned smokey eyes and drove a responsible car. Perhaps my wires were crossing the places I've lived, seeing as who I was that day appeared to be much more like a woman in the South than a woman in Southern California, but when you spend so much of your life just trying to be who you think other people want you to be, some wires are surely bound to short circuit.

Greg laughed at himself as we handed our menus to the waitress.

"You got it," she said, and she walked away with the order I wanted to take back.

While I admired how easily Greg seemed to be himself, what I didn't enjoy was just *how* easy it was for him to be himself. I often find myself in this place, inspired by someone until I find out more about them, like just *how* successful and confident they are. If they are too successful or seemingly too confident, I turn on them. I get embarrassed and jealous, and they go from being "so funny" to being "so annoying." Whether it was my own insecurity or the fact that maybe Greg was a little too confident about being himself, everything he said seemed to be a put-down, as if what he was really saying to me was *how could you possibly be so insecure? What is wrong with you?*

Everything I said, he questioned. When I said I really enjoyed working at a coffee shop, "Really?" he asked with surprise. "*What* do you like about it?" His tone suggested he'd caught me in lie—I couldn't possibly *like* working in a coffee shop, right? While at one point in my life I really did enjoy working in a coffee shop, after a total of ten years in different shops, I had stayed long past the season of enjoyment and was visibly miserable every day. But I didn't want him to *know* I was miserable, stuck in a comfort zone of making almond milk lattes for minimum wage and little to no tips. I felt the eagerness to impress him well up inside me, I tried to drown it out with my sugar-laced coffee, but to no avail.

"Well, I get to meet cool people like you." I heard myself say it and even I cringed. *Tone it down, JJ.*

His questions about everything kept coming.

"Why do you like this? Do you *really* enjoy that?" While a more secure me may have thought he was just getting to know me better, the insecure me was put off by so many questions, perhaps because I didn't know the answers. Given my bag full of three glass water bottles, my sweet coffee concoction, and my Atkins-based break-fast order, it was fair of him to question me, but still, he didn't *know* those things weren't me, or did he? Had he figured me out? Whether he did know and thought I was lame for lying, or he didn't *know* and thought I really was an IHOP whore, I'm sure he sensed my own discomfort… with myself.

I wanted to write him off as a jerk, that would be the easiest thing to do, but the jerkiest thing he was doing was questioning me (most likely out of sincere curiosity), which in all reality, is what I should have been doing myself—questioning my own behavior. I didn't stop to question anything, to take a look at the cake-faced girl in the mirror and wonder who she was, because that would have meant facing the truth: that even still, after all these years, breakups, self-realizations, and therapy, I *still* didn't know who I really was, and even more so, I still didn't know how to love myself. It's much easier to think of someone else as a jerk than to see yourself as lost.

When the date ended, Greg walked me to my Uber. Though he was nice in saying goodbye, it was *very clear* he would not be calling me, that we would, in fact, never see each other again. I got in the Uber and promptly began to process the entire date with the driver, who listened just as intently as my therapist/best friend—"Who you should totally meet," I told my driver.

"I think you're really funny," the driver said, and for the first time that day, I felt like myself.

"Maybe just text him and say you weren't really yourself," the driver said. "Let him know that wasn't really you." Whether or not this was actually good advice, I felt like my Uber driver had a point, plus he was an unbiased dude driving me home, not one of my friends who think I'm the best thing in the world and that Greg should have been totally grateful to have gone out with me.

When I got home, I walked in the front door and literally shook my whole body, as if I were shaking off whatever carnival creature or IHOP whore it was that had possessed me.

"BLUUUUGGGGHHCCCCKKKK!" I yelled as I walked in the door and shook myself like someone being slain in the spirit at a Pentecostal church. I walked into the living room and fell face down onto the floor. The whole house was quiet, no one else home to ask me how it went or tell me not to text the guy less than an hour after the first date.

I laid there for a while, my cheek on the orange shag carpet, looking out through the sliding glass doors of our second floor living room, a home obviously built in the '70s. I grabbed my phone and wrote out my text, essentially apologizing for the date. I'm really not sure what type of person gets home from a first date and sends a text to apologize, but probably someone desperate for one more chance.

It didn't help that I started the text with, "After processing our date with my Uber driver," which is precisely where I wish someone could have stopped me. I continued, "I realized I wasn't myself at all on the date and I just want to say I'm sorry."

I will bless my own heart on that one.

In retrospect, I wish someone had been home, a proofreader of any kind, even the roommate I disagreed with on most issues, *anyone* who could have read the text out loud for me to hear it... *Oh God, that's pathetic,* they hopefully would have said. Or maybe I should have at least gone over the text with the Uber driver; after all, he didn't tell me to mention his involvement, or even apologize, he just said to tell him I wasn't being myself.

Minutes later he texted back: "Get out of your head, it was fine, and great hanging out with you."

Again, I felt like he was being nice, but he felt sorry for me, "Get out of your head?" I read out loud, *what is he? A therapist?* Turns out, as I had learned on our date, he was a kinesiologist who basically can read people's emotions by how they carry said emotions in their bodies. I was doomed from the start.

I laid on the floor, wiping the makeup off with the cardigan I was wearing, forgetting for a moment that it didn't belong to me. If there were a visual for the bottom of a shame spiral, this was it. When one of my roommates got home, she walked into the living room and there was no explanation necessary.

"I see your date went well," she said. She lay down on the carpet beside me and asked if I wanted to talk about it. I was about to start in on the whole story when she said, "Pause."

She started to get up. "I'm so thirsty, let me grab some water really quick..."

"No need!" I yelled as I held up my hand to signal a stop sign. "See that handbag? Open it."

And thus, my story began.

# 4

## PRiNCE\$\$ \$URFER

**WHEN I FIRST MOVED TO CALIFORNIA,** I knew I wanted to go surfing. I spent my whole first summer there watching the surfers from the water's edge or above from the pier; I took pictures of surfers, wrote stories about surfers, but I never actually got out in the water and surfed. Okay, I take that back, I went out a handful of times, enough to say I went surfing all summer, because it was that spread out in between the times that I went, but not enough to actually get any better than the last time I had surfed... in high school. I'm officially at the age where I won't say how many years ago that was (mostly because I can't remember).

Do you know how good you get at something when you go however many years without doing it? I will tell you. Not very good. And let's be honest, even when I did surf, I wasn't that great, mostly because I was much too worried about what other people were thinking, so I spent most of my time paddling myself out of their way. Surf culture can be incredibly intimidating and extraordinarily territorial. People guard their spots in the ocean like those fur-topped guards standing outside of Buckingham palace—take all the pictures you want, but no one is getting in. Hence my hesitation—the guards, which is to say, the guys (more on them in a bit).

With surfing, not only was I afraid of what people thought of me, God forbid I should look stupid, but I was also afraid of getting in the way, of getting yelled at, of putting someone else out because I wanted to learn something new. Not surfing was a form of people pleasing because I knew the surfers couldn't get mad at me if I didn't get in their way; they liked me cheering them on from the water's edge. The trouble is, I didn't like me cheering them on from the water's edge. I mean, sure, to a degree I did, I think cheering people on in life is a good general rule of thumb, however, knowing that I wanted to be out there with them, but wasn't because I feared them, meant I wasn't genuinely cheering them on, I was masking my fear. Knowing I was living in fear made it hard for me to like myself, but other people liked me, so I settled for that, stunting my growth as I put off something I loved for the sake of pleasing other people. It's no wonder I consistently need therapy.

Eventually I got out of my own way and slowly began the process of re-learning how to surf. Even now after years of surfing, I'm still learning new things, and still reminding myself it's okay to show up. I remember one particular morning when I went out by the OB (Ocean Beach) pier. Between the people who hover on the pier, watching your every move, and the crowds that congregate in the water, it wasn't my regular spot, but it looked clean and there were less people than usual, so I thought I'd give it a try. As I mentioned, I surfed in high school... I grew up on the beaches of South Carolina, and sure South Carolina is no San Diego, but there's still surf, mostly in the winter or during hurricane season... if you look real hard, it's there. I remember thinking surfing was the coolest thing, I don't even know why, as I'm sure it's different for everyone, but I knew I wanted to be a surfer from as early as I can remember. The trouble with that desire was, for as rare as surfing was in the South at that time, it was even rarer for a surfer to be a girl.

Guys are highly encouraged to pursue three things in the South… sports, business, and women. Possibly even in that order. Girls on the other hand aren't so much encouraged to do any sort of pursuing. Girls are taught how to act and how to look and how to be ready when a fella comes-a-knocking, but not much else as it relates to life pursuits… especially when it comes to sports, or business, or other women. (Keeping in mind, all of this is from the perspective of someone who grew up in the South in the '90s, I understand perhaps times have changed… perhaps…).

But little girls like me grow up and move away from home and sometimes forget all about the things they once loved and the person they had hoped to be, or at least this one did. After years of living away from the ocean in cities like Chicago and Portland, I discovered a bit more of who I was outside of the South and how I felt about the expectations set upon me. I found my voice and I learned how to speak my truth in grace and love, but firmly when necessary. I learned that the way I'm wired is no accident, the things I love might have been placed specifically in me, and engaging in those things would bring life to my soul no matter how trivial they might seem to the rest of the world.

After seven years away, the ocean began to call my name, and she lured me back with her nostalgia and a desire for something more. I moved to San Diego in the summer of 2014 and realized I had accidentally relocated myself to the exact place I had always wanted to live but had never thought possible. I was finally going to be a surfer.

Except nothing is ever as easy as simply stating: I'm going to (fill in the blank). There are a lot of factors involved, especially with surfing. There's board sizes and balancing, knowing how to paddle and recognizing when to get up, not to mention the hazards and distractions of other people flailing around in the water who are also trying to learn... or they are already experienced enough to run right over you should you be in their way. And of course, there is the wonderful, magnificent, all-powerful, unpredictable ocean.

I started surfing shortly after moving to California at the age of thirty-one. I started surfing where most adults who learn later in life start: in the whitewash. The whitewash is where the waves have already broken and tumble harmlessly into shallow water upon the shore. I'm a quick learner, so after about the entirety of a day, I decided I was ready for more. I deemed myself ready to paddle beyond the rushing waters of the whitewash. The ocean thought otherwise, as if the waves themselves were Gandalf the Grey proclaiming at my every attempt, "YOU SHALL NOT PASS!" It was humbling—actually, it was embarrassing—but it sounds more grown-up to say it was humbling.

On this particular day, when I finally got past the break, I realized the waves were a little bigger than I had anticipated from shore. I'm constantly trying to push my comfort zone with surfing because I constantly want to get better and the only way to get better is to challenge what you think your limitations are. That said, there's also knowing your limits and when it's time to lay down your pride and admit that maybe you just aren't as strong as the ocean or the expert surfers in the water (and drowning to find out might not be worth it). I'm often wrestling between the two, usually not realizing my limits until I pass them and find myself flailing in the water beneath the power of a wave I was not prepared for.

"These definitely aren't princess waves," I said under my breath as I paddled out, trying to avoid some of the glares coming in my direction. *Is it my surfboard?* I wondered as I tried to smile and act like I wasn't fazed by the conditions. My surfboard often sticks out like a sore thumb because it's the only one in the water that's bright pink with a huge rainbow across the top. But wait, it gets better... flying over the rainbow is a unicorn, and riding upon the unicorn, in all her girly glory is a pretty, pretty princess. It's a 7'9" fun board and it is definitely fun, but given its size I can't duck dive it (when you duck the board under the oncoming wave), so when I'm trying to get past the break, especially on big days, you might see my board flying through the air as it shoots up out of the water and I shoot down under the water. What can I say? Sometimes the princess likes to go flying without me.

When I finally did make it out past the break, I discovered a whole separate obstacle I had not accounted for, likely the real reason I was getting all the glares... the guys in the lineup. The lineup is where all the surfers sit on their boards past where the waves are breaking. There they wait, mostly (if not always) dudes, hungry for waves, staring each other down, and even more so, staring down any newcomer who tries to paddle into their territory. It's not the most welcoming feeling, and it's probably even harder to overcome than the threat of a wave. Without saying a word, the guys make it clear that you are not to get in their way. It doesn't matter how cute you are or how much cheek you have hanging out of your spring suit, they will run you over. Guys are not surfing to meet girls— guys are surfing to surf. End of story. No debate. And there I was, the only girl joining the lineup, sitting naively on her bright pink pretty, pretty princess surfboard. I wanted to drown.

After nearly four years of living in California and trying to surf (off and on again), I had almost given up multiple times because I felt like I was never going to get any better, and getting stared down or run over by more experienced surfers was wearing me down. However, this last year I decided I wasn't going to quit. I didn't care how good I got or not, I didn't care whether people laughed at me or tried to box me out, I was going to learn to surf because *I* had always loved surfing, and I wanted to do it instead of just talking about doing it. Plus, I knew I was never going to actually get better if I didn't keep trying. As with anything, the good ones don't get good overnight, they get good because they keep trying.

And so, day in and day out, I'd show up to the ocean's edge, a little scared and a lot excited, or a lot scared and a little excited depending on the size of the waves, and I'd battle past the break into dude territory, sit on my pink surfboard, and I'd wait for my wave. With consistency comes muscle memory, strength, and even a little self-confidence. Over time I slowly began to figure out what was going on and where I needed to be in order to catch the wave. I began to care less about the intimidating dudes, and more about perfecting the craft.

The few months leading up to that one morning at the OB pier had been my favorite months surfing because I had pushed my limits and paddled past my fears and allowed myself to just enjoy the thing that I loved without being swayed by onlookers and nay-sayers. Not to mention I'd *actually* been surfing—all the effort had paid off because I was actually riding the waves and not just trying to survive them.

Even though I continue to feel more and more confident in my ability to surf, the ocean is different every day. Just because I'm surfing well one day doesn't mean I'll have the same waves the next day. As soon as I think I've mastered it, the ocean is like, "Nope. No, you don't." So, it is still kinda humbling, and still kinda embarrassing, but now, it's mostly just humbling because I know what I'm capable of, so I don't have to be embarrassed. If the ocean is calm one day and has other plans the next, so be it.

So, there I was out in the ocean by the OB pier, people were gathered above to watch the surfers, all the dudes in the lineup understandably giving me the look of "Why are you here?" I paddled around for what felt like half an hour, unsuccessful in my attempt at each wave that came my way. Finally, I saw a wave forming on the outside and it looked rather large from far away, so I could only dread how much bigger it was going to be by the time it reached me. I knew I was in the perfect spot for where the wave was opening, giving me a perfect right, which is my favorite direction. As far as surf etiquette goes, it was technically "my wave" as I was in position for it and had yet to encroach on anyone else's wave. But sometimes etiquette gets thrown out the window when it's the perfect wave—sometimes it's every man for himself, and seeing as I literally lack the balls, I often lose out on the race to a wave. I knew the guys were hungry for this wave, they were nearly foaming at the mouth, and I saw them starting to paddle toward me so they could box me out and cut me off, without a single care that I was already in the perfect spot to take this one.

I didn't even have time to hesitate, I just took a deep breath, said to myself, *here we go*, and paddled, hard, as if I was being chased and refused to be caught. I saw myself at the top of the wave and instead of looking down at how far I had to drop, I looked out and popped myself up as fast as I could. It was the most amazing feeling as I dropped down into the wave and rode nearly all the way to the base of the pier, somehow managing to weave in between dudes the whole way. As the wave died out, I sat myself down on my board and turned it around to paddle back out. I heard cheers above me and I looked up to see a family standing there on the pier clapping and cheering. At the very end was a little girl no more than four or five years old with sunglasses and blonde pigtails. I could hear her yelling, "It's a girl, it's a girl, she's surfing!" and she waved to me. I waved up at her and smiled. My heart felt happy.

As I paddled back out past the break and re-joined the lineup, the guys were all sitting quietly. Even if you do a good job, they aren't going to tell you that—surfers are not exactly a celebratory crowd, at least not the more seasoned surfers. They want to ride the waves more than they want to make new friends, and certainly more than they want to congratulate someone else's good ride. Almost immediately, another wave came along and with a newfound confidence, I went for it. I rode it in a way I had yet to ride until that day… it was as close to magic as I think there could ever be. Even I was like, *how is this happening?*

I paddled back out to the lineup again and sat a minute to catch my breath. As I was trying not to obnoxiously smile ear-to-ear. I heard a little voice screaming from the pier, "PRINCESS SURFER, PRINCESS SURFER!" I looked up and there was the little blonde girl in pigtails, frantically waving to me, wanting me to wave back to her. My heart nearly exploded out of my chest and onto the princess on my surfboard. I smiled and waved back at her, overjoyed by the thought that maybe, just maybe, that little girl saw another girl doing what she loved. Even if I was out there all alone among the dudes, that little girl saw me doing something seemingly hard and scary. Maybe she got to see for herself that girls can do tough things too and they don't have to be limited by social norms or opinions of others. Maybe that little girl said to herself, *I could do that too!*

And it wasn't just that I did something for that little girl—she did something for me, too. She celebrated me, even if she didn't know that's what she was doing. She celebrated me when no one else did. She made me feel like it mattered, all the work I put in, all the fears I faced, all the mocking, all the scoffing— all of it was worth that one moment to be the one girl who caught the big wave and passed all the guys on the way to shore. It reminded me that I want to live my life more fully, doing what I love not only because it gives me life, but also because it encourages other people. And I want to celebrate other people more, because it feels good to celebrate and you never know what a clap or a wave or a smile might do for someone.

I saw myself in that little girl up on the pier. I used to be that little girl, looking out at the waves wishing I could surf with the big guys. Sure, it wasn't some record-breaking event, nor was it even such a big deal for some surfers, but it was a big deal for me. It was a big deal to get to be the person who showed at least one little girl that she could do it… whatever her 'it' is, she can do it.

I've never been much of a princess girl, but yesterday I was someone's princess surfer, and that is a title I will gladly accept with a smile.

# 5

# ON-AGAIN-
# OFF-AGAIN

**I HAVE AN ON-AGAIN-OFF-AGAIN RELATIONSHIP** with my overall dental health. When I was in sixth grade, it was decided that I needed braces, severely. I'm sure it was decided much sooner than sixth grade, based purely upon being called "Buck Tooth" and "Bugs Bunny" on the playground, but sixth grade is when the professionals stepped in and said,

"You need help, Bugs."

I was the kid who always wanted glasses and braces. They seemed like a rite of passage I needed to experience in order to grow up properly. Unfortunately, I had perfect vision up through college, so "Four Eyes" was not something I got to experience hearing as a young child. Towards the end of my college career, I was driving a friend home one night, pulling on the corners of my eyelids and squinting to help me read the street signs and my friend noticed.

"I think you need glasses," she said.

"Really?" I asked, knowing I already had the perfect frames picked out for years. I went in for a vision test and I may have intentionally blurred the lines a little by misreading the little letters on the chart. I knew it was an "E," but I still said "B" and in the blink of any eye, I had glasses! I wish I had the foresight then to realize glasses were inevitable anyway—it was going to be a lifelong process of your vision getting progressively worse as you age little by little, but I didn't want to finally get my glasses at eighty. I had wanted them since I was nine, and I had already waited a whole twelve years to get them, so at twenty-one years old I already felt glasses were long overdue.

My braces journey though, that was a long-suffering process, and for some reason, I loved every step of it. The journey began with a spacer, it looked like a little metal spaceship that was attached to the roof of my mouth. There was a key that went with it and every night I had to insert the key into the spacer and turn it—this was "spacing out" the roof of my mouth. Apparently, all my teeth were jammed together because they had no space, hence the big buck teeth, pushed out, front and center. While I hated the process of my mother inserting the key into the spacer in my mouth and turning it until my spacer clicked, *and* that I nearly gagged every time, I did love the praise I got for being so tough. *Really, I didn't do much, just survived a gagging! Ice cream? Yes, please.*

After my evening key-crank, I was rewarded with ice cream for being such a strong girl, whether I cried or not. Not crying was not the true determinant of strong girl status, not choking on my mother's fist as she spaced out the entire roof of my mouth was what made me a strong girl, and strong girls got ice cream. The spacer ritual lasted for what felt like years, but to a sixth grader with no concept of time, it was probably the equivalent of a couple of months. After the spacer, my mouth was finally ready to be braced. I got to leave school early and miss the rest of the day because I needed straight teeth, and that is a perfectly acceptable excuse to miss math class.

I had braces for four years and experienced everything there is to experience with braces, except for kissing. I never kissed a boy while I had braces because apparently boys did not think my braces were as cool as I did, even when I color-coordinated them. My favorite color combination was turquoise and purple, in honor of the Charlotte Hornets. It was the '90s and the Carolinas were not well known for their professional sports teams, except for the Charlotte Hornets, who were as important to a kid in the South as the Chicago Bulls were to a kid in the Midwest. While Chicago had Michael Jordan and Scottie Pippen, we had Larry Johnson and Mugsy Bogues, who was at the top of his game in the '90s, despite the height disadvantage.

The first boy who noticed me after I got my braces off had already expressed an interest in me while I still had the braces on. One day he complimented my sweater vest, that alone should paint a picture—braces and sweater vests—but this boy *liked* my sweater vest, so I overwore it in an attempt to keep getting his attention. We wrote notes to each other and often had a middleman do the exchanging of the notes for us. By the time he actually asked me out I had gotten my braces off, but I knew it wasn't just because of my perfectly aligned, slimy new teeth, or the sweater vest, apparently.

I maintained my perfectly straight teeth well into college, always getting my regular cleanings because that's what you do when you're a dependent on your parents' health insurance. This is where the off-again part of my dental health relationship begins: college graduation.

I'm sure there is a lot one learns about "the real world" during their college years. The trouble is, if I did learn things about the real world, I don't remember them. I do remember learning about Rasputin and Monet and that my religious studies professor had a strong distaste for the story of Jesus.

"If I knew I could be God for all of eternity and all I had to do was suffer for a few hours, I would do it, too. Who wouldn't!?" she'd ask and look for people in the class to agree with her. There was one Jewish kid who would always agree, and he became her favorite student. Despite their religious differences, Jesus not being the Son of God was their common bond. I always thought it was odd that she'd ask that question, as if she were jealous of Jesus, like he was some annoying older brother who got all the attention. On top of the fact that she was completely missing the point of the story (in my opinion). But in college I had the confidence of a box tortoise, often retreating into my shell whenever professors posed any question at all, let alone one involving my opinion on the salvation of man.

When I graduated college, semi-ready to face the real world, I was armed with a full-length history report on how Rasputin brainwashed the Romanov family, my own attempt at replicating a Monet painting (thank you art class), and a newfound understanding that just because someone was "religious" did not mean they liked God, or his son, for that matter.

What I did not understand was that, upon graduation, I would have to figure out my own health insurance, as well as schedule all my own doctor and dental appointments, not to mention all my eye exams, and prescription needs thanks to my decision to see a "B" instead of an "E" on the eye chart. I really wish I would have seen that coming.

About ten years went by before I saw another dentist. Ten. Years. I was twenty-two when I last had someone "tickling my ivories" (an expression I was also late to learn meant playing the piano, not a dentist working on your teeth). And so, I was thirty-two before I ever made a dentist appointment myself.

On-again!

The only reason I made the appointment to begin with was because my dog had gotten ahold of my retainer—the retainer that I was supposed to wear to bed every night *for the rest of my life* so my mouth wouldn't shrink back to its pre-spacer days and reunite my two front teeth so closely they'd be forced to take back their leading roles.

While I may be slow to accessing the professional side of dental care, I am profusely diligent about my nightly routine. This one night in particular, I accidentally drank too much— not enough to miss the nightly routine of brushing my teeth and putting in my retainer, but just enough to get sick in the middle of the night and project vomit, along with my retainer, across the room. I woke up the next morning to my dog *chewing* on the vomit-covered retainer. That retainer had been with me ten years! It was one of my longest running relationships and one of my proudest accomplishments up to that point, and in one night of realizing I can't drink whiskey straight, it was ruined.

The dog was okay though, and I tried to save the retainer by boiling it in hot water, but I didn't take into consideration the fact that it was plastic, so the moment I dropped it into the boiling water, it morphed. Which is to say, the dog wasn't even the one who really ruined the retainer, but me, I did. I ruined the retainer. I remember when I was anxious about turning thirty, people would tell me, "Don't worry, thirty is the new twenty!" And I do think that's true… but it's not because we're still cool, it's because we still don't know what we're doing.

I made the dentist appointment to get a new retainer and they scheduled me for a cleaning as well since, you know, some time had gone by since my last one. I waited in the chair for the hygienist to come in, tapping my feet to Celine Dion playing overhead... *"I'm the one who wants to love you moooooooore!"* Immediately, I was transported back to middle school, back to missing a whole afternoon of school because I needed straight teeth, as well as ice cream afterwards to make me feel better about how hard the whole process was. I smiled when the hygienist came in.

"Oh, wow," she said. "You have such beautiful teeth!"

I put my hand to my mouth the way Miss America does when she is announced as the winner.

"Oh really?" I said as if I didn't already know my teeth were beautiful from the nearly five-year process it took me to get them that way. I wasn't looking for a continued compliment so much as I just didn't know what else to say. I couldn't just say, "I know, right?"

"Yes," she said as she walked over and sat down next to me. "Really beautiful teeth."

"I'll be sure to let my parents know," I joked, "They paid for my braces."

She laughed as she got prepared and put on those microscope-looking goggles to get an even closer look at my beautiful teeth. I continued tapping my feet to the music with an added dose of confidence. As she zoomed in on what I now thought of as my *perfect* teeth, I got another "Oh, wow!" from her, except this time in a different tone, a little less peppy, a little more question-y. She poked around with her little scraper stick, then she leaned back.

"So, I guess it has been a while, huh?" she finally said.

*How could she possibly know that?* I thought, while also trying not to laugh because of just how long it had actually been, and how quickly she figured it out, not to mention how bluntly she announced it.

"I mean, yeah it's been some time," I admitted.

"How long?" she asked.

I was caught off-guard, I mean, was she even allowed to ask that? I don't really know the doctor/patient rules when it comes to dentists, but isn't there like a confidentiality thing?

I panicked. I was suddenly embarrassed and with '90s love ballads still playing in the background I fully regressed back to middle school behavior and... I lied. I knew my answer had to be kinda long since it was "so obvious" but ten years was too long to admit to.

"Like... five-ish years?" I said.

"FIVE YEARS!?" She yelled practically loud enough for everyone out in the waiting room to hear.

*Now I know that definitely breaks confidentiality,* I thought to myself.

"Well, honey, no wonder," she said, "you have enough tartar in here to make a sauce!"

I don't even know how to spell the sound effect I made in response, something to the effect of "bluuugghhccck!" (Also, I apologize if I just made anyone uncomfortable. I also will never eat tartar sauce again.)

The most disturbing part of her proclamation was how *undisturbed* she seemed by what she just said. I think it's a top five, if not a top three, grossest comment I've ever received personally, and she said it as if she just noticed I had flowers printed on my shirt. *Honey, you have enough flowers on that shirt to make a bouquet!* I was waiting for her to follow up with, "Bless your heart," but seeing as we were not in the South, that sweet but shaming adage didn't seem to be a part of her vernacular. Backhanded compliments, though? She'd fit in well in the South.

After she scraped away at my teeth for an uncomfortably long time, she held up her little scraper stick to show me some of the tartar she'd removed, like she felt personally satisfied with the amount of her collection and needed to show someone for validation.

"I know you weren't scheduled for a *deep* cleaning," she said, "but I went ahead and did a little extra since it was so bad." She waved the little scraper stick around while smiling proudly. I was conflicted because she did do me a favor, but she was *not* paying me a compliment—not with that *I-got-all-your-tartar-sauce* smile. *Am I on the West Coast?* I asked myself, feeling an insane amount of deja vu.

I looked at the little clump of tartar tucked into the hook of the scraper stick. It looked like a little lamb, caught in the hook of the shepherd's rod, the loving shepherd who had rescued it from the crevice it had fallen into. *The Lord is my shepherd, I shall not want*, I thought to myself. I was equal amounts of amused and disgusted.

Eventually, the dentist came in and took a mold of my mouth for my new retainer.

"I heard you had quite the cleaning," he said, and I thought, *Okay, that for sure had to break confidentiality.* "Guess we won't have to wait five years till we see you next, huh?"

I laughed like a kid who got away with lying about doing their chores.

"Yeah, five years is waaaay too long!"

He asked what color I wanted my retainer to be, and I probably should have picked a more adult color, say something neutral, but I was still in my regressed state of '90s love ballads and lying to adults about my life choices, so I chose turquoise and purple.

"Do you want it to glow in the dark?" he asked, laughing.

"Oh my gosh, yes, you can do that!? That'd be awesome!"

It was at that moment that I realized he was being sarcastic.

"Oh, you really do?" he said more matter-of-factly. "Sure. We can do that."

He gave a final look over my teeth and the results of the hygienist's work.

"How old are you?" he asked.

I wasn't sure where this was going. I looked at his left hand and there was a ring. *Okay... married, so not a pickup line,* I thought. It's funny how as a kid someone can ask you how old you are and it's just a conversation piece that you will proudly answer. *Six!? Wow! What a big girl!* But, as an adult, if someone asks you how old you are, it's like, *hang on, who wants to know and how single are they!?*

"Uhhh, thirty-two," I said.

"Ohhh, okay. Wow. That explains it," he said.

I asked exactly what it explained.

"Well, you look so young."

With that remark I felt my confidence revving back up.

"Oh, thank you," I smiled.

"Yeah, when you walked in," he said, "I would have guessed you were 25."

My Miss America hands started reaching for my face again.

"Oh gosh," I said as I covered my mouth in disbelief, "Really?"

"Yeah, but looking at your teeth," he sighed, "your teeth are *definitely* in their thirties." *And he patted me on the shoulder!*

"From here on out, you're gonna need to take care of those old ladies, okay?"

I dropped my Miss America hands. *Did he just call my teeth old ladies because they were in their thirties!? Am I paying for this appointment? Where am I, really?*

Before leaving I was reminded to floss every night.

"Just floss the teeth you want to keep," the dentist said, like every other dentist before him.

I laughed to be nice, but I didn't think it was that funny. Nope, not funny, not after all their other comments. My mouth was exhausted, and my self-esteem was shot, I just wanted my Charlotte Hornets retainer so I could leave as soon as possible. My mom was not there to drive me home or get me ice cream or call me strong. It was just me, alone in my car, wishing I hadn't tried so hard to grow up so fast, wondering if I'd even grown up at all.

Off-again.

It would be another five years before I went back to the dentist. Not a *made-up* five years, an *actual* five years. And naturally, I went to a different dentist, if for no other reason than I had moved to another state.

I told this hygienist the *real* truth right off the bat.

"I know it's been forever and I'm incredibly embarrassed as to what you will find in my mouth, but just do whatever you have to do."

She X-rayed my mouth and then examined my teeth.

"You have a nice smile," she said, but I wasn't going to trust any compliments until the microscope-looking goggles came on. She was kind and didn't make any disturbing noises while looking at my teeth. She scraped here and there and then sat back.

"Here's the thing," she said, "you're going to need a deep cleaning, which is much more thorough and requires an additional appointment."

I thought back to the hygienist who had "done a little extra" when she so aggressively scraped away at my teeth even though I didn't pay for a deep cleaning. *Oh, that was actually really nice of her,* I thought.

When the dentist came in to affirm that I needed a deep cleaning, I asked if they could just scrape it all now. She said it was an entirely different appointment that involved numbing my gums. I asked her how necessary the appointment was, thereby setting myself up to receive what she had to say next.

"Well, the bacteria have crawled into your gums and built up condos."

"Oh, God," I said out loud. *Condos? That might be worse than the tartar sauce.*

"Yeah, they're trying to put down roots, but we're gonna need to evict them ASAP!" She said it like she was a Ghostbuster ready to blast some slime that I was not the cause of, but the victim of, and I felt oddly comforted. My bacteria-busting dentist then pulled her eye protectant glasses up and looked at me, frankly.

"It will be intense, but your mouth will be numb, so you'll be fine. Plus, you seem like a strong girl."

On-again!

# 6

# FLiPPiN' VANAGON

**PEOPLE ALWAYS ASK** how I met my husband, Josh, and more often than not, I give them the short version.

"We met at a friend's house."

I'll share some more stories in this book about us dating and getting engaged, but as far as how we met, I like the long version much better...

In January of 2018, right after New Year's, my sister, Betsy, and I took a trip to Florida to run in the Disney half-marathon. We had planned the trip about a year prior, knowing we'd both be home in South Carolina over the holidays, likely laying around on our mother's couch, in need of something motivating to get out of the house. "Let's start the year off being active," she said.

"Moving into the future!" I replied. Cheesy, but motivating.

We assumed January in Florida would be the perfect place to run a half marathon because it wouldn't be as cold as somewhere like Chicago or Boston or wherever else marathons take place. What we didn't account for was the freak winter that overtook the south that year... it even reached Florida, which was unheard of! Snow and ice... *in Florida!?* Not possible. Except it was. It was the weirdest winter in the Southeast's history, at least the weirdest one since I've been alive. Growing up, we didn't get snow in South Carolina. Okay, we actually did get snow once when I was a kid and everything shut down: schools, grocery stores, *church*, everything! Nobody knew what to do with it, let alone how to drive in it. On top of which, it was not some snow dump like you'd typically see on the news in the Midwest, this was a light dusting, a sprinkling, if you will, like powdered sugar on a donut. But for South Carolina—it was a statewide emergency—SHUT HER DOWN!

Since we hadn't seen snow in the south other than that one time when we were kids, Betsy and I were incredibly excited to possibly have a white Christmas. But the snowstorm was delayed, probably somewhere in the Midwest, and it didn't hit until nearly two weeks *after* Christmas—the day we were supposed to drive down to Florida. Once again, it wasn't so much a snow *storm* as it was a snow *dusting*, but without the proper equipment to clear the roads of every fallen flake, my mother was understandably worried about us driving. "I don't think you should drive the van out in this weather," she said. "We don't have the equipment for the roads and it's nasty out there." We assured her we'd be fine, scraped the ice off of the van windows, and began our journey south. We got about ten minutes down the road when I hit an ice patch. Although I grew up in the south, I had lived in Chicago for four years, so I know, once you hit an ice patch, you're done. You can't jerk the wheel, you can't slam on the brakes. You just have to make like Elsa and let it go.... LET IT GO!!! And I did, after a quick attempt to correct the wheel, it immediately felt like an over-correct and I knew there was nothing I could do. I let go of the wheel and yelled out "I'm sorry, Betsy, I'm so sorry!"

"It's okay," she yelled back. "It's okay."

And we braced ourselves for impact.

The van went off the road, hit the shoulder, and began to tumble. All I could hear was loud noises as we flipped over and over. It felt like ten minutes, but it was probably only ten seconds, and then all of a sudden, we stopped rolling, and it was dead silent. Everything was pitch black, but then I realized my eyes were still closed, my whole body still clinched. We opened our eyes and discovered each other each upside down, dangling from our seatbelts... the van had landed on its roof. I remember I was scared but I also felt kinda like an astronaut. I wanted to say, *Houston, we have a problem*, but it didn't feel like the right timing.

"Betsy, are you okay?" I asked.

And thankfully she replied, "Yeah. Are you okay?" I told her I was fine.

"Can you reach the camera?" I added.

She laughed at me for wanting the camera while we hung upside down from a car wreck, but once I realized we were both okay, my first thought was, *I need to document this!* Betsy, dangling from the ceiling, tried to reach my camera. It had flown up towards the front on the passenger's side, her fingertips were just barely able to swipe the side of the camera.

"It's okay," I said, and together we counted to three, unbuckled our seatbelts, and dropped to the floor—technically the ceiling.

We crawled out of the van, not a scratch on us, *or the van*, not a single dent, not even a broken window. The van was a 1984 Volkswagen Vanagon, the one I used to live in, as referenced in my first book (shameless plug). I had sold the van to my dad once I realized I was not cut out for van life, and so every time I went home to South Carolina, there she was waiting for me to drive her.

(Yes, the van was a she.) She was fun to drive, but apparently not on ice. She was tough, though. I still couldn't believe there wasn't a single scratch on her as I walked around and checked for damage because after all, she was upside down! The tow truck actually did more damage flipping her back over than when we crashed. Even the firefighters who showed up on the scene told us if we had been in a compact car, we probably would have been smushed (a technical term for badly hurt or maybe dead).

"It's the worst car you could have been driving on icy roads," one of the firefighters said. "But it's the best car you could have been in to flip over, because that thing wasn't going to bend *at all*."

And so, in a way, that old van protected us. And apparently our mother was right… about everything, but mostly about the roads. Question authority, but never question your mother.

As people were driving by the crash site, all they could see was a green VW bus upside down on the side of the road. Pictures and comments started popping up on Facebook. People wrote things like, "Oh, looks like Shaggy lost his way" and "Cheech and Chong went up in smoke!" While we were still standing at the crash site watching the tow truck flip the van back over, I randomly got a text from someone who asked if I had flipped my van… followed by pictures of it already posted on Facebook. *Really Y'all!?* I thought to myself. *You're going to post pictures of a crash on Facebook for a stupid punchline!?*

"Oh, my God," Betsy said. "We'd better call mom and tell her that we're okay, so that she doesn't see it online first."

We were fine. The van was fine, but we almost didn't go down to Florida because we'd gotten in this wreck and were a little shaken. I actually told Betsy I didn't think we should go, but she was adamant.

"I already paid for the hotel *and the race*," she said. "We're going!"

I kinda resented her determination, but we rented a car and what should have been a seven-hour drive turned into a thirteen-hour drive because "the roads were so bad" (i.e., there was no equipment to clean them up and the locals didn't know how to drive in snow, especially in Florida). We passed a number of other cars that had hit ice and slid off the road just as we had done the day before, so we drove even slower than most of Florida's population, aka the retirees of America. When we got to Florida, all the news reports repeated phrases like "coldest winter in Florida history." I'll never forget the "breaking news" that we heard as we slowly rolled into Florida.

"This just in… the iguanas are falling off the trees!"

That's how cold it was, the iguanas couldn't stick to the trees, which apparently was cause for statewide concern.

We made it to Disney World and picked up our race packets just before the orientation ended. We got to our hotel room by 9 p.m. and Betsy said she wanted to catch the first shuttle in the morning to the race line, which left at *3:30 a.m.*

"No way," I told her. "Absolutely not. I've done races before, we don't need to be on the first shuttle, you end up waiting around for two hours for the race to start. It's literally *freezing* and I'm not standing in the cold with a bunch of fallen iguanas."

But it was Betsy's first race, and she was a little gung-ho, as most first-timers are, so she insisted on catching the 3:30 a.m. shuttle.

"You should listen to me," I retorted, adding the always-helpful line, "you never listen to me."

This led to an all-out sister fight about every issue since childbirth. I think it was a mix of exhaustion, nerves, and a little post-family-holiday tension thrown in, but we just went at it, yelling at the tops of our lungs. I tried to shush her. "The neighbors will hear us!"

I whisper-yelled, but it was like we were an old married couple and she just yelled louder.

"I DON'T CARE ABOUT THE NEIGHBORS," she screamed.

I told her she was being selfish, which was *not* a good word choice on my part, especially because she had paid for the hotel *and* the rental car, which she very quickly reminded me, followed by "I'M LEAVING, GO FIND YOUR OWN WAY HOME!"

"YOU'RE CRAZY!" I screamed back.

And we just went at it until about 1 a.m.

After that we both finally calmed down and talked things through. I conceded and agreed to take the 3:30 a.m. shuttle, which meant we'd be going on about two hours of sleep. We caught the first morning shuttle and sure enough, we had to stand around and wait in thirty-seven-degree weather until the start time at 5:30 a.m. on the morning of January 6th, 2018. We huddled as close together as possible, not only with each other, but with other people from the shuttle—while, you know, trying not to be creepy.

After an hour and a half of waiting in the cold at the race sight, Betsy quietly said, "You were right."

I smirked a victory grin without rubbing it in her face.

"I know," I said quietly to myself, "Oh, I know."

The race started at 5:30 a.m. It was still dark and still very cold. I hadn't packed any winter running gear because I thought Florida would be warm, so I ran in my peacoat for the entire race. What Betsy and I didn't know was that it was a race for a cause; you were *supposed* to come to the race all layered up and shed your layers along the way, and all the clothes left along the course would be donated to charity. If we had known that we would have worn stuff we didn't want rather than wearing our favorite winter clothes on top of our summer running clothes.

I faced an inner battle as I ran: *Do I shed my coat for someone less fortunate than me?*

And then I felt the cold, and the answer was: *Noooooooo, I do not.*

Despite the challenging weather in Orlando that year, I will say, Disney World is the best place to do your first half marathon because just as you start to feel exhausted and think you can't take another step, you hit the Magic Kingdom and your inner child just bursts from within and comes to life.

I remember screaming, "OH MY GOSH, MY CHILDHOOD! THE MAGIC!"

Not only do you get a second wind of excitement, but you also get tears because you're wondering how your childhood went by so fast and now you're in your mid-thirties, completely winded by your half-jog. As a grown-up in Disney World, you start to get a little existential, but just as you spiral into the deep space ponderance of human existence, you get distracted by waving to Buzz Lightyear and you keep running. It's perfect for people who can't sit with their feelings.

After the race, we returned to our hotel room, and we could hear the next-door neighbors arguing through the wall. We figured they must have also done the marathon and were functioning on a similar level of exhaustion. Betsy said she would have asked them to be quiet but didn't think she had the right to since we had probably kept them up the night before. We turned on some white noise and passed out for the rest of the day. That night, we limped our way around the Magic Kingdom as we inhaled food from various buffet lines.

Betsy flew out the next day, but I had two more days before I would fly back to California, so I stayed at a friend's house. The house was actually called "The Magic Estate" because it was this big mansion in Orlando and about nine people rented it out along with my friend—including a dolphin trainer, an illusionist, a professional paintballer, a magician, and a few other "eclectic" types. I had long heard about The Magic Estate and *before the race* I was looking forward to staying there, but after the race I was just hoping none of her roommates would be home because I was not in the mood for people at all. I was exhausted—from the race the day before, from the fight the night before that, from the thirteen-hour car ride before that, from the wreck before all of it—I had nothing left. On top of that, my friend had recently shared with me that she had another friend staying there who was also about to fly back to California.

"So, we'll have a big group here tonight," she said. "It'll be fun!"

Despite the optimism in her voice, it did not sound like fun.

Betsy had a friend who lived in Florida, who gave her a ride to the airport, and then was kind enough to give me a ride out to The Magic Estate. On our way there, I told her everything I had heard about the house, and we were both excited to see what the place looked like. When we pulled up to this run-down mansion, all the lights were off, the yard was overgrown, and it was dark and gloomy looking.

"Wow, The Magic Estate doesn't look so magical!" she said.

We both laughed, but at this point, I was feeling skeptical.

"I don't know if I want to be here," I said. "I may text you tomorrow to come back and pick me up."

She told me she would check in on me the next day and assured me I would be welcome to stay with her if I wasn't "feeling it" at The Magic Estate.

I walked into the cold, dark house, slightly relieved that no one appeared to be home, but also thinking, like, *WHY IS THE HEAT*

*NOT ON!?!* Probably because it was Florida. Apparently, everyone at the house was taking a nap on a Sunday afternoon, hence why it looked so dark. While I knew a bunch of people lived there (who also had visitors staying there), I only knew two of them: my friend, Jena, and one of the magicians who I had met before through Jena. Jena was all excited to see me and she could tell I was tired, "Hey girl! How are you? What do you need? What would be most helpful for you right now!?"

I took a deep breath, "I need… to not talk to anyone, to not meet anybody new, or be asked about who I am or what's my life story. I've got nothing left to give."

I was physically exhausted from the race, and mentally and emotionally exhausted from everything that happened surrounding the race—the fight, the drive, the car wreck. I couldn't be "on" and I couldn't fake excitement about meeting new people, I was just done. I wanted to make it clear I had no interest in socializing because I figured as soon as nap time was over, the house would come alive with a bunch of thirty-something-year-olds, rested up and ready to chat.

At the very moment I finished saying, "I've got nothing left to give," one of the guys, the one who was also visiting from California, walked around the corner.

He looked at me and said "HEY! I'm Josh! Who are you?"

Before I could even answer, he proceeded to sit down, as if he were going to stay a while, and he asked me what my story was.

*Oh God,* I thought, but then, when I looked at him, I felt something, I didn't know what it was that I felt, it was just "something." *Huh,* I thought, realizing I was actually curious to talk to him. However, given what I had just told Jena about my emotional capacity, she quickly jumped to my rescue.

"JJ and I are going to have a girls' night tonight and go to a movie."

The three of us ended up chatting for a bit before Jena and I left for our movie. But as we left, I had to admit to myself that my plans to isolate had started to sound less appealing. Though I had just met this Josh guy, and we only exchanged a few words and, more importantly, a few movie quotes (movie quotes *are* my love language), I didn't want to leave his presence.

I wanted to skip girls' night.

I wanted to stay and talk to Josh.

But since we had just met, I knew I couldn't just blurt out: *I don't want to leave you.* As I've gotten older, I've learned it's better to be a little less creepy and a lot less clingy with guys... a real perk of dating in your thirties as opposed to dating in your teens and twenties.

When Jena and I returned from the movie, I was anxious to get back inside the house and talk to Josh. I tried not to analyze my thoughts, I just paid attention to them. I noticed how much I wanted to talk to Josh, especially given the fact that I had planned on talking to no one for the next two days.

And it happened. Josh and I ended up talking all night, well after everyone went to sleep, just talking. We talked about everything from where we grew up and where we went to college to all the things people say not to talk about at a dinner party or on a first date—which mostly entails therapy, religion, and a few minor political references. He talked about his work in photography and videography. I shared how I recently got into comedy and how often I wanted to quit. At one point I noticed the room getting brighter.

"Did someone turn a light on?" I asked.

Josh laughed, "No, that's the sun."

Jena made fun of me the next day and blatantly called me out.

"I like how you showed up here like 'I don't wanna talk to ANYBODY!'" And then you were little Miss Chatty Cathy until 6 a.m.!"

I gave her a kind glare. "Well, things change!"

My sister's friend texted me the next day to see if I had survived my night at The Magic Estate.

"Do you still want me to come pick you up?" she asked, "You're welcome to come stay at my place."

I texted back immediately.

"Nah, I'm good. The Magic Estate turned out to be magical after all!"

Josh and I spent one more day in Florida together before I had to fly back to San Diego.

He dropped me off at the airport and said, "Well, I'll see you soon, either in San Diego or Santa Barbara!" He was living in Santa Barbara at the time, which was about a four-hour drive from me.

"Sounds good to me!" I smiled.

I boarded my plane grinning from ear to ear, knowing something was different, but still hesitant to call him "the one." (I've prematurely called someone "the one" more times than I care to admit). As I started to analyze the last two days in my head, I found myself texting one of my friends...

> Either I just met "the one," or I just had some kind of weird Christian fling 😬
>
> 😂 What do you mean?
>
> Well, I met a guy, and we shared our hearts all night long... he really touched mine. 😂

He touched your heart? 🫤

Hahaha, yes, a lot of heart touching,
hence the weird Christian fling.

She laughed at me, and I laughed at myself. Lots of 😂🤣😂🤣

I think he likes me, but how do we ever
really know?

For the next two days, Josh and I texted each other non-stop. I told him I had a show coming up that weekend that I was kind of nervous about.

When the day of my show rolled around, Josh wished me luck and said he wanted to hear how it went. I showed up at the venue and waited for the show to start. It was a 'showcase' show, which meant a number of comedians would be performing one after another, each for around the same amount of time. I was slated for a middle spot, which is the sweet spot for a showcase show; the audience is warmed up and ready to keep laughing, but the show hasn't dragged on so long that the audience starts to get tired and anxious to leave. I performed well enough to feel good about, but nothing to write home about.

When I stepped off stage, Josh was there, standing in the back of the room. He had flown in to surprise me! It was the grandest romantic gesture I had ever been on the receiving end of, especially since we had only known each other a total of four days at that point. It felt like I was in a movie; like one of those sappy rom-coms I always yell at while watching because they're so "unrealistic."

I texted my friend that night.

He definitely likes me 😍

How do you know?

Because he's here! He flew across the
country just to surprise me! And I'm not
even creeped out!

😂 I think that means you like him too!

The year before Josh and I met, Betsy convinced me to sign up for a Disney race. She even made sure we signed up early so we could train all year for it, which we barely did. Then, we almost didn't even do the race because of the icy roads and the accident. Then, I almost didn't even get dropped off at The Magic Estate because my inner introvert was screaming at me to isolate myself and to not be around people. And then, I met Josh—the guy I would eventually marry. There were plans in place, a full year ahead of time, which led to us meeting (plans in place for him, too, because he had booked a wedding to shoot that same weekend). Josh and I both lived in California and yet we both *happened* to be in Florida at the same time, and we both knew the one same person whose house we both stayed in. Is that really just a coincidence?

I might not know how "fate" or "destiny" or "God's plan" works all the time, but I do know there is good out there for us. I also know there are "roadblocks" that can keep us from the good, sometimes they are our own selves keeping us from the goodness that is available to us. I admit, I get in my own way, *all the time*. If it wasn't for Betsy demanding to get her money's worth out of the race, I would not have been in Florida that weekend. Betsy's personality type played a much-needed role in helping me show up for my own life. It's bizarre to think about all the tiny little details, the miracle it really is to meet a person you like, and who likes you, *at the same time!* Half of the battle of relationships is just liking each other *at the same time*. My mind is still blown.

All that to say, you never know. You might be having an off day, off week, or off year, but who knows, not only what tomorrow is going to bring, but also what the next hour is going to bring? We all have those days where we wonder, *"What am I doing?"* And then you get that email or that phone call or that random invite to run a Disney race… whatever it is, it just shifts something in your spirit and changes your course.

I had planned to do this race for a year. I spent half a day driving there and a few hours running it. And then, in a matter of seconds, I went from "I don't want to talk to anybody!" to "Hi, I'm JJ… Let me tell you my story!"

You just never know.

# 7

# PREACHER'S KID

**I THINK I GOT MY PEOPLE-PLEASING GENE** from my dad. My mom certainly has her own amount of it, but there's something about the family my dad grew up in that shaped him for a lifetime of making sure people liked him. Despite not wanting to, my dad followed in his father's footsteps of going into ministry. Though it may seem like he was doing so to please my grandfather, my grandfather was never around to please. As a traveling music evangelist with the Billy Graham Association, Papa was off traveling the world for the sake of the ministry. So, if I had to guess, I would think my own dad going into ministry was more about making my grandmother happy, and her ability to give a "praise report" in her annual Christmas card about just how many of her children have gone into "the ministry." *Yea, and most of them are miserable*, I wish someone would have said to her.

My dad is much better about his people-pleasing now, not caring so much about the opinions of others, but then he's also had seventy-two years to get there. Life lessons really do take that long... sometimes they take a whole lifetime. I am both encouraged and depressed by that thought. I hope it doesn't take me thirty-four more years to care less about the thoughts of other people, most of whom don't actually care about me, but "better late than never," as my dad always says.

Growing up, my dad was the fun dad. He was the parent you went to when you wanted something—a new toy, a sleepover, a pizza for dinner instead of another casserole.

"Only if your mom is serving eggplant," my dad would say, "then I promise we can get a pizza!" He knew mom wasn't serving eggplant because he *hated* eggplant, so it was a nice way of making us think we *could* possibly get what we wanted without it ever actually happening. We'd beg our mom to make eggplant on occasion.

"We *love* eggplant," one of us would say, but she'd see right through it.

I would have to think about it harder, but in my instant memories of childhood I don't recall hearing my dad say "no" very often. "Let me think about it." "Let me talk to your mother." "Go ask your mother." These were the responses we heard without the finality of *no* in them. They left room for hope—hope that we just might be able to go *out* to eat for once, or order a Coke instead of water, and these careful responses meant that he never had to be the one to disappoint us.

In addition to no soda or junk food in the house, we might have been the last family in our entire hometown to get cable and internet, but not because we didn't *beg* with all our might. "We'll think about it," Dad would say, but I'm pretty sure he never thought about it, at least not until the two oldest of us (Bonnie and I) were out of the house and off to college.

I remember coming home from college one weekend and my younger sister Betsy, who was a senior in high school at the time, was watching something on MTV.

"How are you watching that?" I asked her. "Did you record it somewhere?"

She told me Mom and Dad had finally relented and gotten cable. When I confronted them about it, clearly disturbed that there were more than three channels available for viewing as soon as I *didn't* live at home anymore, Dad said, "Well, we thought about it, and it seemed like time."

"You thought about it *for ten years* and *now* it seems like time?"

"Well, we can't live in the dark ages forever!" Dad joked. "Plus, it gives you a reason to come home more often."

While Dad may have been the "Yes" man, he definitely *wasn't* the one you wanted to discipline you. In the early '90s, spankings were still very much a thing and a perfectly acceptable way to discipline your child. There were whispers of it *not* being the best idea to hit your child, but those whispers were so faint it would be another ten years or so before parents actually became divided on the issue. Because Mom was the one home with us more often, she was always the one who was on the receiving end of our bad behavior—our fights with each other, our temper tantrums. If there was ever a "problem child," it was probably me—the middle child. Though there are four of us Barrows children, I was/am smack dab in the middle. There's Bonnie, the oldest, a year later came me, and another year later came the twins—Bobby and Betsy. At one point, my mother had four kids under the age of four. She should win an award. Sibling alliances and rivalries would form and change and more often than not, I was the one stirring the pot, switching sides and calling names. Whenever things got too out of hand, my mother would sometimes take it upon herself to spank us, which, honestly, was always our preference.

Before each spanking, she would lay us over her lap, put her hand on our backside, and pray.

"Lord, help them to know this hurts me more than it hurts them."

As a kid I remember thinking, *how is that possible? What a crock of a prayer!* As an adult, although I don't currently have kids of my own, I do understand it doesn't feel good to have to be the disciplinarian, and so it hurts more *emotionally*. She could have clarified. So, to recap: Dad was who you went to when you wanted something, and *Mom* was who you wanted when you had to be disciplined.

If we were ever so bad that Mom felt we needed punishment beyond her ability, we'd hear: "Wait till your father comes home." Even for kids who have a really good, really loving father, those words are terrifying. Dad was kind, but he held nothing back when it came to a spanking, wanting us to really learn the lesson, perhaps so he wouldn't have to do it again, but with me, there was always an *again*.

There were two different styles in which Dad would approach the spanking. One style would begin when we were told to wait in our rooms. Then we would hear him snapping his belt straps together as he walked down the hall, the sound growing louder and louder the closer he got to our rooms. This style of punishment gave us time to think, time to employ an approach of our own, like stuffing a shirt down the back of our pants for padding and hoping he wouldn't notice. If it wasn't a belt, it was a switch, and oftentimes he'd have us go outside and pick our own switch, which I always thought was dumb because *of course I would look for the smallest switch possible.*

The biggest switch-selecting mistake I ever made was picking a long and incredibly thin switch. I assumed because it was so skinny it wouldn't hurt as much, not considering that its extreme length made it whip-like. Dad looked like Indiana Jones, testing it out in the air as he whipped it back and forth.

"Are you sure you want this one?" he asked.

Thinking *I* was duping *him* I told him I was sure, and to this day I will never forget the sting of that *damn* little switch. That was the first time I realized things could be small but mighty.

Dad's other style of punishment involved much less of a process, it was more rushed, often because we were trying to run from him. This style involved Dad grabbing whatever he could get his hands on, whatever the closest thing was that he could use to smack us on the backside as quickly as he could before we could get away. I was definitely a runner, which meant I definitely got the full gamut of options: a wooden spoon, a hanger, a shoe.

"We got a runner!" I'd hear my brother yell as I dashed through the halls, my siblings taking bets to see how long it would be before Dad could catch me.

In retrospect, there was no way I was getting out of the punishment and running only increased the number of spankings.

"Don't run!" my mother would say, but whether it was at a public pool or away from a punishment, as soon as I'd hear "Don't run," I'd immediately want to.

As a child, you don't have *all* the insights into your parents' lives, which is a good thing, until you grow up and realize your parents are just as human as you, and are, quite possibly, just as messed up as the people who keep asking your parents to pray for them. As a pastor, my dad had to be there all the time for everybody else, helping them with all of their "issues." And for some reason, people expect their pastor not only to have all the answers, but to fix everything for them. And I don't mean like fix their sink or their refrigerator, but to fix their marriage, their jobs, and their relationships with their kids—things that are much harder to fix than a sink or a refrigerator. For a long time, my dad obliged as best as he could, thinking that's what a pastor was supposed to do, "help his flock," meanwhile each year he was writing a resignation letter that he would never turn in.

I remember Sundays being a heavy day. We'd return home after church, much later than everyone else because in a Southern Baptist Church, the pastor has to stand out front after the service and greet everyone as they leave… Every. Single. Person. My siblings and I would wait—running around outside, getting into trouble, begging to go home and eat lunch. A few times people commented on our "behavior." When I think about it now, we were just four hungry and bored kids, watching our parents meet everyone else's weird need to shake the pastor's hand, so we did what any kid would do and ripped all the roses out of the church flower beds. Harmless. And if we felt we had waited too long, there was also the occasional stealing of the communion bread to satisfy our hunger, which was quite delicious because it was always purchased the morning of, so it was always soft, never stale.

"Thank you, Jesus," we'd say, not yet aware of what a pun was to be able to intend one.

By the time we finally got home for lunch, Dad would sit at the table, stare out the window and say, "I'm so glad that's over."

I used to think it can't be *that* hard to be a pastor—after all, you only work one day a week. I later realized that as a pastor, you work 24/7, you actually *never* stop working, because so long as a church is made up of people, there will always be something for you to do: a wedding, a funeral, a baptism, a relative in the hospital, a prayer request, a soccer game. Yes, I remember a family requesting that my dad come to their child's soccer game as a "representative of the community." All of this in addition to creating a totally original, never-before-heard take on scripture, the actual breath of God, which he needed to relay in layman's terms for a congregation of "dumb sheep," as Christians often call themselves, *week after week*. And giving a sermon is not like comedy where you get to perform the same set, week after week—giving a sermon means writing a completely new one-hour special, week after week... for twenty-seven years. My father, for all his faults and all his goodness, I'm surprised is as sane as he is.

My mother, as the pastor's wife, didn't have it any easier. It's not like she got to sit back and watch Dad do all the work. She was also on display, and so were her kids, which meant how we behaved reflected my parents' parenting ability, and, therefore, their ability to lead a church. Back then, a woman was not allowed to be a pastor, which is a shame considering what a gifted teacher my mother is. While my dad wanted a break, my mom wanted to speak, but that was *not* allowed. Her work involved remaining silent, politely smiling, and playing the part of the pastor's wife. She was the go-to role model for other mothers' questions about how to raise their kids.

"Do you let your kids do [this] or [that]?" she was often asked.

When we were really little (and there were four of us, remember), my mom, raising us with no help, would often find comic relief in putting on a tv show, usually Pee-wee's Playhouse with Pee-wee Herman. She laughed, we laughed, and for a moment she could breathe (plus Pee-wee hadn't been convicted of any sketchy misdemeanors yet).

My mom relayed this parenting strategy to a group of mothers who were sharing things they found helpful in parenting—the fact that she found great relief in watching Pee-wee Herman with her kids. You would have thought she had told them she was teaching her children the ways of the Taliban by how disgusted they were.

"How could you *possibly* watch that trash?" one of the mothers responded. "And *especially* to let your kids watch it! Bless their hearts."

There it was.

That statement, "Bless your heart," carries with it the sweet sting of a Southern woman riding sidesaddle on her high horse. In other words, she's not being nice to you; she's *shaming* you and being nice about it.

I remember being in high school when my mom got a phone call from another parent of a girl in the youth group. The mother was very disturbed that her daughter had asked her if she would buy her a *thong*.

"Absolutely not!" the mother said.

"Well, the Barrows girls wear them!" the daughter replied.

As soon as they got home from the mall, the distraught mother called my mother, the pastor's wife.

"Do you actually let your girls wear those things?" She asked with only the slightest bit of judgment in her voice.

"I don't *buy* thongs for my daughters," my mom said. "But what *they* buy and what *they* wear is up to them." She was basically saying "mind your business" without saying "mind your business." I was so proud of my mom, a Jersey girl transplant figuring out the way Southern women communicate, a mix of sweet and sour that leaves you questioning how they actually feel about you.

I didn't grow up in the limelight by any means, but I think for any preacher's kid, there's this unspoken expectation, mostly by the community, for you to look, think, and behave a certain way. Maybe that has changed over the years, and maybe struggles don't have to be as secretive as they used to be, but there is still a very weird expectation placed on a pastor and his family. I don't have an answer for it, nor do I have a suggestion on how to get people to "expect less," although that may be a more realistic mindset to have about most pastors: *Expect less and you might get more!*

I know people will argue that pastors have chosen to take on the role in which people expect more of them, but somehow the expectations have got to lessen! There is a day in and day out expectation for a pastor to teach, grow, lead, *and* entertain his congregation, addressing each and every individual need they have, all while being an exemplary husband *and* father. And we wonder *why* so many pastors crack? Seriously?

I'm not excusing poor behavior by men or women in leadership roles. They need to own their choices as much as we need to own ours, but we also need to check our expectations and the pressures we place on leaders, who are as human as we are, to be perfect role models.

My dad resigned from pastoring the same year I entered rehab. He said that seeing me get help gave him the strength to finally walk away. He had spent a lifetime helping and pleasing so many other people, whether or not he did it all well, I don't know, but I know he tried. When he left pastoring, I realized that it's never too late to start over, and that you are only as stuck for as long as you chose to be. His resignation also meant I wasn't a preacher's kid anymore, and while I struggled for a hot second with my identity (seeing as how my excuse for everything had always been: *Sorry, I'm a PK!*). Ultimately, I felt free. When my parents eventually divorced, there was no more pretending we were the perfect family. I no longer felt responsible for how people saw my dad or my mom. It was hard and freeing all at the same time.

While my parents, like many parents, have done some things right and some things wrong, I will always see them as *parents* who never stopped loving their children. In a world where that is not always the case—parents who love their children unconditionally—I have abundantly more than I could have hoped for in life. I may have gotten a people-pleasing tendency from my parents, but I'm also a runner, at least emotionally, meaning as soon as I recognize that tendency to please, I run. I'm working on communicating better when I do run, like actually saying *no* or *I can't* instead of just ghosting the asker, but at least it feels like progress—baby steps, if nothing else. And though baby steps are the longer, more scenic route through life, often causing you to arrive a little later than planned…

Better late than never.

# 8

## ¡CE, ¡CELAND BABY!

**IN APRIL OF 2018,** Josh and I went to Iceland for a photography workshop that Josh was helping lead. The first three days in Iceland were spent with the photography group, running all over the island as they snapped photos of beautiful landscapes. I mostly sat in the car to avoid freezing. Apparently, photographers will do whatever it takes to get the shot. I am not a photographer and therefore will always be more interested in staying warm than freezing out in the tundra for a photo. After the three days of the workshop, Josh and I and another couple, Montana and Nicole, took off to caravan around the country. Montana and Nicole were in a Sprinter van and Josh and I were in a camping car (a car with a pop-up tent attached to the roof). Josh and Montana had been good friends since their early twenties, and Montana's wife, Nicole, was one of the first people to make me feel welcome into Josh's group of friends.

Entering friend groups in the dating world can often be an awkward, if not unpleasant experience, but Montana and Nicole quickly became like family to me. Their teenage daughter, Hailey, had come along with them on the trip, so they all camped *inside* their Sprinter van. When Josh told me we would be sleeping not *inside* our car but in a tent *above* our car, I was not only prepared to be freezing, but I was also prepared to be angry at Josh for making us sleep *outside…* *in Iceland.* However, between my fifteen-degree Marmot sleeping bag, the canvas tent, and the memory foam mattress, I was actually quite warm and comfortable and therefore completely unable to say to Josh, "I told you so."

I was sick the first few days in Iceland and so I was tired and uncomfortable as I tried to recover. I was also dealing with some lingering stomach issues that kept me perpetually plugged up. By day two of driving around, I felt gross, and I really just wanted a shower and a bowel movement.

The most misleading thing about all the photos we had seen of Iceland were pictures of people lounging in steamy, natural hot springs. All the hot springs we visited were either A) too hot for human skin or B) more lukewarm than hot, so you were still freezing while sitting in the "hot spring." Multiple times I cussed the facade of Instagram for making hot springs look like an enjoyable experience. When the five of us stopped at a natural hot spring that (yet again) was much too hot to get in, we cooked dinner, and the girls played Uno while the guys talked about the workshop.

The next morning, we all drove over to a community swimming pool that also had clean showers and indoor plumbing. *Praise the Lord!* We were excited to find out there was an actual hot tub at the community pool, and so "hot tubbin'" became the first order of business. The locker rooms split off into men's and women's sides, which seemed normal enough. As I began to unpack my bag to change into my bathing suit, I noticed signs all over that roughly translated to "must shower naked before entering pool area." I thought it to be more of a suggestion than a rule, until the locker room attendant stopped me as I was walking right past the showers. She explained that showering first was required. She pointed to the communal shower where all the women were showering naked and told me I had to clean off before I could use the pool area. She was literally the guard in between me and the pool, and it was clearly her job to make sure I cleaned every crevice of my apparently dirty body so as not to pollute the pure Icelandic pool waters.

While it was clearly not a big deal for most of the girls and women there to shower naked in public... well, public in the privacy of the women's locker room, I have never been one to feel comfortable changing in front of people, let alone showering in front of them. While I've come an incredibly long way to learn to love the body I am in, at that point I hadn't yet taken the additional step of feeling so free in my body so as to prance around naked in a private but public locker room.

"Off!" ordered the locker room attendant as she pointed to the showers.

All I could do was laugh at the absurdity of it so as to avoid crying. She went back to her desk stationed strategically alongside the showers, between the lockers and the entrance to the pool area. I tried to come up with a way to sneak past her, but it was unavoidable.

"Okay," I said under my breath, "when in Iceland..." I walked to the showers, dropped my towel, and joined the other four naked people rinsing off under the wall of shower heads. *At least we're all naked*, I thought.

Two of the women hopped out and just as I began to realize that no one was even paying attention or cared that I was naked, I heard the other two people giggling. They were middle school-aged girls, and they began to practice their English.

"Naked," one said, and they both laughed. I turned around to see both of them looking at me.

"Naked," the other one said, directly to me, and they laughed and laughed.

I wasn't sure what I was supposed to do in that situation. Playing it cool would have been to laugh with them, but it would've been weird to laugh with them and point out that they were also naked, right? I mean, not only were they strangers, but they were also underage, and I was the only other one in the shower area.

The other option would have been to stand up for myself. I was having flashbacks of being laughed at for being underdeveloped—not only in middle school, but also in high school *and* in college. Without a curve to my name, I was often called Gumby or Surfboard or French Fry. Those names distanced me from ever really feeling like a woman. But these giggling little schoolgirls didn't know my background, nor did they understand that I was boldly exercising vulnerability and trying to walk in my power, naked. What was I going to do? Scold them for laughing? Make fun of them and ruin their self-esteem for the rest of their lives? No. When in doubt, just don't engage the underage, especially in a shower.

*Let 'em laugh, you'll live*, I told myself, and I got out of the shower as fast as I could. The "security guard," as I had come to call the locker room attendant, gave me a nod as if to indicate her approval that I was officially cleaned and cleared to use the pool. I don't know if it was the individualistic American in me or the independent woman in me who wanted to make her own choices, but I wanted to act like I had some power in the matter. I wanted to say something like, *I showered because I wanted to, not because you made me*, but in all actuality, I only showered because she made me.

I was relieved to finally get out of the locker room and into the outdoor pool area. I joined Josh in the hot tub and we both sighed in relief to feel warmth around our bodies while still sitting in the cold outside. Montana and Nicole joined us. I asked Nicole if she had met the "security guard." We both laughed at how odd different cultures can seem when you're traveling outside of your country and comfort zone, and how we in turn probably seem just as odd to the people in Iceland. As the view of the mountains and the cold air hovered above us, I quickly forgot about the whole showering thing. Josh took note of an ice tank in the pool area and decided to go test it out. He and Montana both got in, then Nicole. I debated it, but I really didn't want to be freezing cold again. Josh said it was mind over matter and I tried to think about my love for surfing and how much surfing is a mental sport, almost as much as it is a physical sport, especially in cold water, and especially when you get held under crashing waves.

Josh said I should do it, and I said I didn't like being "should-ed on." He corrected himself and said I *could* do it.

"Go, baby, go!" he added.

"I will, but not if I'm feeling peer-pressured," I said.

"It's not peer pressure, it's love pressure" Josh replied. We laughed and Nicole joked that "love pressure" didn't sound much better.

I finally decided to get in. After feeling so sick and lethargic, I wanted something to jolt me awake, to make me feel alive, to make me feel strong after feeling so weak and tired. As soon as I lifted myself out of the hot tub, I was already freezing from the cold Icelandic air. I shivered as I ran to the ice tank, a much taller, yet smaller tub that resembled a hot tub, except it was filled with freezing cold ice water.

I stepped in calmly, took a deep breath, and sank my entire body down into the icy water. I focused my mind. I started to feel a little lightheaded, so I tried to take deeper breaths. *Remain calm,* I breathed in. *Remain present,* I breathed out. I thought about how I always want to push myself more and actually believe that I really am stronger than I think. I can handle more than most people think, I just need to believe it to be true.

I sat in the tank longer than anyone else as Josh cheered me on from the hot tub. My thoughts turned back to surfing and how much I wanted to get back in the water. I could no longer blame cold water as an excuse for why I hadn't been surfing lately, especially since I surf with a wetsuit (they don't talk about how cold California waters are in the movies). I calmly got out of the ice tank and smiled as I ran back to the hot tub.

"See baby, I knew you could do it… like a boss!" Josh said as he kissed me.

While Josh had suggested I *could* get in the ice tank, no one had *made me* do it. I did it because I wanted to prove to myself I could, and I felt like I snatched a bit of my power back. My whole body tingled as I sank back into the hot tub.

After a while, we got out and went to the locker rooms to take showers, the second time around feeling a little less shocking than the first. I had braved a security guard, laughing schoolgirls, and an ice tank—I was more confident than my first encounter with community pool rules. After showering I was clean and happy, and felt more rested than the previous days. I got dressed, put on my favorite sweater and hat, and met up with everyone outside.

I noticed Josh looked particularly cute. He was wearing my favorite red flannel of his. Josh and Montana said we needed to get product shots that day for the companies who had let us take their products on the trip. Since the first part of the trip had been a photography workshop, a few companies had paid to have pictures taken of their products in Iceland. When I commented on how nice Josh looked, Josh said he wore the red flannel for the product photos. We headed out to find the right spot for the photo shoot. Montana, Nicole, and Hailey followed behind us. The winds were particularly high that day and as we started to go further up one of the mountains, the winds picked up even more. We were next to the ocean and when Josh pulled over to talk to Montana about what they should do, I stayed in the car and watched the boats rocking back and forth in the harbor.

Josh got back in the car and asked if I would mind if we turned around and went back a ways because the winds were too high. I didn't mind at all and sat content in the front seat, staring out the window. We drove back down through a canyon, and Josh stopped in a few different spots, none of which seemed just right, much like baby bear looking for the just right chair or the just right bowl of porridge in the story of Goldilocks... too hot, too cold, too windy, too cloudy. After so many stops in search of "just the right spot," I remember thinking, *these must be some really important products.* We finally picked a side road that was gated, but the gate was wide open. It led us through a field that had mountains on one side and the ocean on the other. Earlier that same day Josh had asked me which view I preferred: mountains or ocean? I had said both and it looked like he found exactly that.

We parked and just as they got all of their equipment unpacked, it hit me... I had to go to the bathroom. For the first time in the whole trip, my "regularity" kicked in and I knew I had to take advantage of the moment. My bowels were ready for movement, but I didn't want to make everyone pack up since they had just found "the perfect spot." I told Josh I needed to go so badly that I might run off in the hills.

"Yeah, we might be too far away from a bathroom," Josh said, "and I don't want you to miss the chance, go baby go!"

I ran up the hill and found a pile of rubble that I could hide behind. As I approached the rubble, there in the middle of it was a toilet! No other evidence of a home having ever been there, just a big pile of rocks and a toilet. It was like a sign from God. The hills were alive with the sound of me rejoicing, finally relieved to be going to the bathroom, *and* with the most epic bathroom view I'd ever seen—mountains and ocean.

At the exact same moment that I was taking care of business, a van drove up to where Josh had parked the car, and a man informed Josh that we were on a private road on private property.

"Everyone has to leave now," he said, in a loose English translation.

Unbeknownst to me, Josh pulled out a ring and told the man, "I'm about to propose to my girlfriend, she's up there about to come down."

The man's eyes widened; his jaw dropped. "OH! UH, OKAY," he said. "GOOD JOB, GOOD LUCK! Close gate when you are done!"

Excited to be relieved, I ran back down the hill, holding out the roll of toilet paper in one hand with it streaming behind me.

"I did it, I did it!" I yelled as I came running down, thinking the most glorious part of the trip had just happened. I had no idea what had taken place while I was gone, or what was about to happen when I reached the bottom of the hill.

When I got back to the car, Josh grabbed my hand and asked if we could go take a few pictures by the water since it was such an epic view. He took me out to the field near the water and he took my sunglasses off to fully capture our faces in the photos. We hugged and he started to pull something out of his pocket. I thought, *oh my God, it's happening,* until I realized it was an AirPods case. He opened the case to pull out two portable earphones. I laughed to myself and thought, *of course*. He wanted us to dance by the water, which I thought was sweet and romantic… and suspicious. But Josh is always romantic, and so it wasn't totally unlike him to do something really sweet and meaningful.

When it comes to proposals, Josh and I both knew we wanted to get married. We had often talked about our married life, much more than we had ever talked about a wedding, so timelines of when we would get married never really came up. I knew Josh would propose one day, I just didn't know when.

As he pulled out the AirPods, I had a moment where I thought, *this is it! It's happening!* but I told myself to let it go, as this could just be Josh being romantic and I didn't want to ruin the moment by being disappointed if it wasn't what I thought it was.

He put one earphone in my ear and one in his and then he hit play. It was our favorite song, the one we had danced to in my kitchen the first time he came to visit me in San Diego. I smiled and hugged him.

"You're so sweet, this reminds me of that first time we danced in my kitchen in San Diego."

"Me too, baby," he said as he spun me around and danced with me. He pulled me in close and held me and asked if I remembered what I was thinking that first time we danced in my kitchen. I wanted to say, *that's when I knew I wanted to marry you,* but I didn't want him to feel like I was trying to make it be *that* moment if it wasn't. We danced and the song ended. *Oh,* I thought, *this must just be Josh being Josh wanting to have a romantic moment in Iceland. It's still wonderful, but also if this isn't it, WHAT THE HECK!?* He took a deep breath and hit replay.

"Well," he said, "that moment is when I knew I wanted to marry you."

"Wait what?" I said snapping out of my thoughts.

Josh started to tear up. "You are my favorite person, and I love doing life with you, love all of your emotions, your high ones, your low ones, and your feisty ones… I love all of them. And I'm sorry if this process has taken longer than you would have liked… but it was never about me not being sure. You are the perfect woman for me, the best person I have ever met, and I want to spend every second, every hour, every day, every month, every year with you for the rest of our lives."

We both started crying, and I tried not to interrupt him by saying, *WAIT, ME TOO! YOU'RE MY FAVORITE PERSON TOO! THAT'S WHEN I KNEW TOO!*

Then he got down on one knee and opened a box with the most beautiful ring I had ever seen.

"Jennie Joy Barrows, I love you so much. Will you marry me?"

It happened so fast, and I was trying to register what was happening in my mind while trying to take it all in.

"YES, OF COURSE!" I blurted out. "I'M SO GLAD I WENT TO THE BATHROOM FIRST!"

We both laughed and cried. All I could say was "thank you," over and over again. He put the ring on my finger, and I jumped in his lap as I cried.

"I really am so glad I went to the bathroom first," I said through my tears. We laughed and hugged and kissed.

"I know, baby," he said, "I couldn't have planned it better." He picked me up to turn me around and there was Montana and Nicole and Hailey, photographing and videoing the whole thing. We held our hands up and yelled. They cheered as Josh picked me up and spun me around.

We took our time hugging and kissing in the field. I wanted to be present so I could fully remember it all... but it's still such a blur when something so wonderful happens.

# 9

# FELT BOARD JESUS

**WRITING COMEDY IS HARD.** Preparing for a comedy show is hard. All of it is hard ... not only trying to write new stuff and figure out when to work it into the routine, but also just getting your whole routine down, especially if the new stuff doesn't work, is hard. What a mix. I have also heard that I am apparently not supposed to say it's hard because that will create the self-fulfilling prophecy of it being hard and of me not being able to do it. So, I'm supposed to say things like: "I got this" or "I can do this" and "This isn't that hard." While I know that's true—I *can* do this, I also know that doesn't mean it's not hard.

Josh got home last night from Texas. He was there for a week, shooting a wedding, followed by a commercial shoot, followed by another wedding. He's got some kind of viral junk going on, so he slept upstairs last night. He doesn't want to make me sick, and I certainly don't want to get sick before my show this weekend, so though I've missed him, it only makes sense. I'm also currently dog-sitting for my brother's corgi, Benny Boy, and I can hear Benny groaning in the other room. He's either stretching or whining because he wants to get into the bathroom so he can eat my tampons. Dogs are so weird. One moment while I see if the dog needs to relieve himself.

(Insert elevator music interlude here.)

Okay, Benny did indeed need to relieve himself. I took him for a walk, which led me to a random thought (walks will do that to you, you get out to walk your dog or clear your head and suddenly you find yourself reminiscing about Blockbuster Video).

My random thought train started as follows… I miss video stores. We had an old school mom and pop video store in my hometown of Pawleys Island, South Carolina, and for the life of me I can't remember the name of it because we just always called it the video store. It was before video stores became a chain, so even Blockbuster Video was a thing of the future back then.

I used to love going to the video store to see which new posters and cutouts they had set up, would it be *Ghostbusters*? Or *Harry and The Hendersons*? *Harry and the Hendersons* was a childhood favorite of mine. Friday nights were reserved for television classics such as *Step by Step* and *Family Matters*, thanks to T.G.I.F., but almost every Saturday night we went to the video store to pick out a movie. Between four kids and two parents we had to agree on one movie, which was never easy, but all part of the ritual.

From Friday night into Saturday morning cartoons (which was also the only morning we were allowed to eat sugary cereal), leading up to Saturday night at the video store, weekends were sacred to this early '90s kid. To this day, I can't imagine a better way to spend a weekend. The only thing that put a screeching halt to all the fun was church.

Sunday morning would inevitably roll around, and we'd all have to get up, get dressed, and go to church. All the kids would tumble into church with their parents and then be dismissed to children's church. I remember near the end of sixth grade being so excited that soon I wouldn't be dismissed with the little kids to go to children's church. Soon, I'd be in seventh grade, and I'd get to stay in *big church*.

When that day came… I regretted it, terribly. *Oh my gosh, how can this be so boring? I'm supposed to just sit here the whole entire time?!* The following week I watched the kids get dismissed to children's church, my younger brother and sister still in that age category.

"I want to stay here," my sister whispered.

"No, you don't," I said. "We just sit here the whole time!"

"Come with us!" she said, but it was too late, the children's church teacher scooted her along. I could almost hear the dramatic music from one of our Saturday night movies building to a crescendo as my sister and I reached our hands toward each other in slow motion, a tear in each eye.

"Save yourself," I mouthed to her as she was pulled away.

My third Sunday in big church, I got a little too impatient with the pastor and without knowing he was actually nearing the end of his sermon, I held my fist up in the air and pointed to my wrist as if to say *hurry it up!* He did not like that one, especially since the pastor was my dad. Shortly after that incident, the church started a "Sunday School" for kids who were too old for children's church but too young to actually grasp the weight of big church, sort of like middle school for church.

I loved Sunday School. I loved the singing, the crafts, the felt board Jesus. Felt board Jesus was soft and cuddly and so relatable, minus the fact that he was made of felt. When you're a kid, you don't realize that your Sunday School teachers are only in their thirties (some only in their twenties), possibly also trying to navigate their faith and understanding of felt board Jesus. They just seemed like grown-ups who knew it all, even when you asked "why" in response to everything and they simply replied, "Because God loves us."

*But why does he love us if we're so bad?*

"Because he's God."

You get a lot of "because" responses and not a lot of "that's a great question" or "I don't actually know" responses in Sunday School. They seemed like valid responses, and back then, I never once thought to question them. *Oh, okay, "because." Cool.*

I remember one week we were going to perform in big church, and someone had the bright idea that our Sunday School class should *stay after the performance* and partake in big church all together, not just sing and then be dismissed, but sing and then go take our seats *for the rest of big church.* I very carefully plotted who I would sit next to, picking the girl with the fluffiest Sunday dress (we still dressed up for church back then). I promptly fell asleep on her lap, my head cushioned by her skirt fluff, a string of drool dangling from the corner of my mouth, threatening to leave a slime trail on her dress if she were to move a muscle.

Time is also a bizarre concept as a kid, you have no baseline, no framework. A half-an-hour sermon can feel like two days, and Monday mornings meant you had an eternity of school days to endure before your next epic weekend of TV, movies, and sugary cereal returned. And when the weekend finally did arrive, it was over just like that, only to wake up Sunday morning with a sugar hangover while getting all dressed up to face felt board Jesus.

I look back on it all now and wonder how it went by so fast. I know everyone has their own version of "the good ol' days," some more questionable than others, but those were mine—video stores, '90s television, sugary cereal, and felt board Jesus. I had no idea those were my good ol' days when I was living in them. I don't think many people do realize they are living in their good ol' days, perhaps even right now.

If I'm honest, my high school and college years didn't look too incredibly different from my childhood. Replace a T.G.I.F. party with an actual party, the video store with the movie theater, a sugar hangover with an actual hangover, and felt board Jesus with a cute youth pastor who incentivized kids to come to youth group with donuts, and BOOM, yet another decade of good ol' days, complete with the Spice Girls and a Delia's catalog.

Still, I don't think some of my most pressing questions were ever answered, perhaps because I never asked them out loud. I was afraid of how I'd be seen if I had questions about this God who loved us so much, yet according to the Bible metaphor we were just dumb, dirty sheep.

"He leaves the ninety-nine sheep to go get the one."

*Yeah, but why?*

"Because He loves us."

*But why?*

"Because."

I'd get so confused.

One week the message was: We're created in God's image, we're children of the King!

The next week the message was: We're wicked, we're sinful, we're dumb, dirty sheep.

I resonated more with being a dumb, dirty sheep than a daughter of the king. I was definitely a late bloomer, in many ways, I still am, and I wasn't exactly the brightest crayon in the box. I was average, but nothing to write home about. I was neither exceedingly popular or ridiculously good-looking, nor was I a complete ugly duckling who had to develop grit and master another skillset like math or sports to try to impress people. I was called names but not so badly that it kept me from showing up. I mostly just tried to ignore name-calling so as to not draw more attention to the names. I was simply somewhere in the middle, lost in a sea of mediocrity, unaware that "mediocrity" was even a word at that time, and just hoping that while life wasn't "bad" maybe one day it would be better.

But what do you do with kids in the middle? Kids who aren't functioning in either extreme of the "social" food chain; kids who are neither at the top in need of humility, nor at the bottom in need of encouragement? Kids who seem just fine, and so really, there is no need to address anything, no extra attention required, just a sigh of relief that they aren't too difficult or too emotionally high maintenance. I felt capable of more, but *more* wasn't what was expected of me. I was seemingly just an average kid, somewhere in the middle of life's extremes. I don't know what I wanted, I just know I wanted something… more.

I *was* that kid, and I still don't know what to do with the kids in the middle, but I know they matter too—the easy ones, the agreeable ones, the ones that everyone is so thankful for. The other day even my dentist commented.

"You are the easiest patient I've ever had."

For a brief moment, I felt like the most talented person in the room. One could look at my high school record and think I did it all—I was homecoming queen, class salutatorian (which I had to google how to spell), and editor of the yearbook. I don't want to minimize these accomplishments, but none of these do I boast about too loudly because if you were to dig deeper, you'd learn there were only six students in my graduating class at a small private school founded by the parent of a kid who couldn't graduate public school. So yes, I can thrive as a big fish in a small pond. After all, being a senior in a ninth-grade math class, I still managed to come out second. But any expansion in the pond real estate and I'd probably rather find the nearest dangling fishhook and go out on a high note. Second of six is my version of a gold medal. *Remember me in my glory*, I'd say as I swam towards the shiny silver glimmer.

On the one hand, even still, I really am "fine." I am neither the best at what I do nor am I the worst at what I do. I have a home, a husband, an occasional dog-sitting job, and I am grateful for the life I have, especially if I play the comparison card. Someone else always has it worse, so who am I to complain... about anything. I am fine.

And on the other hand, sometimes I don't feel "fine." I certainly don't feel like I have it all together, and I still have so many questions about how life works. Questions I didn't want to take up space by asking because I liked that people found me "easy" and "agreeable," but I still want to know why—in regard to so many things. Some "whys" are personal, and some are bigger life pictures. *Why, God? Just, why?*

I suppose the difference is, not only am I no longer afraid to ask the question, but I also don't feel like I need the answer. I just need to feel the freedom to keep asking. Without debate, without judgement, without "because." It's in the wrestling that I find the most peace; a peace without answers, and a comfort to be myself, to be confused with a God who, for some reason, always loves me. While I know people will push back on this, especially church people, I still don't resonate with being a daughter of the King, nor do I resonate with being a dumb, dirty, sheep. I don't think God sees me or expects me to behave as either of those. I think I'm just me, in a complicated relationship with an Omnipotent Being, who despite many of humanity's failed attempts to represent Him, and the rest of humanity's refusal to acknowledge Him, I just can't help but love Him. Some days I have no idea why, it's not the moving stories or the image of the cross or the repetitive worship songs. It's not even His soft, felty hands, it's simply just…

Because.

# 10

# AUNT FLO

**ENGAGED LIFE, GOTTA LOVE IT, RIGHT?** I don't know, do ya? It's a lot… meeting everybody, coordinating times to hang out with people and be intentional by calling families, staying in touch with friends, and making sure everyone feels important to you as a couple. All of that plus planning a wedding and hearing everyone's opinion on who should be on the guest list. Phew! I don't know if this is everyone's engagement experience, but it was mine. Probably because I was about to marry an enthusiastic extrovert who loved to include everybody in everything, especially a big life event like getting engaged. I knew Josh was extroverted from the moment I met him, but when we got engaged, it was like the floodgates opened and all of a sudden people came out of the woodwork who we needed to get together with. Many of them were wonderful, but as an introvert, it was exhausting. I was in a constant state of needing a nap. I'm sure marriage will be much easier, right? (Insert sarcastic smile here).

If there's one thing I do know, it's that marriage does *not* make things "easier." I'm not unsure about getting married, not hesitant in the slightest, I'm just frustrated by the expectations placed on us to make sure everyone else feels so involved in our life and process. Or maybe everyone else is just living their own life, and this is me overthinking it all because it's actually the extrovert I fell in love with who's been making all the plans to hang out with everybody.

Josh had friends in town this past weekend, so naturally they wanted to hang out. I think if we're all being honest, they wanted to hang out with Josh, but because I now come with Josh as a package deal, they *have* to hang out with me, too—other than that, I'm not sure how much they'd want to. I feel that way about a lot of Josh's friends, I don't think they actually care to know *me*, but of course I can't say that. I have to smile and be the worthy, perfect fit for Josh (or so I overthink, thanks to my own insecurities that rear their ugly heads no matter how many therapy sessions I've paid for).

Josh told me his friends wanted to grab lunch with us over the weekend, so he picked me up around noon-thirty to go to a restaurant to meet his two friends and their one small child. At least that's what I thought we were doing. On the way to meet them, I saw a text come through on Josh's phone, and Josh responded with "almost to your house!"

I asked if we were going to someone's house instead of a restaurant, and Josh filled me in (for the first time) that the couple we were going to meet for lunch was staying with some *other* friends and we were *all* going to hang out at their house, and we would "eventually" get lunch together.

I could feel myself getting irritated. Maybe because I was preoccupied that morning and didn't eat breakfast, and by the time I realized I didn't eat it was close to lunch and I knew we were *going to lunch* so I still didn't eat anything. By the time Josh picked me up I was *starving*, only to find out we were hanging out with *more* people than I had anticipated and not exactly eating lunch right away. So, I was, you know, frustrated. My tone expressed my frustration as I asked a few clarifying questions. Josh didn't really know all the answers because he said we were all going to meet up and then decide. He couldn't understand why that was so frustrating to me. To him, it was as simple as people getting together and hanging out, then figuring out when to eat, eventually.

But there were two levels of discomfort for me in his plan: people I *didn't know*, and not knowing when I would eat. I'm what you call "a grazer." I eat small meals or snacks every two hours and when I don't eat, or at least know when I will eat next, I go *insane*. Some might call this 'hangry', the hungry/angry combination, but honestly, I get something worse than hangry, I get *insangry*. I was already well on my way to *insangry* when Josh told me we would now be hanging out with a total of five adults and three children. In addition to the two of us.

The math was simple. That was waaaaay more than the two adults and one baby I was originally prepared for. Therein lay my third discomfort: *additional people I was not mentally prepared for.* As an introvert, I not only need a certain amount of time to charge up for social interactions, but I also need to be mentally prepared for whatever type of social interaction I am walking into. As simple as it may be for some, being blindsided on the way to a social inter-action with the information that there are additional people at said interaction— well, that's the quickest way to give an introvert an anxiety attack.

This is a huge difference between Josh's personality and mine. There is no right or wrong, just a difference, and hence why we often try to communicate before we assume. While I was feeling frus-trated, I could not *assume* Josh had intentionally held information from me about additional people, he just didn't think about it being an issue. Josh will always be a "the more the merrier" kind of guy, which is a great quality, people *love* the guy who includes everybody, I do too. But some of us are just not wired like that—always wanting to include everybody in on everything— and it's okay, we're all wired differently.

While I used to beat myself up for not being more "inclusive" in regard to inviting lots of people into my personal space, Josh has actually encouraged me to be myself and acknowledge my needs— most of which include a little more alone time than Josh sometimes prefers. I prefer quality over quantity. A big party with surface-level, small-talk conversations on repeat with multiple different people? No, thank you. I can charge up and rally to "make the rounds" as they say, but my first preference will always be an evening with Josh, or a few close friends, or quite simply, me.

Five adults might sound like a few close friends to some, but when compared to my initial expectation of getting to know *two* people, hanging out with five people *I don't know* sounds like a big party. Throw three kids in there and, in the words of D.J. Tanner, *Oh my Lanta! No, thank you.*

While I know this is not going to be a popular opinion, people with young kids are difficult for me to be around at this stage in my life. Especially young parents of young kids who, understandably so, think their kids are the whole world, and therefore believe said kids should be the whole world to everyone else. I have no problem with parents thinking the world of their kids; I have a problem with parents expecting everyone else within a ten-mile radius to *also* think the world of their kids, or even be mildly impressed by them. Some people are just not kid people and that needs to be okay.

That might sound like I hate kids, and I genuinely don't hate them; I just hate when people expect me to get excited about *their* kids and gush over them as if I had the same kind of bond with them. At the risk of being horribly judged... I don't care. And when it comes to babies, I don't think babies are *that* cute. I know, I said it and I'll probably regret it one day, but from where I sit right now, I do not want to see pictures of babies or hold babies or pretend to be impressed by babies—they are just as much a stranger to me as some guy at the bus stop. I do think baby shoes are cute... Outside of that, it's whatever.

Now when it comes to baby pictures of grown people I know, like going to a friend's house and seeing old family photos on the wall or going to Josh's parents' house and seeing his baby pictures in an album, oh good Lord, I could never get enough of that. I like looking for resemblances of the adult person I know in their baby pictures. I even like looking at celebrity baby pictures because I feel like I know them and it's fun to see them before they grew up into the version of themselves that I think I know.

So, I suppose this may come as no surprise, but I have never really wanted kids. I never once thought, *I can't wait to be a mom!* It was often assumed, at least in the culture I grew up in, that I would grow up, get married, have kids. Very much in that order. I thought I was 'supposed' to have kids more than I thought I "wanted" kids. But then I met Josh and for the first time in my life, I thought *I want to have his kids.* Josh changed my perspective on kids, not because of anything he said, but simply because of who he is. I not only want there to be more of Josh in the world, I also want to raise those little Joshes with him. And so yes, my perspective has changed a bit in the last few years—believe it or not, I have softened towards kids—but I still have a thirty-five-year history of not wanting kids that often rears its head when someone expects me to gush over their stranger baby.

All of that to say, this little introvert thought she was going to lunch with two adults and one stranger baby, but she ended up at someone's home with five adults and three stranger babies—technically three and a half; another one was on the way—and that required a different mindset that I didn't have time to prepare for since we were already "almost" there! But it was too late to jump out of the car, so Josh and I got into a heated discussion about it, resolved it, then went inside to hugs and smiles and acted like nothing ever happened.

By now, my stomach was screaming, begging for snacks of any kind as we wound our way through all the formalities of meeting each other and gushing over stranger babies. I was so *insangry* I was considering stealing the baby food directly from one of the stranger babies. Soggy, puréed carrot mush had never looked so appealing. Finally, everyone decided we should walk to a nearby restaurant for lunch. It would have been a two-minute drive, but with all the strollers and car seats to pack and unpack, it was decided we might as well go for a nice little ten-minute walk, right? After arriving, ordering, eating and chatting, I started to feel funny. Like something was about to happen… in the lady department. I went to the bathroom only to be unfortunately correct—*Aunt Flo had come to town*. For those unfamiliar with that phrase: it was *Shark Week*. For those unfamiliar with that term: "This week, starring Daniel Day Lewis, *There Will Be Blood!*"

And there was. A lot of it. A day one, full-commitment amount. On top of that, there was no toilet paper in my stall.

"You have *got* to be kidding me," I whispered. "Hello?" I said kind of quietly to gauge the atmosphere. "Anybody in here?" I asked, realizing there was no way to ask that question (in a public restroom) in a way that didn't sound creepy.

When nobody answered, I ran out of my stall with my pants half down to grab paper towels from the wall dispenser, only to find that *the paper towels were out!* I stood there, panicked, with my pants half down when I heard the shuffle of the bathroom door about to be pushed open. I bolted into the handicap stall just in time before another woman came in.

While I was relieved to find toilet paper in the handicap stall, I wasn't exactly in the clear. Since I didn't know Aunt Flo would be visiting that day, I clearly didn't have any tampons. And not only did I not have any tampons, I also was not wearing any underwear. It's neither here nor there, but I knew I was feeling off that morning and I should have known it was my hormones, but I had been at home lounging around in my sweatpants (free as a bird) before Josh came to pick me up for lunch, and once he got there everything happened so fast that I didn't have time to change. I left the house as is… and it is what it is. It would have been fine if not for Daniel Day Lewis and his feature film coming to town. (Bad joke? Don't get it? *There Will Be Blood.* Okay, moving on). What was I supposed to do?

I tried to secure some toilet paper down there and figured worst-case scenario, I might just look a little funny trying to hold the toilet paper in place while walking—but as soon as I left the bathroom and walked back out to the table, the toilet paper began to slide down my leg. Sweatpants are *not* what you want to be wearing if you have to hold toilet paper in down there, but sweatpants *are* what you want to be wearing if you have wads of toilet paper falling down your pant leg—no one can tell.

I told Josh I needed to leave early to get ready for work and they could all stay, but I was going to go ahead and walk back to the car.

I pulled one pant leg up to tighten the bottom so nothing would fall out. I walked the ten minutes back to the car on the sidewalk of a busy street—one pant leg hiked up my shin, shuffling along with a little hitch in my step, trying to keep the toilet paper from going anywhere other than all the way down my leg. Passersby might have wondered why this little white girl was walking like she had swagger, which I didn't, I just had wads of toilet paper gathering at the bottom of one side of my sweatpants.

I got to the car just in time to cry out of the public's eye. I drove to Target and walked awkwardly through the aisles and grabbed my supplies. My only solace was the self-checkout. I'm so tired of boys ringing me up for tampons—boys, men, no matter what phase of life they are in, they act weird, especially when tampons are the only thing you're buying. Don't get me wrong, I can endure it, but I didn't feel like having that interaction when I was already feeling a little weak, a little vulnerable, a little like toilet paper was clogging up my pant leg.

I went to the self-checkout and let out a sigh of relief to purchase my tampons in private, except in my state of relief, I accidentally swiped the box twice. My kiosk light started flashing the PLEASE WAIT FOR ATTENDANT! signal. *Oh God, no, that's WHY I wanted self-checkout, to avoid the attendant. Dear God, please be a woman, please be a woman.* And then an eager young man with a "ready to help" smile jogged over to me. *Of course.*

"Okay, did you want to put something back?"

"No, I just accidentally swiped it twice."

"Okay I can fix that, let's see, you just wanted the one…. oh, box of… okay, yeah already in the bag. Great. Let me just…" and he kept fumbling over his words as he tried to navigate putting all his codes into the kiosk.

I just stood there silently. There was no need to make small talk at that point, and honestly when a guy starts to act awkward about it, I like to feed into it, like I might just rip him a new one if he looks at me wrong. I'm not saying it's right, but sometimes it's kind of fun to instill the fear of a bloated woman in a young man.

I went home and dealt with what I needed to deal with, put on a different pair of sweatpants, laid in bed and cried until I passed out before having to get up for work.

It was a great day. It was a mess. It was life.

# 11

## ENGAGED AND CONFUSED

**WELL, TIME MARCHES ON.** I've heard it a million times before. I'm not at all surprised that time moves so quickly because I know that it does, and yet I still find myself shocked that so much time has gone by. I'm especially shocked because I feel like I haven't moved forward in life as much I would have liked.

But this isn't about being hard on myself for what I haven't done. This is about moving forward, even if baby step by baby step. There may have been times when the steps should have been bigger and covered more distance, but here I am where I am. I can't go back and change the journey that brought me here, but I can do a few things differently from here on out, like trying to be a little more intentional even in the smallest of places, hoping the small things add up to bigger overall changes.

At the time of this writing, I am engaged to an amazing man: Lord Joshua Daniel Newton. I call him Lord because, well, I fell for an Instagram ad and bought him a square foot of land in Scotland, thereby legally declaring him a landowner and, henceforth, a Lord.

They even mailed him a certificate, so his Lordship is legit! Once we are married, I will officially be a Lady. Look at that, me... a Lady! So, I have a fun relationship with a fun guy (not to be confused with a fungi—sorry, not sorry), and so, I am, as the geriatric millennials say, "#blessed." It's not to say I haven't had my struggles in the relationship department, I most certainly have, and I'm no spring chicken who met her prince charming at a young age and had the big blowout wedding with twenty-seven of her best friends as her bridesmaids—I mean, really, how does one decide!?

I met Josh when I was thirty-five years old, a lot later than when I started planning my wedding at fourteen. If someone had told my fourteen-year-old self that I'd have to wait *twenty-one more years* before I would say "I do," I would have stopped praying things like "Thy will be done," and just begged God not to wait until I was a dinosaur before introducing me to "the one." Josh and I got engaged less than a month ago, and while I feel pretty good for a dinosaur, I am already over the long engagement process while planning a big wedding. Ain't nobody got time for that—not when you're in your mid-thirties and the numbers only go up from there while "the one" is standing right in front of you. I don't know about you, but I am *not* feelin' twenty-two. I'm feelin' tired and ready to skip the big wedding. Sure, time goes by fast, but not when you're newly engaged at thirty-five; time drags on... and weddings start to look like ridiculous, overblown parties meant for everyone else *but* the couple getting married.

The thirties to me are a very awkward age, I often refer to them as "adult puberty." In your thirties, you aren't *that old*, I know, but you aren't *that young* either. Teenagers start calling you ma'am, to which I often wonder, *are you being rude or polite?* I can't tell. Thirty is when the reality of needing to figure out my life set in, sometimes from other people asking me "When are you going to get serious?"—but mostly from myself as I've still struggled to figure out who I'm supposed to be and what I'm supposed to be doing. Perhaps I worry about it way too much, perhaps more than the average person (after all, it's part of my personality type).

For anyone who's familiar with the Enneagram, a personality assessment categorized by nine different numbers, I am a four—The Individualist or The Romantic—and being a four is exhausting. For those who aren't familiar with it, the Enneagram (in my opinion) is a useful tool to help people understand themselves and other people as well. The Enneagram focuses on people's core motivations and fears, and it helps explain the "why" behind our thoughts and actions. It also helps clarify why we communicate the way we do. While there are clearly more than nine different types of people, the nine numbers help describe groups of personality types that have a similar driving force, and within those groups lay the variety of human personalities. It's a lot, but trust me, it's worth the work to "know thyself" and to better understand others.

In some ways, I am most proud to be a four—the individualistic romantic who is usually artistic and creative and strives not only to be unique, but also authentic. We fours are often made fun of for wanting to be different from everyone else so badly—to be not just a snowflake, but a special snowflake. And sure, that's valid, but I think it comes from a deep desire for authenticity, and when you live in a pretty fake world thanks to things like plastic surgery, social media filters, and surface level friendships, being a four means yes indeed, you *want* to be different from all that.

Fours are big feelers. According to some studies they can often be diagnosed as bi-polar (some accurately, some not), but really, they are constantly absorbing the environment around them, and since environments change, so do their emotions. Fours are deep thinkers too, and we get so caught up in our own heads, tangled in our own thoughts as we try to figure out everything around us (as well as ourselves), that our inner world can easily become our external reality, even when it isn't. So, yea, I think being a four is cool, but also, sometimes I don't. I think it's cool to be a four when I want to paint or write or be creative in any way. I think it's not so cool to be a four when I have to walk into a crowded department store and feel like I'm about to have a panic attack from the conflicting emotions that I feel emanating from all the people around me. (Also, I'm a four—why am I in a department store!?)

Sometimes I don't want to be a four because I'm so tired of *feeling* everything and the disconnect that often creates with most people, especially those who aren't also a four. Depending on when you meet me, I could be the happiest person in the world, or I could be the saddest person in the world. I can't be "put into a box," but because I'm a four, I like it that way (and I like to fool myself into thinking I'm not in a box). Note: I am fully aware that because there's officially a "personality type" to describe me, it does mean that there *are* others like me. When I first read my personality type I cried because I felt known, and then I got mad because I was clumped into a category with other people "just like me." The four in me struggles with being a four simply because there are other fours, which is a very four thing to say.

And so as a four in her mid-thirties, struggling to find her place in the world, frustrated that she's not only still struggling, but struggling when she "should" just learn to be at peace and content (*and how has she not learned this by now!?*), wondering how long will it take before she's either okay where she's at in life, or at least okay with herself regardless of where she's at in life? In short, she's conflicted. Okay, I am... I'm conflicted.

I've loved getting to know and fall in love with Josh. It's fun and exciting and romantic and all the good things anyone could want in a relationship. And it's also deep and heavy and hard as two different people from two different walks of life come together and try to figure out how to make life work as a team—a team that is still trying to get to know each other and understand each other, learning that differences are okay and personality types might be a crucial tool in understanding those differences.

As for the Enneagram, Josh is a seven, The Enthusiast or The Adventurer, and boy is he ever. He's always adventuring somewhere, usually optimistic, and perpetually hopeful. He looks for the best in people and knows how to bring out the good in them no matter how grim something or someone may seem. While he's definitely no four, he is the most unique human I have ever met, and that's not just the rose-colored glasses talking. Sevens, all fun and adventure, and always the person everyone wants to be around, often times have trouble dealing with the tougher stuff in life, or at the very least, being aware of the tough stuff. Their endless adventures in search of the next best thing can often be a cover, shielding them from pain or boredom or bad news—the reality that life isn't always as good as they want it to be.

I dated another seven once, when I was in not so much of a good place (neither was he), and an unhealthy four with an unhealthy seven is a disaster waiting to happen. The four needs to process everything, and in their unhealthy state are usually in a pretty dark place. The seven needs to get to the next best thing, the next distraction, not the next reminder that life is hard. The seven usually tells the four to look on the bright side and the four feels misunderstood and overlooked, so the four internalizes, going deeper into the self, while the seven externalizes and runs further away, chasing whatever next is out there to distract them from their problems. Neither four nor seven are completely right or completely wrong, they're just different from each other and therefore unable to connect or find compromise given their misunderstandings of each other's wiring.

While I might have been timid about dating another seven when I first met Josh, I know people are more than just numbers... plus I am healthier than I used to be, and Josh is definitely a healthy seven, the healthiest seven I've ever met. While he may not be the first to notice the tough stuff, he's also not afraid to face it when he needs to. We've had to work on things, learn ways to communicate so that the other person hears it, ways to stay true to ourselves while also being kind to the other.

Josh helps me enjoy life more, to not get so stuck in my head or caught up in my self-doubt. I laugh harder and smile bigger because of Josh. I want to live more life and take more risks. I want to be not so afraid to be me. Like I said, he's good at pulling the good out of people. I help Josh not just see the tougher stuff, but navigate through it, which allows him to experience a fuller type of joy, because he isn't avoiding pain, on the run in fear of it catching up with him. He is at peace with where he is, celebrating all that life has to offer and finding new adventures in the ordinary, everyday stuff.

Josh knows when it's time to go out and live it up, I know when it's time to go home and take a nap. I know it makes him sound like the fun one and maybe he is and I'm learning to be okay with that, but I think we make a good team, and the love I have for him is so full.

On the one hand, I feel incredibly blessed, and I sincerely cannot wait to marry my Lord (not to be confused with The Lord).

Time seems to be dragging until we actually tie the knot. And on the other hand, when I look at my life and how far I've come—vocationally speaking—I can't help but be slightly disappointed that I'm not where I wanted to be by now. Time flew by, and I wish it hadn't.

It's odd living in this tension of complete excitement and slight disappointment. I am overjoyed to share my life with someone, and at the same time, fearful of completely losing myself in the process. How do I join in on living life *with* someone without disappearing into his? How do I make sacrifices and compromises, as all relationships that involve two different people who love each other require, and still stand firm in what I feel called to do as an individual, a creator, a woman, a human with my own voice and something to say—even if that something is *I don't know and that's okay.*

I feel happy and fragile at the same time. Happy to be where I am, and fragile to be where I am, not really firmly planted in any one thing, not really even sure how to articulate what it is I do or what I want to do with it. Sure, I "do" comedy, but I also work a bunch of other jobs just to make "doing" comedy feasible. I don't even know if comedy is the one thing I want to "do."

People have often said to me, "You do too many things, it's confusing. Pick one thing and stick with it."

One? That's all? In the span of a lifetime!? I was supposed to know by now what my one thing is. I was supposed to be well-established in whatever field I chose and have a lot of experience and a huge portfolio to back me up, proof that I am successful at my one thing! My failures were supposed to be behind me. I was supposed to introduce someone to *my world,* not still be in the middle of trying to create it, making mistakes along the way. It's one thing to make mistakes on your own, it's another thing to make them in front of somebody, somebody you love, somebody you want to love you back, somebody you don't want to mess up in front of. It's vulnerable and scary and very much a part of what real love is I think— living in front of someone who sees and loves you even when you're not doing great and you don't have it all together.

Love is being seen in the mistakes, in the failures, in the how well you handle things, even if you don't handle things well, and that person still sees you, still sees your heart, and still loves you for who you are, not in spite of your mistakes or even because of your mistakes, but simply because you are you, and everyone makes mistakes.

I wanted to be more stable in my emotions by now. I wanted to be free of any triggers from past hurts. I wanted to be more solid in my faith. I wanted to have more money in my bank account. I wanted to be an artist or a writer or a comedian by now—like a "real" one, not an "artist" still trying to sell a painting at a bar, not a "writer" still trying to get more views on a blog post, and not a "comedian" still doing open mics and unpaid shows (that end up costing *me* money because parking isn't validated). I wanted to be "official" by now.

And I know, these things don't define me, nor do they determine my worth. I know that I know that *I know*, but I'd be lying if I said these aspirations don't give me a sense of purpose, a means to unleash my voice into the world.

It's easy for someone to look at the adventure my life is on social media—to see the pictures of the good times and think that's all my life is. But it's not. It's a lot of hard work to get to that one happy picture. So hard in fact that all too often I get tired, and I don't feel like doing more to get one moment of celebration, one little victory. And I know the little victories count, I know they add up. People who don't give up are people who have little victory after little victory, with a few little failures scattered in between. They have the persistence to keep going, and eventually they get there, but the reality is, even after they've worked really hard and gotten really tired, even then, upon arrival, there's no time to rest; they must work to maintain how far they've gotten.

Life can be exhausting, and when my over-analytical mind gets ahead of itself and I think about all that it takes just to make it through a day, week, year, and the days, weeks, and years just repeat until we die... I get tired and I ask myself: *What's the point?*

Forgive me—these are happy times! I'm engaged, and I'm blessed beyond belief with a man who not only supports me but supports my questions, my wrestling matches with life, and my search for the meaning of it all. Plus, he's a landowner in Scotland! Not to brag, but I plan to visit our little piece of Scotland one day and I will plant a single flower on our property, which is about all the landscaping that will fit, but whatever. Happy, happy, happy.

Being happy can be fleeting, and I know this to be true because for as happy as I am about being engaged to the most amazing man I could ever hope for, not even that makes all my questions go away, not even that eliminates my concerns about life. Happy doesn't do away with my endless fears about what may or may not happen, my continual confusion about who I am and what I was meant to do.

And as happy as I am to have found my life partner, it doesn't mean I have reached the end of my journey and now I can live happily ever after. I still have a purpose to fulfill as an individual human—whether that's one big thing in my lifetime or a bunch of little things that make up my lifetime. Marriage isn't the end-all, be-all nor is it the determining factor of value for any person, so I know my journey of self-love isn't over just because I found some-one to love me. I have to continue learning to love myself for who I am if I am going to believe I am lovable and trust in someone else's love for me. And loving myself means not giving up on myself and the things that I love—even when I'm tired, even when it seems like it doesn't matter. It does matter.

Happiness fades, but a peace that passes understanding allows for joy to take root even in the midst of the confusion. I'm not just "happy" that I am engaged—I am overjoyed, so in love with someone, still a little fragile in my own skin, sometimes a little more anxious than I'd like to be, but very much at peace with the fact that this whole life thing is a process that I trust I will figure out along the way. I am grateful to have someone who won't figure it out *for* me but will figure it out *with* me.

I wish time would both slow down so I can figure my life out but also, hurry up so I can marry my favorite person. Until then, I must live in the tension of slow and fast, sad and happy, confused and clear. Such is life, such is love, such is the peace that passes understanding.

# 12

## AND THEN... WE ELOPED!

**IN JUNE OF 2019,** long before the world was hit with a global pandemic, Josh and I decided to elope. Little did we know, had we waited a year to make this decision, we would have been heroes, with heartfelt thanks all around for saving lives from social gatherings. But since we were not privy to the mysterious COVID-19 that would hit our world, nor did we desire to wait another year before tying the knot, Josh and I eloped in the hills of Santa Barbara under an old oak tree overlooking the Pacific Ocean. With just the two of us, our photographers and a pastor, our wedding was perfect in every way… minus worrying that our families would secretly hate us for not inviting them. With no threat to their health by attending, how could we not include them in our day?

It's a very interesting thing to merge two families, especially two very different families. I'm not special in this regard as many people have to go through this when deciding to commit to not just another person, but to another family FOR THE REST OF THEIR LIVES. This family merger was not a concept that had crossed my mind very often while Josh and I were dating, mostly because his family was in Alaska, mine was in South Carolina, and we lived in California, so there wasn't a whole lot of intermingling going on. Josh and I would occasionally visit each other's side of the family, each adapting to familial patterns when we visited, but neither of us thought about how each of the families would react when we decided to make a decision for ourselves about OUR wedding, a wedding that neither side of the family was paying for. We were both in our mid-thirties, each with our own bank account and fewer best friends than we had in our college years, so why make a big fuss? Why stress out and pay *sooo* much money for everyone else to have a huge party for one night? We'd rather buy a house one day, or go on an amazing honeymoon, or you know, in my case, do literally anything else other than orchestrate and attend a huge party.

But some people just assume that getting married means a traditional, large wedding ceremony and reception—especially prior to Covid. When there's two families involved, each side knows their own history and the intricacies of their family's dynamics best. In my case, my family knows I'm kind of a wanderer and a free-spirited homebody, meaning yes, I like to get out there and try new things, but at the same time I also like to sleep in my own bed and have a clean bathroom readily available in the wee hours of the morning. I like people, but most of the time, I prefer to be alone. And, having grown up in the South, I *might* have thought that *maybe* one day I'd have a big glamorous wedding, in part to make up for the fact that I never got to be a debutante (which I look back on now and think, *Thank God my parents couldn't afford that*), but it had been a long time since I'd dreamed of a wedding, so long that the dream of a wedding died off and was replaced by the hope of one day just having a life partner—a marriage.

Even that vision got sticky later in life when my parents divorced, but I worked through it, more certain than ever that a wedding was not the end result I'd always thought it'd been when I was growing up... a wedding was just the beginning. After all, Billy Graham himself, America's Preacher, married my parents and not even his blessing came with guarantees. As I got older, I began to question weddings all together—why are we celebrating when the ceremony is the easiest part? Every hard thing I'd ever taken part in—from races to comedy competitions—required that you do the work first, and then you had an after-party. I'm still not sure how that works with marriage yet—at what mile marker should you have the big party? Regardless, weddings had lost their esteem in my eyes, and with the price of everything tripling as soon as you said it was "for a wedding," the whole occasion started to feel like another holiday created by Hallmark just to sell more cards, at least it did for me.

Then there was Josh, who has worked in the wedding industry for the last eighteen years as a wedding photographer. Josh's family is incredibly close, and they know he's also a wanderer, but (unlike me) he is a free-spirited extrovert, meaning he wants to do all the things, and invite all the people. He could travel the world ten times over and make a new best friend everywhere, every time. There would be no doubt for anyone in his family that if the oldest son was to get married one day, that wedding would be one huge party, no mildly important person left behind—the second cousin twice removed (and their "plus one"), the childhood best friend (that no one has seen since second grade), the FedEx driver (who endures the Alaskan cold to ensure every package gets delivered)—these are all potential wedding guests and you can't NOT invite them. While I struggle to maintain the one or two best friends I've had over the years, Josh has a minimum of twenty-three best friends, and that's *my* version of his best friend list.

Just the other day we were walking through a neighborhood we both love.

"My dream," Josh said, "would be to live in this neighborhood with 100 of my best friends in all the surrounding houses." Assuming he was exaggerating, I laughed out loud.

"You have 100 best friends?"

"Yeah," he said excitedly, "I mean maybe not 100 *best* friends, but 100 people I enjoy, and who it'd be cool to live around." Even with his explanation, I couldn't wrap my head around it.

*"You enjoy 100 people?!"*

We both laughed, then he pointed to a corner house and said it could be ours so I wouldn't feel too crowded in between the neighbors.

And so, combine an introvert with some divisive family stuff, and an extrovert with a tight-knit family, and you'll clearly have two conflicting views with their own opinions on how they think a wedding should go. Mind you, even the closest families don't wholly know their child, or their child's partner. It'd been so long since I'd lived at home, my family didn't fully know the degree of how introverted I had become as an adult. I put on a great show, but sometimes just being social is that level of work for me—it's showtime. Not to mention, I still get little jabs about things I dealt with growing up, like my anger outbursts as a child, or my indecisiveness (hence changing jobs a million times over), and other things I've tried to work through and continued to work through over the years—work that my family doesn't see because I don't live at home anymore.

And likewise with Josh's family. They didn't know just how much of a "yes" man he had become, not only to other people, but to his family, addressing their every need and want, and fulfilling it to the best of his ability because he's kind and he cares, but that meant he was also neglecting his own needs in the process. He'd said yes to them for so long that he had to take a beat to think through what *he* actually wanted.

"I never really think about it," he told me once. "It's just easier for me to do whatever everyone else wants."

Josh is generally a content and easy-going guy, happy to "go with flow" or "adjust accordingly," and I believe him when he says he really doesn't mind in regards to anything. But what most people don't realize is the level to which I have to probe to get Josh to unearth what he might really want. Even if he genuinely doesn't care, he needs to be reminded that his preference matters and deserves to be considered. Having shot so many weddings over the last eighteen years, even Josh admitted that he was "kinda over it."

Together, we processed the pros and cons of a wedding versus an elopement, and yes, even I can admit, a wedding could have been fun, but at the end of the day, eloping fit where we were at in life, ready to start our lives together and invest in our future instead of a party. The only thing that might stand in the way of Josh inviting an unlimited number of people to a party is the cost of hosting that unlimited number of people. The man loves to save money. That, and we only wanted to be concerned with each other on our wedding day, not what everyone else wanted or needed.

We were both a bit nervous about telling our families that we were eloping, and they wouldn't be there for our "big day." I think we were both still getting to know one another's families—our quirks, differences, gifts, and so on. When I had met Josh's family, I had entered the picture at a very weird time...

Big life things were happening in the lives of his two siblings—his brother was becoming a father for the first time, thereby producing the first grandchild, and the only family member that would truly matter from that moment on… until the next grandchild arrived.

No one said this, of course, but does anyone need to say it when someone becomes a parent and a grandparent for the first time? No, everyone knows the earth realigns to center around the kid, as it should be and probably will be for me if I have a kid, but since I have yet to experience that myself, I have a hard time realigning my world around a kid, and especially around a kid whose family I just met. I can't remember how or why it happened, but somehow, someone, myself included, thought it would be a good idea to meet Josh's entire family the very same week the first grandchild was born.

We all flew to Colorado to meet Josh's new nephew, the first grand-baby of the Newton family. Josh's brother lived in Colorado, and so his parents would fly down from Alaska and we would fly over from California and all meet at the same time—me and Josh's parents and their first grandchild. In retrospect, this was a horrible idea—new girlfriend and first grandchild both seeking love and approval from the same family—who will win the hearts of the family!? But little did I know the first grandchild and I were not even on the same playing field… and so I packed my bags for a weekend in Colorado to meet my boyfriend's family: first time grandparents and parents whose lives and sleeping habits had just been drastically altered by the arrival of grand-baby numero uno.

In all honesty, the weekend went really well. There was no dramatic turn of events, no "Oops, I dropped the baby!" story to tell. At the time, I genuinely felt welcomed in, even if of lesser importance than the new baby, I was nonetheless welcome. As for feeling unimportant, I look back now and see my own insecurities flaring up, my own need to be validated, to be considered as part of this close-knit group of Newtons. I shared some of my family history, too much, if I'm honest. Maybe I wanted them to know I had nothing to hide, or maybe I wanted them to know I wasn't a threat to their family unit; I wanted them to be reassured that their beloved "yes" man wasn't being taken away. My family had been kind of broken for a while, or at least broken up, and so if anything, I was all in to be part of a close-knit family like theirs. When I reflect back on it, upon quieting my insecurities, I thoroughly enjoyed the weekend (as well as some really good Thai food), and I felt like I belonged.

After that weekend, I was added to the family text thread. *I'm in!* I thought with excitement, until all the baby pictures started coming through. *Ohhhh noooo, wrong time to be in.* My phone buzzed all throughout the day with incoming baby pictures and gushing responses to said baby pictures. I promptly silenced my notifications and apologized out loud, as if Josh's family were listening to me silence them. While I may have been timid in real-time group texting (I still have an aversion to group texts of any kind), I did what I thought one should do when entering into a new family—I made an effort. And for me, making an effort looked a little more old-fashioned than group texting. I sent handmade cards and postcards to his family for birthdays and holidays like Mother's and Father's Day. I made cards because I like arts and crafts, but also because it's how I show I care. I believe some call it a "love language."

While I knew Josh had been close with his brother, Tim, and sister-in-law, Ali, before, the reality is ... a baby changes everything. I had never met Josh's family before this baby arrived, so I had no history and no grid for what they were like "pre-baby" or "how much more fun and laid back they were," as Josh would say. I've only ever known Tim and Ali as sleep-deprived parents and Josh's parents as doting grandparents. I've only ever known them to be mostly consumed by the baby changing everything, not that anything is wrong with that, it's just that is when I happened to enter in, and that is what shaped my experience as the newcomer.

Then there was Josh's sister who had her own big life event happening. The first Christmas I went to visit Josh's family in Alaska, his sister got engaged. Because we had been dating almost a year (and at thirty-five that felt like forever), I thought Josh might propose to me during that trip, but when we got the pictures of his sister saying yes in the snow just a day before we arrived, I knew a proposal wasn't going to happen for me. At least that meant I could relax and simply enjoy being there, and possibly have the chance to connect one-on-one with some of his family members. But once again, between baby's first Christmas and sister's engagement, I knew there wouldn't be much time for one-on-ones with the girlfriend. It felt increasingly hard to get close to a group who was already so close.

The hardest thing for Josh to adjust to when he first entered my family was how much TV we watched. We didn't always watch so much TV, in fact my parents were really strict about limiting TV times when we were growing up. But for a while after my parents divorced, they couldn't bear to be around each other, so a few years went by before we ever did anything as a family again. When we finally did start hanging out again with my mom and dad in the same room, it was always hard to know what to talk about, so we'd turn the TV on. The TV became a way for us to be together when we weren't really together anymore.

I remember the first time Josh brought it up, I was so defensive, and although he wasn't intentionally attacking, I bit back.

"Oh, I'm sorry my family doesn't stay up until 3 a.m. to discuss their feelings and opinions ON EVERYTHING!"

And that's coming from *me*, someone who has been ghosted multiple times in her dating career for over-processing *everything*.

In contrast to all the TV watching with my family, Josh's family talked... ALL. THE. TIME. About everything. Ad nauseam. While Josh hoped someone would turn the TV off at my house, I'd pray for someone to turn the TV on at his.

"If I hear one more commercial," Josh would say in South Carolina.

"If I hear one more long-winded opinion," I would say in Alaska.

In retrospect, regardless of where we were, we should have just gotten up and gone outside more—a cool, brisk walk in the woods of Alaska, a warm, leisurely stroll on the beach in South Carolina—but Josh and I were just at the beginning of learning how to be a couple, separate from the families we grew up in. We didn't yet know there was an option outside of incorporating each other into each family's ways of doing things when visiting them. When we were single, our families were used to us partaking in whatever goings-on were occurring. I didn't yet have it in me to suggest to my family to turn off the TV, nor did Josh have it in him to suggest to his family that everyone could keep talking if they wanted, but we were going to go to bed. While Josh was chomping at the bit to have conversations with my family during America's Got Talent or Little House on The Prairie, I was nodding off to sleep as his family's discussion of the Enneagram was only just getting started at 10 p.m.

We learned a lot about each other through interactions with our families, and we still fell more in love with each other. While some family members initially got upset about not being included in our wedding, time is a healer, and eventually, everyone realized it was not the end of the world. That, and grand-baby number two helped smooth things over.

We never set out to exclude our families when we decided to elope, we just wanted to start afresh and set the tone for our relationship, that it was about us. We could love people dearly *and*, at the same time, want the intimacy of sharing our vows with the only two people they were meant for—each other. And our wedding was perfect... for us. And much like our wedding, when it comes to our marriage, we do things our way, we figure out what works for us and what doesn't. Sometimes we talk too late into the night and sometimes we watch a little too much TV, but most importantly, we laugh. We laugh *with* each other and *at* each other. We laugh at ourselves and all our little quirks, for which we often thank our loving families of origin.

# i GOT THE HiCCuPS, HOLLA iF YA HEAR ME!

**WHEN JOSH AND I GOT MARRIED,** part of our marital vows were tested *right away*—you know the part, the "in sickness and in health" part? Yea, that part got tested a week after our wedding day, a *week*, when Josh got strep throat. The strep throat part was fine, I mean not for Josh, but I did a great job taking care of him. I was like *WOW, I am killing it at this wife thing!* And I didn't even have practice.

Practice or not, it was a crazy process to nurse him back to health—taking care of yourself in general, especially the older you get, gets a lot more complicated. No wonder so many people don't do it, it's exhausting. And that's just taking care of yourself, it's even harder to take care of another person as you both age.

I took Josh to the doctor, and the doctor prescribed antibiotics, but they didn't want the *anti*biotics to wreck his entire system, so they said to get on probiotics, but in order for the *pro*biotics to be effective, he needed to get on *pre*biotics. I wanted to make sure I understood the instructions, so I repeated them back to the doctor...

"Okay. He needs prebiotics to feed the probiotics to aid the antibiotics?"

"Correct!" the doctor said.

Who comes up with this stuff? I thought it was a joke. I asked if there was a *post*biotic Josh should be taking to finish it all up.

"No such thing," the doctor said, clearly not getting my sarcasm.

And as if a cocktail of biotics wasn't enough, there was the timing of it all—Josh had to take the prebiotics an hour before the probiotics and the probiotics 4 hours before the antibiotics, and he couldn't drink coffee within 20 minutes of any of the biotics. WHAT!?!

*Who knows this for sure? Did someone test this?* If so, I'd like to read about the side effects that happened within 20 minutes of drinking coffee. I swear doctors just come up with things thinking, *This will keep em' busy!*

And that's not even the weird part. The weird part was the side effects of the biotics. For Josh, they weren't the normal side effects like nausea, diarrhea, or itchy scalp. Josh got what was medically described as "excessive hiccups." A whole week of NON-STOP HICCUPING. And no, it wasn't merely a hiccup here, a hiccup there over the course of a week—it was here a hiccup, there a hiccup, everywhere a hiccup, hiccup. ALL. THE. TIME.

And it's just hiccups, right? I didn't yet know that nonstop hiccups were a medical issue, so at first when he kept hiccuping, I lovingly said, "Okay, for real, just stop it. Cut it out. Can you just stop?"

But he couldn't stop, no matter what he did. He'd just have to retreat to another room and hiccup alone. But no matter where I went in the house to get away from the sound, it was all I could hear.

HICCUP!

ALL. DAY.

After two full days of hiccuping, Josh started doing these breathing exercises, and I don't know if he looked them up or made them up, but I'd be in another room and could hear what sounded like a drunk Darth Vader. We tried everything, and I say "we" because I was just as affected. He tried holding his breath, breathing into a paper bag, drinking water upside down. I tried running him over.

He ate a spoonful of sugar, a spoonful of vinegar, and a spoonful of cinnamon. We used half a bottle of peppermint oil, and by the way, for all you essential oil people who say there's an oil for everything—NO, there is not. You were probably already thinking it... *Should have tried peppermint oil.* We did. I was dropping it in his mouth, rubbing it on his neck, I was even anointing his head with it. I tried getting Pentecostal for a hot second, laying hands on him, praying... *"In the name of Jesus come out!"* HICCUP. *"In the name of Jesus go back in!"*

I tried scaring him, jumping around corners, screaming sporadically. But nothing. This lasted for *a week!* Seven days. He couldn't eat, he couldn't sleep, I couldn't stand him, and I felt horrible. One night I told him to hold his breath, "And then just keep holding it," I said, only kinda kidding.

All jokes aside, I did legitimately get scared because I went down the black hole of Google (Web MD over here) and I found out that the longest case of hiccups ever recorded lasted *sixty-eight years!* I thought, *this is it. This is my fate. I took vows. I can't leave him.* I started planning my future as a motivational speaker for debilitating diseases. Sure, it was only hiccups, but it was so much more. There was no sex, and this was week *one* of our marriage. I guess technically there could have been sex, but have you ever had sex with someone who can't stop hiccuping? It's like trying to get turned on by a squeaky toy... it just feels wrong.

*I am doomed*, I thought. That's where my mind went—to the absolute worst-case scenario. My husband is either going to have hiccups for the rest of his life and we're going to be on Oprah for it, or he's going to have to hold his breath until death do us part.

By the end of the week, we were both kinda on edge. I was annoyed and I felt bad that I was annoyed because I knew he couldn't help it, but deep down I was still kinda wondering if maybe he could. He was not only annoyed, but also in pain and completely confined to the house. He hadn't been able to leave or even talk on the phone, and he's the extrovert in the relationship. We were both exhausted and lamenting, *WHY ARE THE HICCUPS RUINING OUR LIVES?* It seemed so simple—hiccups—and yet they were completely interfering with our day-to-day living. Not only could he not sleep (which I felt horrible about), but trying to sleep next to him was a nightmare.

One night I could hear him doing his little breathing exercises in another room, followed by HICCUP, and I actually started to worry that maybe he was making it worse by getting all Darth Vader on his diaphragm.

I went into the room and said, "Hey, what if you're stressing your body out because it's not used to breathing that hard? It could be making it worse!" He replied that it was the only thing that *did* help, followed by HICCUP.

"*CLEARLY NOT!*" I snapped.

We ended up getting into a big fight, the biggest fight of our week-old marriage at that point. Josh isn't a yeller, he's very patient, it takes a lot to set him off. Believe me, I've tried. So, after a few of my snide remarks, Josh finally broke.

"I'M SORRY, OKAY! I'M SORRY I HAVE THE HICCUPS, I'M SORRY I CAN'T HELP IT, I'M SORRY IT'S ANNOYING, I'M SORRY *I'M ANNOYING* AND YOU DON'T WANT TO BE AROUND ME, I'M SORRY I DON'T KNOW WHAT TO DO! I'M NOT TRYING TO ANNOY YOU SO IF YOU'RE SO ANNOYED WHY DON'T YOU JUST GO IN THE OTHER ROOM AND CLOSE THE DOOR BECAUSE I DON'T KNOW WHAT ELSE TO DO! I'M SORRY I…"

"Wait a second," I interrupted. "Shh!" We both paused for a minute, and then two minutes turned into three… and it was silent. Not one hiccup.

It was the best sound in the world, and I breathed a sigh of relief.

"Apparently I just needed to make you angry," I joked, "You're welcome!"

And the hiccups were gone.

At dinner that night, we laughed about it all. Our first week had been exhausting. We went to bed, I kissed him goodnight, turned out the light, and closed my eyes. Marital bliss was back.

I laid in the darkness with a smile on my face, and as if life itself were saying "not so fast," I heard…

HICCUP.

# KINDA FUNNY
# (AND KINDA NOT)

# 14

# THE POPS
# OF COMEDY

**I HONESTLY DON'T KNOW** how someone gets started in stand-up comedy. I suppose some see other comedians perform and think to themselves *I could do that,* or *I want to do that.* Others may have heard their parents listening to comedians on vinyl and wanted to make their parents laugh the same way. I guess it depends on the era in which you grew up, whether you were around a radio, a record player, or scrolling through TikTok on a cellphone. I've had other aspiring comedians want to "pick my brain" about how to get further in the business and I'm always caught off guard by their questions. Don't they know that I am also still aspiring... for some God-forsaken reason? Not only do I not know *how* people start doing comedy, but I don't know why many of them *keep* doing comedy. It truly is a horrible business... at least for someone like me who has yet to see their name on a theater marquee.

I've tried to the best of my ability to respond helpfully to someone who asks about my craft, but honestly, I feel ill-equipped and pretty certain I didn't give them the information they were looking for, as if I know the way to some magic portal but *I'll never tell!*

I got into comedy by accident, pure accident. It was the year before I met Josh, I was thirty-three, living in Ocean Beach, San Diego, and going through a really rough season of life. Though I had made my rounds in rehab during my twenties, life comes in waves, hard seasons hit again, and there it was—a really hard season coming back to taunt me. The benefit of being "older and wiser" was that I had enough tools in my tool belt to recognize when I was heading down a dark path, and I knew what I needed was help. I was in much need of consistent therapy, if for no other reason than to process some of the stuff in my head.

Yes, I journaled, but journaling only seemed to increase the feelings of despair whirling about me. It's not like a weak mind is able to journal something profound and go, *AHA! Let us go forth and make change!* I talked to friends, most of whom wanted me to cheer up and not be such a drag, which only made me further suppress what I was feeling. I knew I couldn't cover the cost of a weekly therapy session, not even a bi-weekly session. I *maybe* could have saved up enough for once-a-month sessions, but it was tight just paying rent in Southern California. Going to a therapy session for just one visit seemed pointless, plus no one would accept me as a patient if I started with: "I just need one visit." I'd rather buy groceries.

It's not that I felt sad, it's that I felt nothing… an absolute abyss of nothing. There was no point, no purpose, no reason for being, life just… was. There was nothing specific that sparked it, which is perhaps the most maddening part, but that's how depression works. It creeps in when you think you're doing well and reminds you that your life is empty, and everything is utterly meaningless.

It's the voice that whispers: *There's no point. No one cares. Let's get this over with.*

On top of all that nothing, I felt stuck, stuck in the nothingness. I was drowning, like Atreyu's horse in *The NeverEnding Story*, giving in to the sadness.

Since I was aware I was stuck, I was able to pinpoint that everything I had been doing up to that point wasn't working. I was in a comfort zone of hopelessness. I was working in a coffee shop, which is always the second thing I do when I don't know what to do with my life. The first thing I usually do is go back to school—I went to art school in Portland, seminary in Chicago, and I had gotten accepted to grad school in Pasadena when I realized I couldn't afford to keep going back to school. So, I went back to being a barista. I had been a barista in multiple states over the course of ten years, it was a comfort zone. I knew the coffee shop would always be there for me. But there in my comfort zone, I was miserable. Every time I looked at the coffee grounds swirling about in the pour over, I'd hear Atreyu's voice in my head, *"Don't give in to the sadness"* and I'd watch the coffee grounds sink to the bottom.

"Try not to say that in front of the customers," my boss would say, as she patted me on the back, me completely unaware that the thought was actually coming out of my mouth.

The biggest myth about a comfort zone is that it's comfortable. While it may seem to be comfortable at first, it's only a matter of time before you feel so restless in the comfort that you realize how horribly uncomfortable your comfort zone is. Ironically, the only way to get out of any comfort zone is to do something uncomfortable, which is the last thing you want to do when you're feeling hopeless, but probably the most necessary.

*I'm in a comfort zone,* I remember thinking. *What can I do to get out?* I thought maybe I could take a cooking class. I like cooking, I like it a lot actually. It had been a while since I'd cooked, but I thought maybe a cooking class could jumpstart me back to my days of being a chef (yes, in a former life I was also a lunch lady, but you have to read my first book for that story). I Googled cooking classes and found several offered here or there, but nothing stuck out to me. *So, what, I just go once, make a meal, and that's it?* I convinced myself that would never help me in the long run, and I ruled out the cooking class (but I still plan to take it someday).

I thought about a workout class. Maybe I could do an eight-week-program or buy a certain number of visits to a gym with classes. Exercise is sure to make you feel better, even if you aren't dealing with why you're miserable in the first place, it at least tricks your body into thinking it's happy for a while. But it was hard for me to work up the energy to even go to a workout class, on top of which, I felt like the gym would only be a momentary distraction from the things I needed to process, persistent inse-curities that had grown into what felt like crippling anxieties: I was going nowhere, my life was meaningless, and after ten years of experience, still unable to make a heart or a leaf in the foam of a latte, being a mediocre barista would be my life's achievement. I was also most likely going to die alone, just to add insult to injury.

Along with the cooking class, I ruled out the exercise class if for no other reason than it just felt like more instant gratification and not actually a healthy path to getting mentally unstuck. Plus, the last time I used food and exercise to process my emotions, I ended up in rehab with an eating disorder. And I was promptly put on exercise restriction.

I don't remember exactly what it was, but I started Googling completely random topics—*how to get unstuck, how to get out of your head, what makes people happy,* and *leaving your comfort zone.* The most common thing that came up across everything I googled was *improv comedy classes.* I knew what improv was, I had briefly dated a guy back in Chicago who had been taking improv classes at the time. He took me to an improv show once and I remember being fascinated with everyone onstage just playing off of each other. I kinda fell in love with the idea, but then the guy stopped talking to me and I fell out of love just as quickly.

Years later, I took part in an improv workshop in Portland, Oregon. I remember the teacher telling us to go around the room and point at objects while yelling out the name of something else. People were pointing at chairs and yelling...

"LAMP!"

"GRASS!"

"COW!"

The teacher told us as soon as we felt stuck just to yell out anything, anything at all, that the only way to keep yourself from freezing was to just keep going. I had yelled out as many random things as I could, but the game seemed like it would never end. I thought surely the teacher would be distracted by everyone else now pointing at lamps and yelling...

"FUR!"

"CAT!"

"BURRITO!"

I began wondering what words were triggering other words for people. I was lost in thought and stuck in my ability to come up with new words when the teacher spotted me.

"Keep going!" she said.

Clearly frozen, unable to think of something I hadn't already said, the teacher walked over to me. *Oh, God,* I thought, further distracting myself.

"The only way to get yourself unstuck is to just say something, it doesn't matter what it is or if it makes sense, just yell it out!"

I pointed to the bar, about to say "BAR!" when I remembered I wasn't supposed to say what it actually was, but I had already formed the B-sound in my mouth, so I had to say something that started with a B. But as I rolodexed my mind for words, the teacher yelled at me again.

"*Just say something, anything at all!*"

I stared at the bar, still pointing at it, and in a voice louder than I had used all day, I yelled it out.

"BUTTHOLE!"

The room fell silent. I quickly put my hand to my mouth and looked at the teacher.

"It's okay," she said. "Now, just keep going! Keep going, everyone!"

"FART!" I heard another guy yell while pointing to a table, clearly triggered by my word choice.

At the very least, the exercise reminded me not to take myself so seriously, as I so often do, but I also learned the importance of doing *something* instead of doing *nothing* to get yourself unstuck, hence improv's mantra of "Yes, and…" (In improv, you are supposed to say *yes* to whatever scenario is created, *and* you create from there. You don't shut down an idea just because it's foreign to you.) And third, I realized that I'm still prone to calling people a butthole when they are getting on my nerves, feeling like the name was directed more toward my teacher than toward the bar I was pointing at. Nonetheless, the butthole had a point, and I was grateful to her for teaching it to me.

That was the last time I had done improv, about five years ago, and now here it was coming up in my Google search for happiness. As I hovered my cursor over the improv classes wondering if I should click on one, I recalled that last experience, remembering it as incredibly uncomfortable, yet oddly exciting. I felt nervous as I looked through the list of different theaters offering classes. Nervous is good, nervous is *something* instead of *nothing*. I hadn't felt nervous when I was looking at cooking classes or exercise classes. My nerves caught my attention and signaled to my brain that for the first time in a long time, I felt alive. I went through my usual excuses: *I've never done it. What if I'm not good at it? I'll never be on SNL, so what's the point…* and then I chose a class and signed up anyway.

I wasn't signing up to be famous, or even to be funny, I was signing up to get unstuck.

The class started a couple of weeks later through National Comedy Theater in San Diego. It was a six-week course, and I showed up mostly nervous and a little curious. I can't remember exactly how this next part happened, if I had selected the wrong class or if I went to the wrong classroom, but when I told the teacher I was there for the improv class he told me the improv classes were all full and had been full for a while.

"This is a stand-up comedy class," he said.

Without the slightest idea as to what that meant, I thought to myself, *it's probably the same thing*, and I stayed.

This is how accidental comedy was for me… not only did I stumble upon it through a random Google search while looking for happiness, but I also didn't even know the difference between stand-up comedy and improv. I mean, I knew stand-up was a thing. I had seen clips on YouTube of people telling funny jokes on a stage, but I didn't know it was like a *THING*; an art form with a long history and levels of status earned from years of hard work. I certainly didn't know it was a job, nor did I know it was how most sitcom stars started their careers. I thought Ellen was just … Ellen, a sitcom star in the '90s who got in trouble for being gay and then years later widely accepted by the public. I didn't know she was originally a stand-up comedian. I thought Jerry Seinfeld was just a character on the TV show, *Seinfeld*, who sometimes told jokes at a night club. I didn't know that that was his *job* on the show, or in real life for that matter! And perhaps even more importantly and certainly more horrifying to the comedy world, I thought Robin Williams' big break was the movie, *Mrs. Doubtfire*. I had no clue about his *Mork and Mindy* TV days and, well before that, his stand-up.

The comedy world was foreign to me, and here I was about to take a stand-up class, thinking it was improv.

As the class began, I thought the biggest difference between these two categories of comedy—improv and stand-up—seemed to be that one involved a group of people working together, and the other involved just one person working alone. In improv, you play off of each other, sharing the stage with your teammates while people in the audience watch, sometimes shouting suggestions for topics, hopefully laughing in between. In stand-up, it's just you, sharing the stage with a spotlight that is on only you, engaging the audience enough to hopefully hold their attention, but not so much as to get them to engage back, unless it is laughing or applauding. You want the audience to like you, but you don't want them to talk to you. It's very odd, and yet it makes a lot of sense, especially if you've ever told a story to a group of friends and there's always that one friend who interrupts with a question right when you are about to tell the group what you did.

"So, what'd you do?"

People who ask questions in the middle of the story, not even for the sake of clarification, but just because they can't wait to find out the rest, have always kinda irked me. This alone was reason enough for me to prefer stand-up over improv...

"So, I talk and they just... listen?"

"Well, yes," my teacher said, "and hopefully they laugh."

The first day of class blew my mind. I came in the door as a dry sponge, practically useless, but the longer the class went, the more I absorbed until, by the end of the class, my sponge runneth over. For our first exercise, my teacher had us take turns getting onstage and share why we were there.

"Why are you taking this class?" he asked. Tony was the teacher's name, a big Italian guy who used to be a bank manager and had been doing comedy for the last twenty-plus years. While he may have respectfully listened when students made their attempts at being funny, his face did not lie. "Get outta here!" I imagined him saying in a Sopranos-*style* voice when something wasn't funny.

Each person took a turn and shared their reasons.

"I've always wanted to do comedy."

"It's on my bucket list."

"I love Steve Martin."

"I want to be a comedian!"

*Oh God,* I thought, *I don't think I am supposed to be here.* It was clear to me that people had put a lot of thought into why they wanted to take a stand-up comedy class. For some of them it was even a steppingstone to the career they wanted. Seeing as how I had just learned that stand-up was an actual career choice fifteen minutes prior to the exercise, I didn't know what to say when it was my turn onstage. I kept trying to think of what would be a "good reason" in the eyes of—well, in the eyes of I'm not sure who. In the eyes of the class? Or my teacher?

When I stepped up onto the stage, I just stood there. I had nothing. I started to feel a little panicky, similar to the feeling I had when I first discovered the class, and I reminded myself that was why I was there, not to be famous or funny, but just to get unstuck.

I grabbed the microphone and took a deep breath.

"I'm here because… well, honestly because I needed therapy, but I couldn't afford it."

The room laughed and I was surprised. Tony pointed his pen at me.

"That's funny," he said.

"Oh, I was being serious." The class laughed again.

"And that's what makes it funny," Tony said. He explained that often what makes something funny is its relatability, in fact oftentimes, the more honest, the more funny.

WHAT? My mind was blown. Again. *You mean to tell me I can get onstage and talk about my insecurities and people will think it's funny because they can relate!?*

I've heard comedians talk about their AHA moments in comedy, when they knew they had "caught the bug" so to speak, often after a big show or a loud crowd. Sometimes I'm still not sure if I have "caught the bug" yet, I still feel like a fraud given my late-in-life stumble into stand-up. But if I were to have had an AHA moment, that first class was would have been it… *I can talk about being insecure for a living and not have to pay a therapist for it? Let me get my journals.*

Okay, I'll admit, I wasn't completely sold yet. I was curious, but I certainly wasn't looking for comedy to be a career. Especially because, after that first day, I realized how funny everyone else in the class was. I've often been called funny, but I don't know how intentionally funny I was trying to be, so I always thought I was more weird than funny. I remember when I was fifteen, I was dating a boy and his mom told me she asked him what his favorite thing about me was.

"He said he loves how funny you are." At fifteen, that was not the answer I was looking for.

"You mean he didn't say I was pretty?" I asked.

"Oh, you *are* so funny," she laughed.

But as per usual, I was being serious.

Even if people had thought I was the funny one in various friend groups, I now found myself in a group of people who were *all* the funny ones in their group. It was like making the varsity team by the skin of your teeth, knowing you'll never actually start a game. What I didn't know at the time was just how much a stand-up comedy class was *not at all* considered the varsity team in the world of comedy—it was the equivalent of peewee football at best, a few friends and family cheering you on for trying, knowing you won't get much further than an elementary school football team. But it would be a while before I discovered the hierarchy of the comedy world. For now, I was in new territory, only able to grasp one uncomfortable experience at a time. I often tell people that had I'd known anything about stand-up comedy before, I don't think I would have ever pursued it. I'm pretty sure I had to be naïve in order to move forward in this industry.

By the end of our first class, I was convinced I had made a huge mistake. Though I had my moment of laughter, which I enjoyed, mostly because it caught me off guard and *any* emotion is heightened when it is caught off guard, I had no idea how to recreate that moment. Nonetheless, I took the homework home and decided I would at least look it over, I could decide later if I would go back the following week.

Our comedy homework was pages and pages of questions about our life and our feelings, asking us to recall times when we felt embarrassed, how it made us feel and why. It was literally therapy. I remember sitting in the kitchen filling out the questions, some of which I had to really dig deep for. When you face why you feel the way you feel about something, it's bound to stir up some emotions. I remember crying as I was writing out one of the answers when my roommate came into the kitchen.

"Are you crying? Are you okay?" she asked.

"I'm fine," I sniffled. "I'm just doing my comedy homework."

I think the reason we had to figure out our experiences, and analyze why we felt the way we felt, was because we had to be able to connect to our own emotions if we wanted to connect to other people's emotions. What I started to learn was that stand-up comedy was not merely getting up on stage and saying whatever comes to mind and hoping it's funny. It's hours and hours (and *hours*) of work off the stage, and if you aren't just relying on the shock and awe of a generic sex joke, it's even more work.

I went back the next week and we each took turns reviewing our answers onstage.

"That's funny," Tony said in response to somebody's answer about having a fear of peanut butter. "Now expound on that. There's a story in there—what is it?"

He gave us notes on what was funny about our childhoods, these deep-seated insecurities, all of which I had no idea were funny until other people would laugh because they had a similar awkward experience.

"Expound on that," Tony would say, and that was pretty much our homework for the next week: taking these long answers, picking them apart, and expounding on one or two sentences that had resonated with other people. "When you come back next week," Tony said, "I want you to be able to share without looking at any notes."

While the degree to which I take things too seriously can sometimes be an unenjoyable experience, especially for other people, that homework assignment was one time when taking things too seriously served me well. I spent the whole week writing out what I would say *over and over again,* memorizing it day after day. Tony had told us that we could email him during the week with anything we had, and he'd be happy to look it over and make edits. Toward the end of the week, I emailed him "my speech," which is what I was calling it because I didn't yet know in comedy it was called "a set." He emailed a final revision to me on Sunday morning and our class was that afternoon. I spent all morning and all afternoon going over my "material," a term I also learned to use instead of "comedy homework." It does sound more professional, I suppose.

Our class started at 1p.m.

"Okay, who's up?" Tony asked.

Someone volunteered to go first, and Tony said they could take their notes on stage, but to try not to look at them. After three people went, I realized I had taken the assignment way too seriously, no one had their material memorized, everyone was just "um-ing" and "uh-ing" while looking at their notes, there was a lot of "um, yeah, and so, uhhh..."

My classmates seemed to enjoy the fact that everyone was struggling together to remember what they were going to say. I immediately felt embarrassed, like the teacher's pet who the rest of the class doesn't like just because she understood the assignment.

I struggled, trying to decide if I should pretend like I didn't have my material memorized. I didn't want to be the dork who tried too hard to excel at publicly processing her emotions.

Then Tony called on me.

"JJ, wanna go up?"

"Suuuure," I hesitated.

"It's okay if you don't have it memorized, just try to do what you can," Tony encouraged, and I laughed awkwardly as I stood up.

The student who had gone before me was still onstage, waiting to introduce me. We were taught to never leave the stage empty. Once you finish you wait for someone else to volunteer and then you introduce them, shake their hand, and essentially, "hand the stage off."

The guy who was handing the stage off to me was Scottish with a thick accent.

"Remind me your last name," he said off the mic.

"Barrows," I whispered.

"Please put your hands together for Miss JJ Barrrrrowssss!" The class clapped and I enjoyed hearing my name pronounced with such a long R. We shook hands and he handed me the mic.

"Well, I..." I paused for a moment and looked out at everyone waiting for me to say something. Though I wanted to fit in with everyone else, I reminded myself why I was there, to get unstuck, not to stay in a comfort zone where I make everyone else feel comfortable with me.

I put my notes down on the stool beside me and I recited my speech, which is to say, I performed my material, straight from memory, as if it were a live show and I was interacting with the crowd. I had yet to know about crowd interaction or how live shows even worked. I didn't have direction yet on *how* to deliver the material, I just delivered it in a way that felt most natural to me, like I was talking to people for the first time, even though I already knew what I was going to say.

I'm not saying it was perfect by any means. I have a knack for adding way too much trivial detail to any story: *And then he put yellow mustard, not the spicy stuff, on his sandwich, I think it was roast beef, then we left for the beach.* No one cares about the mustard, or the sandwich for that matter, leave it out and get to the point, what happened at the beach?

So, I ended up reciting just over fifteen minutes from memory, telling stories from my childhood, growing up as a preacher's kid, learning things way too late in life, things I had always been insecure about, but that people found humorous when I was able to make fun of myself about it. When I finished my classmates applauded, some in disbelief, a couple in annoyance, but most of them seemed to have thoroughly enjoyed what I shared.

"How did you do that?" Tony asked. I couldn't yet tell if he was asking in a positive tone or an accusatory tone.

"Do what?" I asked.

"I sent you your edits only this morning, how did you get all of that memorized *and* perform it like you've done it a million times before? I didn't teach you that."

*Oh no, was I in trouble?*

"I don't know, I just kept reciting it over and over and since I knew it, I just felt comfortable sharing it."

"Do you have a photographic memory?"

He kept asking questions, trying to understand I think, but I couldn't read his tone. I didn't think I had a photographic memory; I was pretty sure I would remember if I did.

Finally, he clarified, "That was amazing, I mean honestly, really good. I seriously can't believe you just did that. It's rare."

I felt embarrassed that the attention was on me, and I was getting it in a way the other students hadn't. Yes, I wanted to do a good job at whatever I did, but I didn't want to make other people uncomfortable with how well I did it. Again, this was just a class, it's not like I went on AGT and blew their socks off, but for my first few baby steps out of my comfort zone, it felt about the same to me.

People came up to me after class and told me they loved what I shared, impressed by how well I shared it.

Tony pulled me aside.

"Look, in the ten plus years that I've been teaching comedy, I've never seen one of my students do that *and* do it so well, especially this early on. We have work to do, but you got something, kid. If you do the work, you could really do this."

He looked at me as if he had discovered a secret, and I didn't realize how much I wanted to feel seen, like someone had finally noticed the potential I often felt but mostly only hoped I had. I'll never forget his words as long as I live:

"You got something, kid."

By the end of the six weeks, our class size had dwindled from twelve to six. Most people, not realizing how much work it was to actually craft even just a five-minute set, ended up leaving the course halfway through. Upon completion, we had a graduation performance that was coupled with the level two class, a class you could only move on to with approval from Tony.

There was one woman in level two who caught my attention: Lisa. She was funny, natural, and so confident. She had married later in life, gotten pregnant on her honeymoon, and become a mom of triplets at *forty-five*! To me, her material was flawless. At the end of the showcase, we all took pictures onstage.

Lisa leaned over to me and whispered, "Hey, you were awesome. Are you going to take level two?"

"I don't know… you have to get approved to take level two and I don't know if I can yet."

Lisa laughed. "Oh, you'll be approved. Yeah, you're taking level two."

It was just a small theater hosting a graduation showcase of about thirty-five people, where a level two student complimented my performance, but given how late in life it had taken me to show up for my own life, it may as well have been a performance at Carnegie Hall with Carol Burnett waiting just offstage to congratulate me.

After the show, I was invited to be an opener for a performer at The Comedy Store in La Jolla. The *world-famous* Comedy Store (mostly just famous for its L.A. location, but still famous nonetheless). I went from an audience of thirty-five people at a graduation showcase to an audience of 250 people at the Comedy Store, my second show ever. Tony, my teacher, came to the Comedy Store and again, he pulled me aside.

"I could fit in my pinky nail the amount of people who have the natural talent you have. You've really got something, kid. If you decide to do this, it's all yours."

I *killed* my show, which is a good thing, and another term I learned in my early days of comedy. I was nervous as all get out before I got onstage, and then as soon as I got the mic in my hand, I don't know how, I just let er' rip. Hearing so many people laugh at once was such a thrill that a few times I almost forgot what I was supposed to say next. All I could think was, *Oh my God, they're laughing!* Tony hugged me when I got off stage.

"You're a killer."

I will never forget his encouragement, the genuine look of someone who believed in me. I have parents that love me and friends who enjoy me, plenty of people who think I'm creative or quirky, but the look of someone who truly believes in you is a compliment and a feeling unlike any other. Whenever I doubt myself, I remember Tony.

"It's all yours," I still hear Tony say in the back of mind. "All you gotta do is want it, and it's all yours."

I took three courses from Tony, and still think I need to take more (are we ever really done learning?), so I have felt connected to him over the years. Whether he ever claimed me or not, I took to calling him "Pops," dubbing him my comedy father because he looked after me and believed in me.

At the time of the Comedy Store show, I didn't yet know what it meant to "want it." I didn't know you *had* to want it because it was going to get hard and you would want to give up, no matter how much natural talent you have or how well your graduation showcase went. Having a few good shows doesn't seal your fate in the world of comedy. But I didn't know that yet. I was just having fun, dumbstruck by the rush from my own untapped potential I had stored up for so long. Kinda like the excitement of a Champagne bottle popping open, I was experiencing the high of a good show, oblivious to the long road ahead... a road I'm still on, still unsure how to answer people when they ask me how to get further down the road.

I'm flattered they think I've gotten far enough to know, but without much insight to offer, I proverbially pat them on the back and tell them, "You just gotta to want it."

# 15

# SHE'S NOT READY

**BY SEPTEMBER OF 2019,** I had been doing comedy for just over two years, paying more attention to the comedy world and making friends in the industry. During that time, a comedian friend of mine posted a video of a podcast interview he had recently taken part in. Since I was interested in his comedy career, I watched the whole thing without skipping ahead ten seconds at a time. Towards the end of the interview, he talked about a female comedian who was about to film her first Dry Bar Comedy Special.

"I don't think she's ready," he said, as he sighed aloud, "but she got the opportunity..." and he threw his hands up as if to say, "What can ya do?"

Based on what he shared about the female comedian, I knew who he was talking about. He was talking about me. I've always thought this guy was so great on and off stage, really funny, plus kind and encouraging. One time he told me I should consider doing a one-woman show. You can't get more encouraging than that. At the time I was a mere seven months into doing comedy, so it may have just been a kind gesture, a "keep trying and maybe one day."

I was no threat to his decades of experience, so perhaps his compliments may have been given more freely. I had often felt encouraged by the things he said, naive to the idea that anyone might have any kind of issue with me. But upon hearing him bother to mention *me* as "not ready" on *his* podcast interview, I felt a brief moment of confusion. *Why would I matter to him?* At the same time, I also felt the wind knock out of my sails and a little whisper in my head that said, *yea, JJ, who do you think you are?*

I've often felt that way with the different things I've pursued in life—I lack the experience and the time required to be taken seriously. Perhaps the problem is that I've tried so many different things that that's where all my time went—starting over with something new instead of staying in one place, perfecting and mastering a craft. I don't know. I do know that I don't think I would have gotten here, doing comedy, without having done all those other things first, without having something to compare comedy to—be it level of talent or level of enjoyment. I wouldn't have gained the confidence I had from all my previous efforts in order to try the next thing, which eventually led me to trying comedy.

So, I'm late to the comedy game. I'm thirty-six years old with less than three years under my belt and I know I need more stage time. I know I have more work to do, but being late to the game doesn't mean I don't get to play. It doesn't mean I don't get to try, I don't get to show up and throw my hat in the ring as a contender.

I don't talk about the toxicity of the comedy industry much, at least I haven't as it relates to me personally. I describe the comedy industry as "hard," "rough," and "competitive," but I don't say "toxic." I avoid using toxic as a descriptor because I think the word is overused and therefore, its power is watered down, the word no longer serves its purpose. I once posted a video joking about my husband enjoying anime, to which a large portion of the anime world responded in my comments.

"Don't be toxic! Let him enjoy himself, you're the problem!"

Wow, it's a joke between me and my husband, a joke that *he is in on*! Calm down, children. And hence why I don't want to be associated with the trolls who cry TOXIC! The other part of why I don't talk about my issues with the comedy industry is because I don't want to ruffle any feathers, I don't want to lose stage time from the "gatekeepers" I might piss off if I call them toxic. Perhaps I *am* part of the problem. Either way, I often stand quietly on the sidelines as I watch a bunch of older white guys hash out their "ish" with people getting more opportunities in comedy than them. These guys, who may be a bit bitter that their twenty years of doing comedy is getting them the same opportunities as my three years gets me, say things like, "it's because you're a girl," and they dismiss my talent as needing to fill a quota. I don't want to appear too pompous too soon, God forbid I be proud of my talent, but all jokes aside, I do want to own my story, my worth, my value, and my talent, and not apologize for what's God-given. I'm a hard worker, don't get me wrong, but I'm also gifted. I'm tired of pretending I'm not so that other people will feel more comfortable.

Whether it was a human experience based on life circumstances, where I grew up and the family I had, or it was a female experience in which I didn't learn to own my power, let alone voice it (because that's not what good little girls do), I grew up not thinking much of myself or what I might be capable of. I grew up knowing my place and knowing it wasn't in the spotlight. As a kid I remember doing things good enough to be liked or picked, but never good enough to stand out, appear better than, or make anyone else feel threatened. I didn't want to compete, I just wanted people to like me. People like the underdog, not the guy who wins every time, just look at Tom Brady. He's so good at what he does it's annoying, and we hate him for it. Excuse me, people, other people hate him for it.

Deep down I've always had a desire to win, to be better, to be the best! But if being the best meant beating people out, it meant disappointing someone and probably their entire family too, and, well, I hated the thought. I wanted to win but I didn't try hard enough to actually win, in part so I could excuse my loss. "Well, I didn't try hard enough." That was my safety net that helped no one (including myself). And I held back also in part because I wasn't sure I deserved to win. Surely, the other person was more deserving than I. Surely, I never developed healthy self-esteem.

So that combination of desire and fear has always stuck with me—a desire to be great and a fear of my own greatness. And then later in life, after trying a bunch of things and being pretty decent at all of them, I stumbled upon stand-up comedy and it was something I was really good at it… for a beginner, sure, but still really good.

Why is it so hard for any of us to own our own greatness? Sometimes I give myself pep talks in the mirror, and just as I'm feeling confident, I lean in, visualizing the people who have given me a hard time, and in my best Disney villain voice I say to my reflection: *The audacity you have to be confident!* I follow up with an evil laugh, which always makes me really laugh, and then I remember…

I *am* really good at making people laugh. I think I'm ready to keep doing just that.

# 16

# THE DRY BAR EXPERIENCE PART 1

**IN REALITY,** I'm probably too sensitive to be a comedian—someone who's supposed to make light of things and joke around at the expense of other people's feelings? No way. Not only do I take myself way too seriously, but I also *hate* the thought of hurting someone else's feelings. It doesn't mean I've never done it, nor been prone to *want* to hurt someone's feelings—I certainly have—but once they are hurt, I feel bad. If you've ever watched Season One of *The Real Housewives of Beverly Hills,* you know what I mean (if you haven't, you're probably doing way better in life than me; *Real Housewives* is a guilty pleasure I'm not exactly proud of). For the whole season, I really wanted something horrible to happen to Camille Grammar... nothing fatal, just a little "put her in her place" incident. She was on a high horse, and she needed to dismount (this was my character assessment).

By the end of the season, her husband of thirteen years, Kelsey Grammar (also known as *Frasier* to anyone who knows good television), had an affair with a twenty-nine-year-old and dumped Camille. I did not feel triumphant for getting my wish. The incident I wanted for her was not supposed to wreck her marriage, just maybe land it in therapy longer than necessary, draining her resources, and forcing her to downsize to a smaller mansion. Not that I thought about it too much.

All this to say, I am human, so of course there are countless things I want to make fun of people for. I'm no more "nice by nature" than anyone else, but when I actually see someone's feelings get hurt, I can't take it. I can't take it perhaps because I know too well how it feels, and even if I feel like someone deserves negativity, I've never been able to actually feel good about someone getting what they deserve. A possible exception would be Hitler, naturally.

On top of my "feelings" thing, which BTW you aren't supposed to worry about people's feelings when you are in the comedy industry, there's also the very competitive nature of comedy. *Everyone* wants to book the show, so they'll do whatever it takes to be the one that's chosen. Friends become competitors, men become jerks, and women, women become more foul-mouthed than a Red Sox fan at Yankee Stadium. After all, they have to keep up with the boys, or so they think. It's all very anxiety-inducing.

There's still so much I'm learning about the business. I thought once I had a manager I would be set. I was unaware that a manager doesn't actually book your shows, he "manages" your shows, which means that you have to book shows (that apparently need managing) for your manager to do his job.

"Well, how do I book more shows?" I asked my manager, mildly disappointed to find out that I had signed a five-year contract with someone who wasn't going to book more shows for me.

"You have to get a booking agent," he said, "then you need a business manager to handle all the finances and make sure your manager and agent are getting paid, so you don't have to worry about stuff like that."

"And I suppose the business manager takes a cut as well?"

"Well, they don't do it for free."

How many people does it take for one person to be a comedian?!

So, by the end of 2022, I'd had a manager for two years, but since we signed our contract just two days before the world shut down to Covid, he had yet to manage a show. It's not his fault he went two years without managing a show (right?)—the world shut down. Plus, he doesn't make money unless I make money—so it's not like I was paying him to sit there, but now (at the time of writing this) we're soon heading into 2023 and the world is opening back up, I don't have an excuse for why I'm not performing, and I feel lost again. I was talking to my brother recently who asked about why I wasn't performing,

"There's gotta be places that are having shows," he said. "Jim Gaffigan is on tour!" As if that's a reason for why I should also be able to find places to perform.

"Yeah," I said, "because he's *Jim Gaffigan!*" It helps your case to get booked for a show if people already know who you are.

And in the midst of all this are the people who think I've come so far and must know what I'm doing in the comedy world. Yesterday alone I got five messages from people who wanted to know how to be a stand-up comedian.

One person actually said, "I have quit my job and finally decided to pursue my dream of stand-up comedy, please tell me what open mics you recommend?"

My first recommendation is to get your job back. For. Sure.

I suppose the reason people *think* I know about the comedy business is because once upon a time, I filmed a Dry Bar Comedy Special, which *can be* a kinda big steppingstone in the direction of getting "discovered." I was elated when I got the email announcing that I had been booked to film, drumroll please, A Dry Bar Comedy Special. *Little ol' me?* Thanks to my special, I have, in fact, been "discovered," but like I said, mostly by people who want to know how to become a comedian, or more to the point, how to book a Dry Bar Comedy Special.

"You've inspired me," a girl wrote to me once. "Watching you has made me realize I can totally do comedy." Umm… was that supposed to be a compliment?

The whole process with Dry Bar was very interesting. When you agree to do a Dry Bar special, you agree to work clean. This is not a problem for me as I have never been a Red Sox fan at Yankee Stadium… at least not onstage. In the freedom of my own home, I enjoy a good swear word to really get a point across or get a head turn from my husband. I can see why people use curses for shock and awe—they really do work wonders for getting reactions. That said, swearing is not my thing onstage. I do have some "suggestive" material, some have even called it "spicy" which is comical to me because I'm so far from spicy, I'm milky (weird word, but let's go with it). It's not something I'm proud of, spicelessness, and in fact, I'm often insecure about lacking spice in the gritty world of comedy.

"Who ordered the whole milk?" I imagine hecklers yelling before I get onstage at a club.

I do have a bit that is a true story involving my younger brother saying "damn" for the first time, but that's about as vulgar as I get. None of this I say from a place of pride. I'm not a crusader for squeaky-clean comedy, I just don't like being held accountable to any label because who knows how I'll feel when I'm nearing seventy and a little more tired and a lot more cranky and might want to swear every now and then to relieve my back pain. But as it sits for me right now, I have found it most natural (for me) to just tell my stories without being crass for the sake of a reaction. That said, I do dream of having a private show one day that is a little more "colorful."

While many comedians freak out about how they are going to work clean *and* still be funny so that Dry Bar will film them, this was the one area I finally felt confident in when I was invited to do the special. I knew I could work clean. What I didn't know was the degree to which a Dry Bar comedian needed to be clean, and the systematic process they had in place to make sure their guidelines were not broken.

Once I was signed on to do a show, they sent me a video of the do's and don'ts for performers at Dry Bar.

"There is clean," the host of the video said, "and there is *Dry Bar Clean*."

Even though Dry Bar doesn't promote itself as a religious organization, it's affiliated with a certain religion that has a lot to do with why the company is called Dry Bar. Quite simply, alcohol isn't served (or consumed) anywhere near the premises (the venue where your special is filmed)—it's literally a dry bar. There *is* a bar, but they serve sodas and some kind of flavored milk on ice. The iced milk wasn't half bad, but that's neither here nor there, I'm getting off topic. My whole point was that there is a reason Dry Bar pretty much has its own category of clean comedy.

So, here we get into the categories of clean comedy. For me, there are four categories of clean:

1. Clean
2. Church Clean
3. Family Clean
4. Dry Bar Clean

There is no hierarchy, just differences.

## CLEAN COMEDY

Clean Comedy usually means no sexual content and no big swear words. You can probably get away with "damn" and "hell" if used tastefully or telling a story about kids hearing/using swear words, but you can't use those words often or for no reason.

For example (brace yourself for a cheesy, clean joke): We were getting ready for Sunday School when my son asked, "Can I have some damn Cheerios?" I was so shocked, I spanked him right there, in front of my daughter. When I asked her what she wanted for breakfast, she looked at her brother fresh from his spanking and said, "I sure as hell don't want the Cheerios." This is a badly butchered example of a joke my very conservative Uncle Johnny used to tell, and he thought it was the funniest thing ever. Maybe it was because the kids were on their way to Sunday School, or maybe it was because the kids didn't really know what they were saying, but in a house where you weren't allowed to swear, this joke was okay. However, using the word damn as an adjective like "I ain't paying those damn taxes!"? Less appropriate. Although maybe not in relation to taxes.

In addition, with clean comedy, you *can* be suggestive regarding sexual content, much like parents trying to have a conversation in front of a kid and talking *around* the issue while never actually naming the issue, but you *can't* get all Nicki Minaj or even Dr. Ruth in a joke. In general, sex jokes are out.

## CHURCH CLEAN

In Church Clean comedy, you are probably performing in a church, which means absolutely no swear words and absolutely nothing suggestive. It's clean without the footnotes and euphemisms. There's not much more to say on that. Church Clean is just God Bless America and all that sh*t. Kidding. See that? An example of shock and awe, which you won't really find in Church Clean comedy.

I have plenty of stories that are "clean," but I can't tell them in a church setting. To me, they are harmless. For example, the story about when I learned what the lyrics of a rap song actually meant. In the bit, I'm not promoting the lyrics, I'm making fun of the fact that I didn't know guys referred to girls as "cake," so when I overheard a guy saying he was looking for some cake one night, I chimed in.

"Oh, me too, I love cake!"

I'm making fun of myself, but because it is suggestive, it is not allowed in church.

Also not allowed? The bit about my childhood when I thought shaving above your knee was naughty (because that's what I learned). When a girlfriend told me she shaved *all the way* up her leg, I responded "YOU SKANK!" The joke is making fun of my own ignorance but calling someone a "skank" in church is often a no-go (even if most people say it once they're out in the parking lot).

## FAMILY CLEAN

Family Clean is actually even harder than church clean because the same rules apply to Family Clean that apply to Church Clean— you don't want kids running around yelling "SKANK" after they watch your set, you'll get a lot of emails, I promise. On top of the Church Clean rules, the Family Clean rules add on the awareness that kids are present. You can have a comedy night at a church and not have kids present (hopefully childcare is provided), and so you can still share certain stories you wouldn't share when kids are present, like saying there is no such thing as Santa Claus. Telling a story about discovering that Santa isn't real will *kill* at a kid-less church event, if for no other reason than Christmas is Jesus' holiday anyway. But tell a story about discovering that Santa isn't real at an event labeled "family-friendly" with kids in the crowd, and people will riot.

To me, Family Clean is the hardest of all. Don't swear, don't talk about adult things, and for God's sake, DO NOT TELL THEM THERE IS NO SANTA! Other stories that are off-limits in this category include finding out my mom was the Tooth Fairy, slapping the Easter bunny, and sitting on my sister's hamster, thereby killing the hamster. Though they are technically "clean" stories, parents do not want their kids to hear these stories for fear that their kids may act them out or want to have some lengthy conversation after a comedy show about what happens to pets when they die.

## DRY BAR CLEAN

Let me preface by saying that this is neither a statement nor a position on religious organizations and their affiliations. I have my own faith that may look weird to some people and that is okay. I have no qualms with any specific religion and how they choose to reflect their beliefs. To each their own. This is merely my experience working on a comedy production with a strict set of rules due to their religious background, that is all!

As it pertained to my experience, Dry Bar Clean was like Church Clean *on steroids*. It wasn't as kid-aware because kids were not at the shows, so full speed ahead with the Santa stories! But as far as language goes, you might as well pretend that kids are present, maybe even sitting in the front row, and their mom, let's call her Karen, is also front and center, right there with them, waiting for you to screw up. Speaking of "screw up" don't even think about using that expression with a Dry Bar audience. Dry Bar Clean meant not only should you not swear, but you also shouldn't have swear replacement words (hence, no "screw up"). Though I may not swear onstage, I at least understand the human need to verbally express oneself and have filler words for when the Big Kahuna words feel "a bit too much," as I once heard a woman describe Bill Burr when asked about his comedy. Even "a bit too much" is a gross understatement for Bill Burr, who I think is a Red Sox fan.

Dang, gosh, shoot, and darn are examples of filler words, and seeing as they are obvious replacements for harsher words, they were "technically" not recommended in Dry Bar Comedy. I say "technically" because you had the freedom to use those words, it was just suggested that it might be better for you if you didn't. The Dry Bar video "encouraged you" in a specific direction for how to deliver your material, and then ultimately "left it up to your discretion," which (as they said) "may or may not affect the number of views you get." (More on that later.)

And then there's the oh-so-popular, OMG! While it's kind of a church rule to not take the Lord's name in vain, there is some fluidity in what that means. To actually exclaim, "Oh, my God!" is to be in such utter disbelief that you call upon on your God. I have never understood why the phrase "Oh, my God" was considered to be taking the Lord's name in vain. If nothing else it's a prayer, an exclamation, a declaration—MY God! Do people use it out of context? Sure, but don't throw the pasta out with the pasta water.

And as an extreme side note, nowhere in scripture does it say this expression is the definition of taking the Lord's name in vain.

I'm pretty sure He meant don't kill people in the name of God, don't break up with your girlfriend and say, "God made me do it," and certainly don't hold up signs that say "God hates homosexuals" as if He told you that. THAT is taking the Lord's name in vain—using His name for your own agenda and inability to face your own issues.

"Oh, my God, how am I going to do this?" *That* is calling on my God to help. Not that I have a strong opinion on the usage.

So, back to my point: while there is fluidity in Church Clean when it comes to expressions like "Oh, my God," there appeared to be no fluidity in Dry Bar's version of clean. Not only should you not say, "Oh, my God," you probably shouldn't say "Oh, my gosh," or possibly even my personal favorite, "Holy cow!" To some people, there is nothing holy about a cow, not even the cows possibly present at the scene of Jesus' birth, lying by the manger.

Again, I work clean, "really clean" to some people and "clean, but kinda spicy" to others. Only once have I been called "kinda naughty," but that was by a woman who grew up in a family that wasn't even allowed to watch *The Little Mermaid* because Ariel only had shells covering her "you-know-whats," as the woman called them. After many attempts, some failed, some successful, I have come to terms with the fact that I can't please everyone. I've worked in every venue from clubs and churches to family events and therapy retreats. I know how to be sensitive to a crowd's needs, but *Dry Bar Clean*? This was next-level, and not something even Bill Burr could do. Whether or not you agree with his aggressive style, the man has talent. And whether or not you agree with me about that, the man could *never* do a Dry Bar Comedy Special. To which I'm sure his response would be, "Why would I f—ing want to? F—you, you f—ng F—!" But he would fill in the blanks.

Shall we keep going with the rules?

On top of no swearing and no taking the Lord's name in vain, there was obviously no sex talk, but also no innuendo, no drawing of attention to the female body, and absolutely *no* negative talk about marriage, the last two almost as important as the Lord's name.

I can get on board with the marriage thing. I'm just as tired of hearing comedians do the same material bashing their spouses for the sake of a laugh, but what defines negative talk? What if my husband really did say something dumb like, "Almond butter is really fattening?" Especially if he said it to me while I was in the middle of eating a spoonful of almond butter straight out of the jar. In this case, I would like to point out to my audience that although he is a smart man, every once in a while, he has spontaneous bouts of stupidity.

If I can't even share that true story (never mind the fact that I eat almond butter straight out of the jar), then what shall we talk about? The weather?


I knew I had enough material to fill out my Dry Bar Special, but seeing as "Dry Bar Clean" knocked out my SKANK bit and at least three other of my longer bits, some of which were my favorites, I also knew I had to reconfigure what exactly I needed to do to get my special produced, which was another piece to the puzzle as I discovered. Because your special is a live show, there are two pieces you have to think about: 1) the live audience, and 2) the at-home audience, who will watch the special on TV (if it gets produced). You may get away with saying something in the live audience, they may even like your innuendos, but that doesn't mean the powers that be will actually produce your special. And even if they do, you might get filtered by a system that prevents people from seeing your special because it gets labeled as "GRAPHIC," which, religious or not, if you're simply looking for some good, clean comedy, you're probably not going to click on the one that says "GRAPHIC."

Which mine was, for reasons well beyond my control.

# 17

## THE DRY BAR EXPERIENCE PART 2

**ONCE I BOOKED MY DRY BAR SPECIAL,** I was in just as much disbelief as anyone else. (I used to say, "as everyone else," but then I realized not *every*one cared, and that realization was both a downer and a relief.) I prepared for months, crafting my material, trying it out in different places. The comics who I'd known for the last couple of years, and most often did shows with, hesitated before congratulating me—not all of them, but some of them. They weren't trying to be rude; they just couldn't seem to understand how *I* got a comedy special. *Me,* of all people. *Me,* a girl who'd been doing comedy for less than three years. Fair enough. They wanted to know more about how to get themselves booked than they wanted to celebrate with me. Also, fair. I might have felt the same way if I were in their shoes.

The only comedy friends I never sensed any resentment from were Lisa and Mark. My friend, Lisa Gilbert, is a "mom of triplets" and has always been a class act, not to mention hilarious. My buddy, Mark Christopher Lawrence, is a man who in my opinion needs no introduction, but I'll talk about him anyway. For some reason, Mark has always believed in me, giving me opportunities to perform in many of his shows, some of which even I felt not ready for.

"You got chops, believe in yourself," Mark would remind me. He's been in movies and TV shows, *and* he had his own very successful Dry Bar Special produced, so it meant a lot when he sincerely congratulated me.

I think it's a very human thing to think or feel that if someone else gets what you want, it means you will be left out. Hence why we compete, edge each other out, back stab, black mail, and try to get ahead of everyone else. I'd never experienced this personally until I entered the comedy industry, and I don't just mean experiencing this from other people, I mean experiencing this even in myself. I was caught off guard when I noticed jealousy that someone else got booked for a show and I didn't. I found myself saying things like "How come him or her?" or "Why not me?" I was surprised by my own scarcity mindset, finding it hard to celebrate other people's victories because I thought their victory meant my loss. It's still a battle sometimes. I have to remind myself to celebrate first. Always celebrate first. Notice emotions second. Celebrate, then dive into what those emotions mean.

All of these feelings were at play in the months leading up to filming my special. I was battling my own thoughts and my own insecurities, along with backhanded compliments from other comedians.

"Well, they really needed women, so congrats on being what they're looking for."

*Wha..?!* While I won't blanket statement an entire group of people, here I go…

In my experience, I find the most insecure people in the world to be male comedians, usually middle-aged, and most often white. This doesn't include the guys who've already "made it." Jim Gaffigan, Jerry Seinfeld, Tom Papa, David Sedaris. They are exceptions and the reason why I will not generalize (although, who knows what they were like coming up). But the men who are trying to be *the next* Seinfeld or Gaffigan? Watch out. They will suck the wind right out of your sails while they stomp their way to the top. People always say you have to have thick skin in the comedy business, and I find that to be true simply because of this specific group of men.

Unfortunately, I have given too much power to the voices of these men who want to put me in my place and make sure I know I don't *yet* belong here, maybe I will *if I prove myself* and *if they decide I do*, but I don't belong just because I showed up. It's not that they are outright mean, it's that they are confusingly kind; I walk away unsure if I've just been insulted or I've just been complimented. These men make the sweet sting of a Southern woman blessing your heart feel like a genuine sentiment. They seem to feed off your feelings of inferiority as a woman. I don't know why I've given them so much power in my thought life over these years, but when I have to battle off the voices that tell me I can't, it's often been the voices of these men. There are exceptions, of course, always exceptions (my Comedy Pops, Tony, for one, or my buddy, Brian Apprille, for two), but you know what they say about one bad apple spoiling the bunch? It had never felt truer until I entered the comedy world. I still have to remind myself that I don't have to throw away *all* the apples just because there are a few bad ones in the bunch, ruining my experience.

Show day finally arrived, and I shut out all the noise. I was there, I was doing it, and it didn't matter anymore what anyone's opinion was. I suppose it never really mattered, but it's hard to feel that way when you're on the outskirts of your accomplishments. Show day is still a little bit of a blur. I remember going on a walk down the main street of Provo early that morning. I recited my set as I walked, noticing the "smoke" of my breath as I breathed out into the cold air. I tried to be present, taking in the rustle of the leaves on the sidewalk, a signal that fall was in full effect. I paid attention to the beams of the sun flickering through large tree branches. I stopped in a coffee shop and found it to be a bit more eclectic than the entire town of Provo presented itself to be. There were people with piercings and purple hair, not an unusual sight for most independent coffee shops in any other city, but for Provo, it seemed "eccentric."

As I waited for my coffee, I noticed the guy sitting beside me. He was wearing cat ears and appeared to be talking to himself. At first, I thought it was weird, and then I remembered my walk over to the shop—reciting my entire set, quietly but still out loud. I probably appeared just as odd to onlookers.

Before iPhones and AirPods, people used Bluetooth earpieces to talk on their phone hands-free. You would see people all the time just blabbering away into thin air, and while that's not uncommon now, it was a strange sight back then. I once went to a gas station and in the little mini mart, as I was standing there trying to pick out a drink, a man in a suit opened the fridge beside me.

"Are you kidding me!?" he yelled.

I thought maybe he was mad that his drink was out of stock, but he proceeded to grab a juice and then he yelled again.

"Well, get the damn papers signed today!"

Ahhh, the juice was well stocked, it was just a Bluetooth.

My friends and I used to play a game called "Bluetooth or Crazy?" Was the person walking down the street talking to themselves on a

Bluetooth? Or were they just crazy? I have since added "Comedian" to the list of possibilities.

In the afternoon, I went over to the venue where the special would be filmed. They gave me a tour of the set and helped me pick out what to wear. They told me to bring three outfit options and while I wanted to go all out in crazy colors, I'm always reminded to be thoughtful about how it will come across on video—*will it be too distracting for the eye?* I settled on jeans with a simple rainbow stripe on the side, a way for me to have some color without it being obnoxious, and a light pink sweater shirt, which is basically what it sounds like—a sweater with short sleeves. I was going mostly for comfort, but also for something that wouldn't show pit stains if I lifted my arms. I was already sweating, and I didn't want my armpits announcing my nervousness to the world. The sweater shirt was a loose fit, so it felt like a perfect option.

The people who worked at Dry Bar could not have been nicer. It was a night and day difference from any experience I had up to that point in the comedy industry. At Dry Bar, they actually treated you like you were the talent, as opposed to someone who should just be grateful for the opportunity to be there. They waited on you hand and foot, making sure you felt comfortable, had whatever you wanted to eat or drink, minus the alcohol (again, *Dry* Bar).

They had me film my intro, most of which involved me dancing outside in front of the building. While I appear quirky online or on social media, I'm not as quirky out in public, at least not in the day to day. I may dance at a party or in a group of friends, but in the middle of the afternoon on a sidewalk by myself while a camera crew films me? Not my cup of tea. Someone held out a cell phone playing the song for me to dance to. People walked by unfazed, without so much as a smirk in my direction. I sometimes don't know which is worse, people stopping and staring at your vulnerability, or people acting like they don't see it and couldn't care less about it. I felt awkward but I tried to act otherwise. Had the Instagram account *Influencers in the Wild* been a thing at the time, it's likely I would have been on it.

The night itself was a blur. From what I remember, the first show started at 7 p.m., the later show at 9:30. I met the two other comics who would also be performing. Nic and Eileen were both older than me with more experience behind them, but they were incredibly friendly and welcoming. A producer came in to give us the lineup for the night. I would go last.

"You're the headliner," Nic said with a big smile.

"Hey, that's awesome," he added, and seemed to genuinely mean it. Everything that came out of Nic's mouth was positive and encouraging, I wanted to nickname him K-Love after the Christian radio station known for their "positive and encouraging" music, but I didn't know him well enough yet and wasn't sure if that would come across as creepy. While my experience with middle-aged white men in comedy had been dicey, Nic was a good apple, reminding me that not every middle-aged white man in comedy is bitter and ready to put you in your place. To this day when I think of Nic, I think: K-Love.

Nic was up first, then it was Eileen's turn. They both did really well, but they both came off the stage saying they wished they had done this or that differently, a very common feeling for any comic coming off stage. When I finish a show, I often don't think about how well I did, instead I find myself focusing on what I did wrong or what I forgot. Even though the audience doesn't know I forgot something, *I know*, and I beat myself up for it immediately—sometimes even while the audience is still applauding.

"Don't freak out if you see the clock wind down," Eileen said. "I panicked toward the end and rushed through my last bit instead of just taking my time to finish. They aren't going to yank you off the stage, so just be sure to finish strong." I thanked her for the advice, which I knew was really kind of her to share.

Before the show started, the producers pointed out where the clock would be, a big glaring red light in the balcony, taunting you to either slow it down or hurry it up. Comedy is all about timing, the perfect pace, and the clock is there to hold you accountable. I know I probably would have panicked too had Eileen not given me that warning, so I was incredibly grateful that she offered her insight to help me do a better job. I remember thinking that should I go further in this business, I wanted to be that kind of comedian, the kind that helped others get better.

My first set was, in a word… amazing. It was electrifying (another word). My heart was racing, I was nervous but mostly excited. I had so fully prepared that I knew I was going to kill it (as long as they liked my humor). When I get excited or nervous (or angry or tired or basically in any state of heightened emotion) my southern accent comes out thick. I have never thought I had much of an accent, after all, the beaches of South Carolina are different from the backwoods, but I've lived all over the country long enough to learn that every time I say "y'all" or "tired" without fully pronouncing the R, people always ask me where I'm from. People might not pick up on my accent right away, but then certain words give it right away. That is unless I'm in that heightened emotional state, which is where I was that night at Dry Bar. My accent came out so thick you would have thought I was related to LeeAnn Morgan—another female comedian who's schtick *is* her southern accent (although it's not just a schtick, it's amazingly real!).

People who didn't know me just thought I was a comedian with a strong accent. But later, when my special aired online, comments came in about my accent (among other things). Some people loved my accent, some were unfazed by it, and some just jumped right in with the stereotypical attacks toward someone with a southern accent, taking aim at my I.Q. Close friends and people who *did* know me, however, noticed right away how different I sounded.

"You were just different," one of my comedian friends said to me, "not in a bad way, just different." Thank you?

When I ended my set I got an unprompted standing ovation, something we were told would likely happen since it was a filmed production but seeing as neither of the comedians who'd gone before me got ovations, I wasn't expecting one. Once the first show was over, the director gave each comedian notes for their second show. He came to find me as soon as I got off stage.

"Okay, for the second show," he said, "everything you just did … do it again. That's it, that's my notes. You're gold."

I still feel awkward writing that, like I'm not allowed to speak so highly of myself, but as I know I've said before, I've spent so much time playing small just to make other people feel comfortable, at a certain point I have to be honest with myself: I am not only *good enough*, but I'm also *really good* at what I do. I'll never get better at it if I don't start by owning it.

My second show was equally awesome, though I admit to having felt more of a connection with the first crowd—they were an older group who understood my humor and could relate to my jokes about aging because they'd already been through it. They laughed *with me* because they knew the feeling of transitioning through the decades, but they also laughed *at me* for me thinking I was "so old." They knew how much longer I actually still had to go.

I kept my set as Dry Bar Clean as possible. I replaced every "oh, my God" with "oh, my word." If I made fun of someone it was only myself, and most importantly, I made sure people knew that they were important. I know it's not something you *need* to do or even something you *should* do in a comedy show, but I certainly don't think it hurts to take ten seconds out of whatever you're doing just to let people know they matter and you're glad they are there. I honestly believe the world would be a different place (in a good way) if each of us took a little time to make other people feel important more often. I know I don't do it enough. I didn't do it just for the live crowd that night, I did it for anyone who might see the special at any point thereafter, sometime, someone, somewhere might need to hear those words.

I think I felt so strongly about getting that message across in this particular special because it was so desperately what I wanted to hear at that time. Having entered the comedy arena at a later age, feeling slightly unwelcome and in need of proving myself, I just wanted to know that it mattered I was there, that I was worthy, whether I ever proved myself or not. It was for the audience, *and* it was for me, reminding me that no matter who is on stage or who is in the seats, we are all in this beautiful battle called life, trying to figure out how to make it work.

I got another standing ovation in the second show, high-fiving everyone in the front row as I left the stage. Josh greeted me right away with a bottle of water and kisses all over my head.

"You killed it, baby, you killed it!" I knew I killed it, but I also knew I could do better. I don't mean that in a condescending or self-deprecating way, I just knew I had it in me to keep going and keep getting better.

I waited by the front to greet people as they walked out.

"That was hilarious!"

"You're so funny!"

"You were my favorite."

Those words never get old.

I was relieved and excited and incredibly hungry. I have a difficult time eating before shows, too many emotions going on for me to process food, but as soon as a show is over, I want to throw down, usually with something healthy like sweet potato fries or loaded tater tots. I went back to the green room to eat the meal I was too nervous to eat before the show started. I never seem to mind that the meal is always cold because I waited too long to eat it. Josh will always ask more than once if I'm sure I don't want my food warmed up. He knows I have an aversion to anything that may make me appear like a diva, like asking if there's a microwave to reheat my food after it's been sitting there for over an hour. I'd rather eat it cold than be so "difficult."

"It's not too much," he always says. But not all foods are good reheated in a microwave, so depending on what it is, I have to convince him that I really don't mind it cold.

"I'm not being passive, I just don't like warm mushy fries."

"As long as you're sure."

"I'm sure as long as they don't have an oven."

"Let me go check," and Josh will proceed to go ask if there's an oven to reheat my fries, *because that is way less difficult.*

But on that particular night at Dry Bar, I was not in need of an oven, so after the audience had all trickled out, I went back to the greenroom and ate cold curry; nothing had ever tasted better than in that moment. Everyone at Dry Bar thanked me and I thanked them, and we all hugged like we'd known each other for years. We said goodnight and then Josh and I walked back to our hotel where we met Eileen and her husband in the lobby restaurant. We ordered a glass of wine to celebrate and said a cheers to Dry Bar, which was kinda ironic.

The next day Josh and I got on a plane and that was it. It was over just like any other live show that plenty of people never see, as if the night never happened. Except this night was recorded on six different RED cameras, so it most certainly happened, and it was only a matter of time before it would be released out into the public. We were told it'd be *at least* three to six months before our specials were produced, and that was the "fast track," so to speak. Seeing as it was the end of October, I figured I could wait until January to really start freaking out.

That November, the day before Thanksgiving I got a message from a friend on Facebook.

"Hey, I loved your Dry Bar Special!"

Immediately I felt nervous. What did they mean? Had they watched the live stream the night of and were they just now getting around to telling me?

"How did you see it?" I asked.

Then they sent the link. There it was. There I was—my face on the little thumbnail, my full special—produced in just one month's time.

And that is when the panic set in.

# 18

# THE DRY BAR EXPERIENCE PART 3

**WHEN I SAW** that my special had been produced, I panicked in the same way anyone would—anyone who'd had a night of fun and it had been recorded for everyone to see at a later date. There's a difference between the people who paid to see you perform on the night of a show, and the people who randomly stumble across you online and for one reason or another feel compelled to make comments about you in the God-forsaken comment section. Though it wasn't a Netflix special, available to millions, Dry Bar was the biggest deal for me up to that point, and Dry Bar reached a large audience, larger than I ever have on any of my social media platforms (yes, I've tried them all!). Speaking of, come find me on Instagram: @jjbarrows.

I knew going into my special that it would open doors for me, not only doors for more opportunities, but also doors for criticism, as my reach would no longer be limited to my personal network of people who want to encourage me. That is why I had a plan to wait until at least January (the earliest I thought *maybe* the special would come out, if I was lucky) to panic about things like internet trolls and keyboard warriors, so valiantly taking jabs at people's characters from behind the safety shield of their computer screens.

I was most caught off guard by the fact that I didn't even receive an announcement email from Dry Bar saying my special had been released. There was not even so much as a request for approval of the picture they chose for my cover, a picture that I hated as soon as I saw it.

"WHY would they pick that picture?" I said out loud as I stared at the little thumbnail.

I was in the car and that was the first thing I said in response to my seeing my special available for public consumption. Josh was driving when I got the message and I yelled at the thumbnail like a diva done wrong.

"What picture?" he asked. I showed him the thumbnail photo. "Wait, is that it!?Is that your special!?" Josh celebrated while I sat there, unsure of how I felt.

Obviously, I *wanted* to have a comedy special produced, what comedian doesn't? But *wanting* and *hoping* are so very different from actually following through and doing it. Sometimes it's easier for me to stay in the wanting and hoping phase than it is to tread into the unknown territory of actually putting myself out there.

I was mostly nervous about what people would think—and how people who didn't like me would respond. In a live show, at least you have some control, whether it's addressing the hecklers, ignoring the hecklers, or getting the hecklers kicked out; you have some control over how the night goes and how people experience you. The internet, on the other hand, spares you no feelings and leaves you no control. The moment it's published is the moment your well-intended material is left wide open to interpretation by people from all different walks of life, none of whom seem to agree on anything. Even if you were the birth child of Mother Teresa and Martin Luther King Jr., accomplishing nothing but good for the betterment of humanity, people would find a reason to not like you. I'm not sure why it's this way, perhaps it's jealousy or insecurity. I know I have been guilty of not liking people for no reason other than I've felt insecure around them (which is more my problem than theirs). It's probably true to tell yourself, *oh, they're just jealous* when someone calls you "ugly" or "not funny" or a "wannabe," but it doesn't mean it doesn't hurt.

It's interesting because I've heard the question asked of comedians, mostly to women (I've actually never heard an interviewer ask a man), "Would you rather someone call you 'not pretty' or 'not funny'?"

And more often than not, the women say they'd rather be called not pretty. I agree to an extent. If what I'm trying to be is funny and I am being criticized for not doing a good job at being funny, it's easy for me to dismiss it, either as someone's opinion or my need to work harder. But if what I'm trying to be is funny and someone calls me ugly, which has nothing to do with anything, that reflects a nasty side of humanity that is hard for me to digest: being mean for the sake of mean. I just don't get it. And in that sense, I don't want to be called ugly (at least as it pertains to my comedy) because it reflects the ugliness of humanity in general, that need to find *something* to tear apart in someone. Perhaps it's not my problem to worry about other people, but that is precisely my problem—I always have worried about other people—not necessarily about their opinions, but about their well-being, and the further I have gone into the entertainment industry, the bleaker humanity seems.

After we signed our contracts and finished shooting our specials, we were told we would need to promote the special as much as possible, to send our links out on social media and in emails, to post them everywhere and to rave about our shows *from the rooftops!* Yet I never even received a little celebratory email from Dry Bar letting me know that my special was on its way, let alone that it was already out! I found out from someone who watched it online. I had seen some of the rough cuts about three weeks after the filming, but I certainly wasn't expecting the final to be released the following week! Josh had been asking me if I was excited and absolutely, I was, but I was also confused and nervous and anxious for my show to be out there. But there it was... way out there!

Since Josh and I had been traveling and were just getting home the day before Thanksgiving, I figured I'd wait till the weekend to start promoting it.

In addition, Josh's birthday happened to fall on Thanksgiving that year. We were on our way to a friend's house to celebrate both Josh and turkey when I got the phone call from my mom that my grandmother, Mommom, had just passed away peacefully. We had known her passing might be soon, but I thought for sure I would get to see her at Christmas. My mom, my sister Bonnie, and my brother Bobby were by my grandmother's side when she passed. My only comfort was knowing she wasn't alone.

I had also just published my first book that fall and had written a chapter about Mommom that I couldn't wait to share with her. I wanted to give her a copy of my book in person when I returned home for Christmas, except Mommom didn't make it till Christmas, and since I waited, she never got to read her chapter. I was heartbroken that I didn't get to say goodbye or let her know just how special she was to me. During that time, filming a comedy special really didn't seem to matter, and promoting it just felt gross. I know, life is supposed to go on, and it does, but not taking a moment to feel the loss of someone who's been in my life for *all my life*, I couldn't *not* stop to grieve.

After a time, I returned to my task and promoted my comedy special as much as I knew how, but seeing as it was just me, my husband, and our Instagram accounts as our promotional team, I wasn't exactly sure if we were making a dent in Dry Bar expectations.

November turned into December, and I went home to South Carolina for Christmas, taking part as the comedy act in a church Christmas show three nights out of the week. I falsely assumed that since it was my hometown everyone there had seen my special and I needed to come up with new material. Turns out, only a handful of the people knew who I was, and I should have stuck with material I already knew worked instead of scrambling for new inspiration. After a kinda rocky start, I was able to win the crowd over in the second half, reminding myself every time I started that while it may feel awkward at first, the crowd will like me by the end (hopefully). It helped that I performed in the first half *and* second half of the Christmas show, with other entertainment in between my performances, so the audience wasn't going to get up and leave before I could win them over. To this day, I remind myself of my takeaway from that experience: *never* assume people know who you are, and even if they do, *never* assume they like you.

In January, I was asked to perform at a Church in the San Clemente area. Thankfully, for that show, I stuck to my original Dry Bar material, and I killed my performance. Before the show began and people started arriving, the comics all hung out together in the lobby area. Nic, who I had performed with at Dry Bar, was there and some of the other comics started asking us about our Dry Bar experience. One man in particular who had made comments in the past about me "prematurely" doing a Dry Bar was a part of the conversation. We'll call him Dave. Dave had also filmed a Dry Bar Special, just two weeks before I filmed mine, and he felt the need to chime in on more than one occasion and answer everything *for me.* (He never answered for Nic, though. Interesting).

"So how did you get booked for the show?" someone asked me.

"Oh," Dave said, "it's a known fact that Dry Bar is desperate for women comedians. They don't even really care if they're funny, they just need women on there."

Nic chimed in, "Yeah, well, JJ was the headliner our night and she really killed it. The headliner at Dry Bar, wow, it was really something!" (Oh, how I had missed K-Love.)

"Well," Dave said, "not really. They just had two women and one man perform that night, naturally they needed to break up the flow, so they had JJ go last." Dave just couldn't bring himself to call me a headliner, not after his thirty years in the business and my three— in Dave's world, I was *not* a headliner, I was last.

I didn't quite understand Dave. He had been so nice to me right up until the point I had booked with Dry Bar. That was when he changed his tone with me.

"You better make sure you prepare as much as possible for that." The way he said it let me know he didn't think I was ready for Dry Bar, like there was a "good luck" in his voice but it wasn't a sincere good luck.

I felt deflated after that pre-show conversation with the other comics and the way Dave was controlling my narrative, talking over me, and making sure everyone knew I got the opportunity not because I was good enough but because I was a minority and Dry Bar needed to diversify. I killed my set however, which only made Dave seem more irritated with me.

After that, Dave invited me to be a part of another show—for reasons unbeknownst to me, because I believed he didn't like me. Before the show, he took all the comics out to dinner. Again, everyone wanted to talk about Dry Bar. Again, Dave rolled his eyes. The conversation went pretty much the same way as it had before: people asked questions and Dave talked over me—clarifying the real reason I was offered a Dry Bar special.

"Yeah, but obviously you did an amazing job," another comic named Mike interjected. "There's no way Dry Bar would produce your special that fast just because you're a woman. I mean, the timing is unheard of."

Dave looked like there was too much gristle in his steak and he was having a hard time chewing.

"Well," he chimed in, "yes, they did it fast because they had to have more females on the lineup, they can't just have a bunch of middle-aged men on there. It helps that she's young and pretty and offers a fresh new option for people."

I sat there, stunned and silent.

"Wow!" Mike said, "Way to give the girl a compliment and then run over her with a bus!"

The table finally laughed. None of them seemed to challenge Dave because Dave was the veteran in the group, plus he was the one putting on the show and writing the checks that night, so they just sat there as Dave continued to act more like a petulant child than a grown man.

In that moment, I wanted to hug Mike. I knew he wasn't biased. We had only just met, and he was actually close friends with Dave, so he wasn't saying it just to defend me, he was saying it because he was aware Dave was clearly refusing to legitimize my talent.

Dave fumbled over his words as he tried to defend his comments. Mike called him out again.

"How about her special got released quickly because she's actually really good?" The table was quiet, and Dave sighed audibly.

"Or," Dave said, "yes, it could be that she was actually just good enough to get a special, and it was released so fast because she did it so well, in which case that would absolutely kill me."

Everyone laughed as if he were joking, but I could tell there was a little bit of truth in his words. He had to keep telling himself and everyone else that there was no way I could be that good in just three years when he'd been at it for thirty and we both ended up with Dry Bar specials only two weeks apart.

After dinner we all headed to the venue. I killed my set that night as well, and Dave, though he was the one who booked me, could barely bring himself to say I did a good job. There was a time when I had so desperately wanted Dave's approval, when I looked up to him and his career, when I was flattered by the compliments he'd give me after a performance. But the moment I got too far ahead at a quicker pace than he thought I should, I no longer had potential in his eyes. I was simply "prematurely" advancing because of my gender in a day and age when "middle-aged white men just can't get a break."

Eye roll.

While my Dry Bar Special didn't pick up momentum right away, apparently not even all my friends were chomping at the bit to watch my performance, it eventually grew legs and carried itself to audiences all over. I began receiving messages telling me how much people enjoyed my show, how much it meant to them, and how much they didn't know they needed to laugh *and* to hear that they were important. More often than not, I cry when I read messages like that—messages from people needing to be reminded of their worth. I love making people laugh, but what I love most about using comedy is making people feel seen.

Along with the nice messages, of course, came the mean comments.

"Who does she think she is?"

"Women aren't funny."

"What an idiot."

"This is what it looks like when a youth pastor tries to be a comedian."

Okay, I'll admit the last one was kinda funny, but as a recovering preacher's kid who wants nothing to do with pastoral duties, it stung a little extra.

Dry Bar told us we would get paid based on how many views we got, and this was why it was so important for us to promote our specials. At the time, I was still active on Facebook, and I had received a message that said, "Here's a five-dollar credit for Facebook ads to promote whatever you want!" I remember thinking, *OMG I could totally promote a Dry Bar video to get more people to watch the special!* I genuinely thought it was a great idea, forgetting about the vultures and trolls that lay in waiting out in the public domain. To use the credit, you had to spend at least ten dollars, so I spent the money, and I picked a Dry Bar clip to send out into the God-forsaken untamed world of Facebook.

I remember Josh and I were driving from L.A. back to Santa Barbara when I got a message about my Facebook ad performance. It was apparently "doing well" and had received a lot of comments. This was when I still thought comments were a good thing, so excitedly, I decided to read them.

"Why do people like this even try?"

"I could never be with someone like this!"

"Once again, women proving they aren't funny."

"How pathetic."

The best of all though, was a GIF of a dog taking a dump in someone's yard accompanied by the comment: "I hope this dog shits on your feed the way your comedy shit on mine."

I laugh now typing it, clever. But at the time I wanted to rip open the passenger seat of the car, crawl inside it, and stay there to rot. I started crying and Josh asked what was wrong. I showed him the GIF and the comment.

"And I read some more," I said through my tears.

"Baby! You aren't supposed to read the comments!" Josh said as if he was already privy to the protocol of Facebook ad comments.

"I didn't know," I said. "I didn't think about complete strangers not liking me for no reason." Josh hugged me and told me he loved me and assured me that, of course, those people were either dumb or insecure and had nothing better to do with their lives.

"Which is why they feel good when they tear down others," he declared.

"The worst part is," I admitted, while still crying, "I used a Facebook ad to promote that video, which means I paid Facebook for that guy to shit on me!" Josh laughed as he pulled me in for a hug.

"You can't be funny while you're sad, that's not fair."

Stand-up comedy is hard. It's not like art where maybe someone just doesn't like the colors you're using. It's not like acting where maybe someone doesn't like the character you're playing. Though hard to hear, in the end, the way you act, or what color you paint with, is still separate from who you are as a person. Stand-up comedy *is* who you are, it *is* you, depending on your schtick. But I don't have a schtick, something that separates who I am on the stage from who I am off the stage, it's just me up there, it's who I am.

Mike Birbiglia said it best when he said: "Stand-up comedy is hard because if people don't like you, it's very personal. It's like saying 'it's not you, it's your personality… I just don't like it.'"

Josh consoled me, but I told him I just needed to cry for a little bit, I needed to accept that this was part of the business I was walking into, a business I never even meant to walk into. I started this journey with nothing more than a need for therapy and a random Google search. I clearly had some deep-seated insecurities that had been stuffed away for so long, when I accidentally stumbled upon that stand-up comedy class, it felt good to let it all out in the form of jokes. I never intended to keep moving forward, and I certainly never intended to ruffle feathers along the way, people like Dave or the guy whose dog was virtually taking a shit on my comedy special. I never meant to draw that sort of attention to myself. I found, what I thought, was a good way to express myself that also seemed to help people, whether through laughter or validation of their own insecurities.

Like I said before, I didn't grow up wanting to be a comedian. I knew nothing about this world, and therefore I did not know how thick my skin needed to be to walk through it. Should I keep moving forward? The trick for me was going to be to figure out how to have a soft heart protected by thick skin. I didn't want the barrage of resentment from other comics to turn me into them, a person hardened by the hostility and competition of this industry. Though sometimes it feels like a weakness, I have grown to like the fact that my soft heart is so easily affected by the world around me.

Even at the time of filming my Dry Bar Comedy Special, I wasn't entirely sure I had committed myself to this craft, something I'm quite sure Jerry Seinfeld would call a sin against comedy, not that he would care in the slightest who I am or where I'm headed. I'm pretty sure, if you were to ask him, a man who can write and star in a show about *nothing* for *nine seasons*, what he thought of my view on comedy, his response would be: "Nothing."

Upon the release of my Dry Bar, I had to take a pause and honestly ask myself if comedy was actually what I wanted to keep doing. I stopped sharing about my Dry Bar Special and I took a break from looking for more stage time. Call me weak or thin-skinned for pausing in the middle of a career pursuit I never intended to pursue, but I realized I needed to check back in with myself right where I had left off a few years back, in those dark moments before accidentally stumbling into that stand-up class. Did I ever really address what was going on in my head? Or did I just find another shiny object to distract me for a while? Like with anything, it distracted me only so long as it felt good, but as soon as a Dave opened his mouth or a dog took a dump on my Facebook wall, those original thoughts about myself came tumbling back and I realized that even after moving to a beautiful new place, marrying the most amazing person, and finding success in a field that not a lot of people do, at the end of the day, I'm still just me.

And even if I were to get a Netflix special or tour the world or sell out Chicago Theater (my wildest dreams do not involve arenas), I'd still just be me. If I'm waiting for something or someone to finally satisfy me, fulfill me, or make me feel whole, I will be waiting until my dying day, when God finally shows up and says "Tada!" (I honestly hope that really is the first thing God says when we meet face to face.)

For now, I have some processing to do about what life "in the meantime" looks like for me. But before I pull out my journal and get all existential, trying to figure out the "right" thing for my life, right now I simply have to do the *next* thing.

And right now, the *next* thing involves an online shopping cart and the fleeting distraction of Amazon's two-day delivery guarantee. Tada!

# 19

# GRAPHIC CONTENT (A DRY BAR FOLLOW-UP)

**AS WITH MUCH IN MY LIFE,** I set out to write about my Dry Bar experience with only one story in mind, however the unfolding of the experience led me down many rabbit trails, some perhaps necessary to the story, others perhaps could have stayed in my journal. I am unsure how to go back and include the original part of the story I wanted to share, and so in attempt to finish what I started, if for no other reason than I find it worth including, here is the final kicker in my Dry Bar experience.

As mentioned in "The Dry Bar Experience Part 1," once a comedian signs on to do a Dry Bar Special, they are sent the guidelines for Dry Bar Clean, as well as access to the online portal that shows examples of what other comedians have been "flagged" for. While I may not understand all the ins and outs of the whole system, my layman's terms interpretation goes something like this...

The guidelines are given to you ahead of time so you can properly prepare to have a successful show, which is always great to get set up for success. Much like switching shifts at Starbucks, you don't want to start your shift without the coffee ready to serve. The morning shift sets the coffee up for the afternoon shift, the afternoon shift sets the coffee up for the evening shift, the evening shift for the morning shift, and on and on it goes. You get the picture—the shift before always gets the place ready for shift that follows them. This system makes Starbucks run successfully because every Starbucks and every employee at Starbucks adheres to the same definition of success for the company, hence their consistency across the board.

While Dry Bar is a successfully run comedy production, "successful" according to Dry Bar and much of their religious-based audience is going to look different from comedian to comedian, depending on that comedian's definition of success, as well as their definition of clean comedy, which has its varying layers.

While things may have changed (I cannot speak for what a company does across its lifetime), at the time of my filming, to have a "successful" Dry Bar special, you had to adhere to all of Dry Bar's guidelines in order for your special to not only be produced, but also seen. When producing a comedy special of any kind, there are two different performances going on—there is the live show in which the comedian is engaging the live audience who paid to be there, and then there is the recording of that show that airs at later date for audiences at home. While I have seen innuendos and "borderline" topics come up in the Dry Bar live shows, and even go over really well, it was the TV production you had to worry about in regard to the content you shared on Dry Bar.

In the Dry Bar system if you broke any of the guidelines, your show got "flagged." Depending on the number of times you swore (oh, damn) or took the Lord's name in vain (oh, my God), you might get flagged. If it was seldom enough, only those few sections would be flagged. But if broken guidelines happened throughout, your entire special would get flagged. The purpose of the flagging was for the online audience who set up filters, a form of parental control offered by Dry Bar in their app. People who had the app could look at what comedians have been flagged for and set filters in their app for "no swearing," "no blasphemy," "no graphic content," etc… The app would automatically skip those parts of the special so that the onlooker wouldn't have to be subjected to it. If, however, a comedian's entire special was flagged and people had those filters on, their special, as I understood it, would not show up at all as an option to watch, unless it is labeled something along the lines of "Graphic Content," with a footnote as to what exactly was so graphic about it.[1]

This is important because comedians are paid based upon the number of views they get, but with the flagging system as it was, Dry Bar (whether intentionally or not) had a lot of control over how many views a comedian might ultimately get[2] depending on how "appropriate" *Dry Bar* viewed a comedian's content and therefore how many "flags" a comedian's content was assigned. The definition of "appropriate" is, of course, pretty subjective. So the definition of "success" will vary for a Dry Bar Special because of the varying interpretations of "appropriate."

Once I filmed my special, I had a pretty good idea that I might get one or two flags: a joke about mis-interpreted rap lyrics (sexual innuendo, flagged), and a joke about a southern woman's prayer chain gossiping in Jesus' name (blasphemy, flagged). Apart from those, I

---

1. This, I should say, is information that has been relayed to me from multiple comedians and I am sharing this story from my point of view and my experience working with Dry Bar. I do not know the inner workings of the company, nor am I claiming this to be ultimate truth, just my truth as I understood it based on the limited information I was given.

2. In the Dry Bar app, which is where a large portion of their audience came from at the time.

really wasn't too worried about it. A few people with some hardcore filters might not see a couple of bits. I could deal with that.

My special had been out for three months when I got a message from another comedian friend who was about to film his Dry Bar special. He had been working on his own material and going through the Dry Bar system to see examples of what other comedians had been flagged for. It was near the end of February 2020 (before Covid fully hit the world and there were bigger fish to fry) when he texted me.

"Hey, did you see what your Dry Bar Special got flagged for?"

"No, but I think it's just a couple of bits like my cake joke and the one about the prayer chain."

"No, your whole special got flagged."

"WHAT!? For what?"

"I think you should just log in and read for yourself, hopefully you will find it as funny as I do."

I threw my phone down and went to my computer, wracking my brain for any reason why they would flag my entire special. I logged in and found my name along with the title of my special, "Doodle All Day." The first flag was for LANGUAGE. I had assumed the innuendo would earn that one for me and maybe even the BLASPHEMY flag, too.

"Oh, my gosh!" I joked out loud (yes, I joke to myself).

And then, there it was, after the LANGUAGE flag, in big bright white all capital letters, the mothership of all flags in the church world: SEX/NUDITY/IMMODESTY.

"WHAT?" I yelled. "Nudity!? Immodesty!? What the…"

Underneath were the following footnotes:

- Immodesty
- Female

Pause. Wait? What? Female? Was it being implied there was immodesty in my comedy special because I am a female? The title of the footnote alone was weird, but then I read the sentence beneath it.

- The comedian's defined chest outline is visible.

I literally laughed out loud.

"WHHHAAT? Defined chest? *Defined* chest!? IS VISIBLE!?"

I was annoyed but also kinda flattered... I mean, that is the nicest thing I've ever heard anyone say about my chest! I was completely confused. Never in my straight A life would someone call my chest *visible*, let alone *defined*. Not to mention, even if it were *noticeable*, I was wearing a short-sleeved sweater *(which Dry Bar approved)*. I couldn't have found a looser shirt to wear unless I shopped at Big & Tall. *Who's stretch of imagination included this footnote!?* I thought. Again, I didn't know whether to complain to Dry Bar or send them a thank you note. Was this what it felt like for men to look at your boobs? A mix of disgust and flattery. *Look away! Please look! Look away!* I had never felt that struggle because I never had anything for anyone to look at.

All jokes aside, I began to feel annoyed. If *I'm* being flagged for immodesty simply because I (apparently) have the body of a female, then that means *all* women are being flagged simply for being women. Whether it's our whole special or parts of our special, our comedy is not being seen because we are performing it *in our bodies*, deemed immodest by someone with a different definition of immodest.

And I guess therein lay the problem: Who got to decide which definition was the "right" definition? And was there actually a "right" definition? Or was it just a *different* definition, and the Dry

Bar definition was apparently the definition I signed up for when I agreed to perform with them?

I will be the first to say I still don't think it's fair, especially for people to think my comedy involves sex/nudity/immodesty without even watching my show. At the same time, who am I to tell a company, or a religion for that matter, what they can deem immodest or inappropriate? I can only address my experience as I experienced it, completely unfair to me from my viewpoint, but I don't need to start a crusade against a group of people simply because they have a different viewpoint; not to mention, although I didn't understand the full depth of the system, I did agree to adhere to their guidelines when I signed the contract. Do I wish I had more of a warning or a bit of insight that my body would be an issue? Yes. Can we go back into the past and change it? No. Did I also get a little boost of self-esteem in the process? Kinda... yes, absolutely.

Regardless of the flags on my special *within* the Dry Bar app and community, it has still gotten a lot of views *outside* of the Dry Bar fanbase *despite* Dry Bar's hardcore filters. I'm grateful for the experience while cautious about what I do next. In the same way that I don't intend to *show* my body just to get more views, I also don't intend to *hide* my body just to make sure everyone else feels comfortable. As I've said before, I've played small for most of my life, some of which is just the way I was made (no matter what Dry Bar says), but I'm not going to keep minimizing who I am just so I can fit the mold that will give me a shot. I never fought the flagged-for-female issue, but I also don't plan to shoot another Dry Bar special either, a successful tactic for many comedians trying to grow their audience.

I once heard Cher say in an interview something like *you just have to be willing to do whatever it takes to make it in show business,* and while I love Cher, I don't agree (different definitions, and that's okay). If I were to "do whatever it takes," or mold myself into what others want, in some circles that would mean I'd have to show more skin and be more crass, and in other circles it would mean I'd have to cover up and talk about Jesus. Adjusting to whatever each audience wants only to build my platform and then hopefully one day, I *might* get to just be myself. With that plan, I doubt I'd ever actually get to the part where I'm myself. If all I practice is molding myself into someone else, becoming what people want, then that's what I will become (followed by an eventual breakdown and another stint in rehab, as evidenced by name-that-celebrity). My approach is slower and maybe not a big money maker, but at the very least, I am learning how not to lose myself in the process.

It took me nearly thirty-five years to love my underdeveloped body, and while I don't plan on flaunting self-love through nude photos or performing in my underwear (again, different definitions of body empowerment, to each their beautiful own)—I also don't plan on covering up more or letting someone else restrict my comedy simply because I'm performing it in a female's body.

I don't know what that means for comedy productions in the future, I don't even know how comedy productions work outside of this one isolated experience, but I do know one thing…

Dolly Parton better watch out cause there's another visibly defined chest in town that's ready to take the stage in a short sleeve sweater!

# 20

# SEATTLE INTERNATIONAL COMEDY COMPETITION

## November 2019

**IT'S A RAINY DAY** here in Seattle, Washington. Nothing unusual about that except that I'm here. I live in the land of sunny and 70 degrees year-round— Santa Barbara, California, so the grey skies and drizzle all day of the Pacific Northwest is quite different from my norm. It feels appropriate though. I've missed the seasons and I've gotta say, it's been quite nice to wear a sweater because *I'm actually cold* and not just because I want my outfit to line up with all the seasonal photos of "sweater weather" on Instagram, despite it being much too warm for sweaters in California.

The weather also feels appropriate because I'm just coming off a full week of stand-up comedy performances around the greater Seattle area and I'm exhausted. And since it's raining outside, I don't feel guilty about lying around inside, doing nothing all day. I often struggle with "sun guilt," like if it's nice and sunny I *should* be outside, but it's nice and sunny *every day* in Santa Barbara, so it is very easy to get nothing done because you're always thinking you *should* be outside. But I'm not in Santa Barbara. I'm in Seattle and I'm exhausted and it's raining and there's simply nothing else to do but rest—thank God.

I performed this week in the Seattle International Comedy Competition—thirty-two competitors were chosen out of hundreds and hundreds of applicants around the world. *Around the world.* You may be the funny one in your scene, but when you get thrown in with all the other funny people in their scene, you start to wonder if you actually have what it takes to, you know, be the funny one. Or so was my experience…

When I first got the email that I had been selected to participate in the fortieth annual event of this prestigious competition, I held my breath because I wasn't sure they sent the email to the right person. I'm not saying I wasn't qualified; I had worked really hard all year to tighten my act and perform better. But still, I was only a few years into doing comedy, and as so many middle-aged veteran comics liked to constantly remind me, I needed to "put in more time" and maybe "struggle a little more" and even "suck for ten years" before I would maybe be any good.

Not to mention, comics had applied from all over the world. We had comics from Scotland, Saipan, and Canada in my round of competition, comics who easily made me wish the competition had been limited to Americans simply because of my own jealousy about how talented they were, all of which made me question just how far I'd get.

Nonetheless, I was chosen to take part even when other comics I knew who'd been doing comedy much longer weren't, so in that sense I was both shocked and proud to be competing with some really talented comedians. There were no guarantees going into this competition, except that we would perform for five nights at five different venues in front of live audiences in the greater Seattle area. So, for five nights in a row we all performed in a show that would last up to three hours.

The thirty-two competitors were divided into two groups that would perform separate weeks. There was the first preliminary week with a group of sixteen contestants, and a second preliminary week with another group of sixteen, which is where I was placed—week two. Winners would be chosen from each week and at the end of the two weeks, there would be a third week in which week one contestants and week two contestants would compete against each other. From there, the various judges who had attended all the live shows every night would crown the overall winner, apparently the world's funniest comedian. Let's just say, despite all my daily affirmations, I had a good idea I wasn't quite there yet.

My husband, Josh and I got into Seattle a day early so we could watch the last night of the week one contestants and hear them announce the top five. The comedians were really good, but I also felt like I actually stood a chance. I don't mean that to sound cocky, but instead of scaring me, I got a feeling like, *I can definitely do this.* I was most impressed by the top two and figured they'd be the ones to look out for if I advanced.

The next day, I prepared for my first night's set, which would also be the night I would meet the other contestants in my group. While I often try not to "should" on myself too much, I absolutely *should* have been preparing way sooner than the day of, but between getting bed-ridden sick the week before and our non-stop travels, I hadn't had the time (or so I thought, I'm sure there's always time somewhere) to really settle in and prepare.

The night began two hours before showtime. All the contestants met up for the first time at Comedy Underground in Pioneer Square for orientation. There we were given name tags and assigned our order of performance for the whole week. I was relieved to find out I wouldn't be going first on the first night, but as I watched Peter, the director of talent, make lists for each night, I saw a number one by my name for night four. *Dang it! Well, at least that's 'clean' night*, I thought.

One night of the competition was deemed "clean" night, in which performers couldn't be crass or drop any f-bombs to enhance a joke. I'm not saying that's the only reason performers drop the f-bomb, but if you really think about it, the f-bomb is often what's getting the laugh. To which some might say, "Hey, whatever gets the laugh." Fair enough. I wasn't stressed about clean night the way some others were, in fact, if there were a night in which I'd feel most comfortable going first, it'd be that night.

As night one began and I watched people get onstage from all over—Boston, Canada, Seattle, Scotland, L.A., I got nervous. I got really nervous. *These people are good. Really good.* I was going on fourteenth that night and I was pretty sure I had already seen the top five perform. I watched Andrea Jin from Canada completely murder and realized I had to go on after her. I tuned into my inner Brené Brown and told myself to be brave, to show up, to just "do the breaststroke." Brené has a Netflix special out in which she shares a story about her daughter having to compete in a swimming competition. Her daughter was assigned to do the breaststroke, her least favorite stroke, so much so that she almost dropped out just because she was so bad at it. She did the race, and not only did she come in dead last, but she also got *lapped* by the other swimmers.

When she got out of the water with tears in her eyes, she looked at her mom and said, "I was brave." She did it, she did the breaststroke.

I sometimes cry thinking about that story, just how hard it is to actually show up and put yourself out there, in whatever it is you are pursuing. Some people don't think it's hard because they don't care what other people think of them, but those people are either from Boston or they're sociopaths, so I find them a tad un-relatable (with all due respect to people from Boston, I wish I had your confidence). I watched all these polished and talented comics go ahead of me, and I was tempted for a split second to just drop out, to just not get up there and risk being seen as "not that funny." I wanted to find comfort in not having to be vulnerable. But that's why we're here—to try, to show up for life, to figure it out—what works and what doesn't? The only way to do that, at the risk of sounding like a Nike ad, is to just do it. Just show up. Just try. If Brene's kid can get lapped in the swimming pool, fail so badly in front of so many people, and still see herself as brave for trying (especially while people are watching), certainly I could do the same thing... in the form of telling jokes. I'm not a strong swimmer.

So, I just did it. I followed a performer that was incredibly hard to follow. I had a really good set with an amazing response. Lots of laughs, yay! But as awesome as my set felt, I knew deep down I wasn't in the top five that night. The thing about this competition is that even if you do an amazing job, so does everyone else, which makes it hard to feel like your amazing is all that amazing. I felt like a number, and not a number between one and five.

I continued to perform well each night that week, I even got the encore applause every night, so I knew I was doing great, but so did pretty much everyone else. We were all doing great. The fact that it was labeled a "competition" got into all our heads. Some nights

I felt like I was really "on" and connected to the audience. Other nights I felt like I put on a good-enough performance, but I didn't feel personally connected to the audience. The shows I enjoy doing the most are the shows in which I feel like I'm in my friend's living room telling a funny story, almost unaware that I am actually on a stage reciting lines I have memorized.

I kept feeling like the top five was in my reach, but just barely, like I was swiping for it, but I couldn't quite touch it—so close, but never close enough. Perhaps that's always been my deeper insecurity. *You're good, JJ, just not good enough.* In this business you fake it till you make it, but let's be honest, deep down inside, every comedian in the industry is like a forgotten middle child screaming: "PLEASE LOVE ME!"

We performed in some amazing places like Pike Place Market in downtown Seattle, and even on Whidbey Island. We performed in Auburn and in North Bend. Almost all of which were sold-out shows. The mental battles of competition aside, it was an amazing experience, but if you get caught up in the numbers and the judge's scores of your personality (it's super easy not to obsess over your personality being scored, right?), you can easily miss the amazing part of the experience.

I did the best I could with what knowledge I had up to that point in my life. I showed up, I made 'em laugh, and I repeated it five nights in a row, sometimes switching up material to test the waters with different audiences. I made friends. I know people are "supposed" to say that because it sounds nice, but I feel like I really did make some friends. I genuinely enjoyed the time I spent with the other comedians offstage. I found people whose careers I now follow and enjoy seeing their successes. After that week I can now say things like, "Oh, I've performed with them." When some of them get really big, I'll be able to say, "Technically, I opened for them." Or, even better, I'll be able to say, "Technically, they opened for me."

In my opinion, week two was the stronger group, and I realize I could be biased because I spent so much time with those people, but a few others confirmed my thoughts—they pointed out that a lot of the touring out-of-towners and headliners got placed in week two because of the time frame of the competition, which made sense when I saw one of the week two competitor's photo hanging on the wall of the comedy club we were performing in. Having your photo on the wall of a comedy club means you're a regular headliner there, which led me to my next thought: *I'M IN THE WRONG WEEK!* But at the end of the day, I was proud to have been among them and to have held my own.

And so, here at the end of week two, I'm exhausted. Showing up every night to be judged for your craft is an emotional roller coaster in and of itself. Some nights you're like "I KNEW I could do this!" Other nights you're like "WHY am I doing this!?" But I couldn't be more grateful that I *got* to do this. It grew me in ways I didn't know I needed, it showed me some of my blind spots, it motivated me and encouraged me, and it wasn't *all* hard… I was celebrated, praised, thanked, and was even told I was like Maria Bamford, Mary Mack, and Carol Burnett. I will gladly accept all of those comparisons.

And though I did not advance beyond my week, I genuinely do celebrate all the other comedians… especially our top five from week two. They really did deserve it. They moved on into the semi-finals to compete with the other top five from week one and I'm sticking around for a short while to support the rest of their journey here in Seattle.

At the end of the day, I am so incredibly glad I showed up, which has reminded me to remind others…

Keep showing up!

# 21

## QUITTING COMEDY?

**AT LEAST ONCE A MONTH,** I swear I'm going to quit comedy. Honestly, sometimes I don't know why I keep doing it, that is, until I get onstage again *and for a moment,* I believe it's worth the struggle.

I recently had a show in upstate South Carolina, and I had my normal pre-show jitters, debating whether or not I should even show up to the venue. I'm not proud of it, but sometimes I hope I get Covid before a show so that the show actually *can't* go on. That's what performance anxiety does to me—it makes me wish a virus upon myself. When I realize I'm wishing Covid upon myself is usually about the time I have the thought, *maybe I should quit comedy.*

Leading up to the weekend for the South Carolina show, I drove down to Atlanta to stay with my friends, Jim and Donna, on Thursday night. Josh was scheduled to fly in late that night, but his flight kept getting delayed, so I finally went to bed, tossing and turning until Uber delivered him to Jim and Donna's house at 2 a.m.

The next morning, I got up for my usual morning routine of coffee, reading, and deciding I'm too tired to write. I wrote anyway and worked for a few hours until Josh got up and we both went down to the kitchen for a Donna specialty: an egg sandwich. After we finished eating, Josh said he needed to unpack a few things from the car that I had packed for him and brought to Atlanta. He went outside to retrieve the oversized suitcase full of products and camera equipment for his next shoot. Due to the weight of the suitcase, he was carefully looking down as he walked upstairs so as to keep the suitcase from scratching up against the walls. Just as he used all his momentum to step up and heave the heavy suitcase up with him, he stepped up *into a light fixture*. Not a mere lamp attached to the wall, a bolted-in iron light fixture with sharp corners, which never posed a threat before due to the lesser height of the homeowners, but when matched with Josh's 6'3" frame and the momentum of his forward motion, the sharp iron corner dug right into Josh's head.

I was in the bathroom as all of this was going down, but I could hear Josh.

He was repetitively yelling, "Ow, ow, ow, ow, ow, owwwwwwww."

I came out of the bathroom and called out, "Are you okay, baby?"

There was no response.

"Baby?" I asked again and hearing no response I picked up my pace in pursuit of locating him. He was at the bottom of the stairs, standing incredibly still and seemingly out of it.

"What happened?" I asked.

"I hit my head, I think I really got it good," he said, with a slower cadence than usual. "Can you just look and see if there's a cut?"

As I stood on my tippy toes, he tilted his head down for me to get a closer look and just as I parted his hair to find his scalp, blood came gushing down the front of his head.

Instant panic set in for me as he remained unexpressive.

"Oh, my God, you're bleeding, it's bleeding."

I immediately ran to get my phone to call Donna who had just left the house to walk the dog. As the phone rang, I kept asking Josh what he hit his head on, but he was too slow to respond.

"Donna," I yelled as soon as she answered the phone, "I don't know how to explain it, but Josh hit his head on something and cut it, it's bleeding, and I'm not a mom so I don't know what to do."

Donna said she was on her way back and told me to put something cold on it. Eventually Josh was able to point out the light fixture that had dug itself into his head. A freakishly unlikely accident. I tried to remain calm and not let my racing thoughts and worst-case scenarios get ahead of me, but seeing blood pour out of my husband's head was not an easy sight to take in. I struggled to know what to do or what to say.

I momentarily got caught up in thinking about motherhood. *How can I ever be a mom when I have no idea how to handle an accident?* I promptly scolded myself for going down a negative thought path and said out loud, "I couldn't care less about having kids right now," which seemed to confuse Josh, but he was too out of it to ask questions. Blood was gushing. I was ready to go into bargaining mode with God. *I don't care about kids, I don't care about having anything else in life, I don't want anything else, please, just let my husband live.* I got paper towels to wipe the blood from his head. I told him to hold them over the spot to hopefully stop the bleeding.

When Donna returned, she moved Josh to a chair at the kitchen table where she could get a better vantage point to see his head. Every time she tried to move his hair to see how bad the cut was, he flinched in pain, so it was hard to get a good look at it or tell how deep it was. Once we cleaned up the blood, it looked like the bleeding had stopped.

Donna put on her glasses and squinted at Josh's scalp as she tried to see past his hair. Eventually Jim joined us in the search for the gash. He got a flashlight and the two of them took turns trying to look at it. Donna said she didn't think it was that deep. I didn't care if it was a mere scratch—after seeing blood pour down Josh's head, I wanted him to go to Urgent Care. Josh seemed unable to decide, but he also still seemed out of it. Donna said if it were one of her kids, she probably wouldn't take them to Urgent Care. Granted her kids are now in their thirties, so perhaps that is true, but also knowing those kids are her heart and soul, I highly doubted she'd be so nonchalant. I also highly doubted her eyes were as strong as they once were as she squinted through her reading glasses, so I decided to ignore my queasy stomach and take a look for myself.

As Jim held the flashlight over Josh's head, I tried pulling his hair apart ever so gently so I could see his scalp. Eventually I switched angles, and there under the bright light of a Duracell flashlight, was a gash, a flap of skin pushed to the side like an open curtain. I couldn't tell how deep it was, because I couldn't stand to keep looking, but it was definitely more than a scratch, and unable to shake the image of blood pouring down his head, not a light trickle, but *pouring*, I immediately felt faint. I inched backwards to the kitchen counter where I sat down on a nearby stool. I stared at him, unable to say anything for fear that if I opened my mouth, I'd throw up.

I began to feel dizzy, and I could feel myself swaying. Donna looked at me and started to laugh.

"Are you okay? You're white as a ghost!"

"I feel like I'm going to pass out," I said. I laid my head down on the counter and Donna offered to help me get to the couch. Jim stayed with Josh.

They moved to the bathroom and took turns trying to examine his head more closely in the bathroom mirror. Josh would alternate between being slow and out of it and then suddenly alert and in "go" mode, so it was hard to tell how serious the injury was. All I knew was that, while Josh was the one with his head gashed open, I was the one laid out on the couch with Frannie, their boxer mix, licking my face as if to revive me. I continued to shame myself as a potential future mother while simultaneously telling myself I didn't care about having children, I only wanted my husband to live.

In retrospect, it was not so severe an injury to elicit the "please save my husband at all costs" prayer, but between my fragile stomach and anxious thoughts that thrive when accidents present themselves, I was prepared to give up comedy and tell the painful story of how I once had a promising career as a comic until I lost my husband to a light fixture. The thought of *that* being my story from there on out was what provoked my plea, *Dear God, please save my husband! I can't lose him to a light fixture!*

Donna, being less anxiety-induced and more sensibly detached from the situation, was able to remain unfazed. I was convinced this was because of two things: 1) she had not seen the blood pour from Josh's head like a runny egg yolk, and 2) she had raised two boys who had survived all kinds of terrifying accidents and questionable choices like touring with a heavy metal band. My hunches told me a boy mom has seen it all; they are the person you want in a situation like this to keep you grounded in reality.

As I laid on the couch recovering from where my own head went, Josh held paper towels against his while looking up Urgent Care centers that would take our insurance. In retrospect, yes, that should have been *my* job, but I was too busy reeling out. Eventually,

Josh found one five minutes down the road, but was still somewhat hesitant to go.

"Let's go," I said. I had been ready to go to Urgent Care from the moment it all began.

"I don't want to ruin anyone's day," Josh said. I laughed like a crazy person.

"Are you kidding me? YOU ARE MY DAY! Let's go!"

"Are you going to be okay to drive?" Donna jokingly asked me. I managed to get us to Urgent Care where the not-so-welcome greeting from the staff made us feel that Josh's injury was not so urgent. There was no one else in the waiting room; the whole building was eerily quiet. There were two nurses at the front desk. Holding a wad of paper towels to his head, Josh explained to the nurses what had happened and that his head was currently gashed open.

"We're just going to need you to fill out some paperwork."

Josh wanted to oblige but it was clear he was struggling to stay focused.

"Is there any way I can fill this out after?" he asked, "I'm actually having a hard time looking at this and I can't focus, it's really throbbing." In odd unison both nurses replied no. Their responses were short and made it crystal clear that we were being somewhat irritating for even asking.

I offered to help with the paperwork and as Josh titled his head to look down at the first question, blood started pouring down his head again. I jumped out of my seat.

"He's bleeding!" I yelled, scrambling to find tissue. Both nurses were stunned, at which point I will refer to them as Nurse One and Nurse Two. At first, they both stared motionless, then as I located a box of tissues and approached Josh with it, Nurse One started yelling.

"No, no, no."

I stepped back and watched as Josh tilted his head further and further back to keep the blood from dripping down his neck. Nurse One went for gloves and gauze and Nurse Two just stared.

"Don't just stand there," Nurse One yelled. "Go get somebody, go get somebody!" In a panic, Nurse Two fled to the back. Not even a minute later a doctor rushed out with gauze in hand to take over.

Immediately, the doctor took Josh to the back.

"You can stay here and finish the paperwork," she directed me.

Josh went back, the waiting room fell silent again. I sat alone with my racing thoughts and both of our phones. Since I had Josh's phone, I was unable to text funny emojis to him to lighten the mood and reassure each other that it wasn't that bad.

Nurse One returned, suddenly friendly.

"You don't want to go back there with him?" she asked.

"The doctor told me to stay here while I finished his paperwork," I said.

"Oh yeah, I forgot, she doesn't really like other people back there," she said as she returned to her computer screen.

I wanted to say, "That was an awfully nice try at a conversation," as well as, "See! We told you his head was gashed open," but I kept my comments to myself, as shaming her wasn't going to make me worry any less.

I tried not to think of the scene from *This Is Us* after the Pearson family home burns down and Jack is in the hospital (SPOILER ALERT). He had just been seen by the doctor and all appeared to be well. His wife, Rebecca, leaves to get a snack from the vending machine and returns with a candy bar to discover her husband has abruptly died of cardiac arrest from smoke inhalation. That scene is seared in my mind as it depicts one of my greatest fears: life catching me off guard and taking *everything* away from me. Perhaps my mind goes to worst-case scenarios because, even more than a terrible event happening is my fear of getting caught off guard, thinking everything will be okay, only to be completely and utterly shocked by just how cruel life can be.

I kept telling myself it was just a light fixture, there's no way a light fixture could be life-threatening, but then I'd think about Rebecca biting into that candy bar just as the doctor told her that her husband was dead. *This is what people mean when they say, "You watch too much TV, JJ,"* I thought to myself. I texted my mom and my dad, asking for prayer if for no other reason than to not feel so alone in my thoughts.

My mother was all over it and had contacted her prayer chain in a matter of minutes. I often joke in my comedy set that all a prayer chain really means is "I will tell everybody your business… in Jesus' name." I laughed as she sent me responses from some of the ladies who had already started praying. Although I joke about it often, there is nothing like the audacity of a praying woman before the throne of God. She means business. Though my own prayer life is often lacking, it feels oddly comforting when someone else is praying for me.

My mom called to pray with me over the phone and eventually the doctor came out.

"You can come back now," she said.

I was escorted to the room Josh was in and I saw him sitting up, bright-eyed and smiling. He already looked completely revived, anxious to tell me about what had just happened.

"I got stapled!" he said excitedly. "They couldn't numb it, so it hurt immensely, but check it out…" He pointed to four staples popping out of his head. I was trying to look at the staples while also processing that they had stapled my husband's head with nothing to numb it.

"So, you felt it?" I asked. He nodded his head in a mix of disbelief and excitement.

"What did it feel like?" I asked.

"Like what you'd think it'd feel like to get your head stapled," he laughed. "Very painful."

A new nurse, Nurse Three, much nicer than Nurse One and Nurse Two, commented that Josh handled it very well and it didn't even seem like he felt the pain.

"Oh yeah, it was painful," Josh said again, but he sat up tall and proud. He had handled it beautifully.

The doctor came back in to give Josh his discharge papers and a staple remover. She instructed him to leave the staples in for five days and then to take them out at home.

"Who's supposed to take them out?" I asked.

"You," she said, and she proceeded to show me how, using her fingers as pretend hooks that went under the staples. "And then you just jerk em' right out!"

I felt queasy all over again, but pretended to act like it was no big deal.

We left Urgent Care, Josh with a returned sense of zest for life, and me, just relieved he was still alive and leaving with me. Once the pain from the staples wore off, Josh said he instantly felt better for going to Urgent Care, if for no other reason than he had some peace of mind. I agreed that peace of mind is always worth the price tag… it's the same reason I once gave up living in a van rent-free in exchange for renting four walls and a door that locked at night… peace of mind.

We drove back to Donna's where everyone breathed a collective sigh of relief. We re-enacted the day's events over dinner; me laid out on the couch, white as a ghost with the dog licking my face.

"All while Josh bled to death," I exaggerated.

We laughed, and I thought about how good that felt, to laugh, and once again I found myself saying, *Okay, God, I won't quit comedy.*

# THAT'S LIFE
# (AND OTHER
# SPIRITUAL STUFF)

## 22

# DiNNER PARTY POOPER

**I CAN'T SLEEP.** I know, probably not the best way to convince someone that what you're about to write is worth reading.

"Hey, I wrote something really profound after replaying the day's events over and over in my head and decided that I *should* in fact return those napkin rings to Hobby Lobby. Once I made peace with that dilemma at 2 a.m., I felt sharp enough to write a chapter in my book... you should read it!"

Or so my case would go.

I did all the things one is supposed to do when they can't get to sleep. I tossed and turned, I turned on a heating pad, I lathered myself in lavender oil (a few drops too many because I think the smell woke up my husband). I finally got up and left the room to make some peppermint tea and sit by the fire. I'm currently trying to avoid the chicken salad in the fridge if for no other reason than 2 a.m. just feels like an insane time to eat chicken salad. Oreos? Maybe. But chicken salad? Why is *that* what I want right *now*?

As I laid there in bed trying *not* to mull over the past day's events, I couldn't help but play them over and over again. I realized I hadn't felt this way since I used to perform. Covid wiped my schedule clean and so it's been almost a year since I've been onstage. I'd almost forgotten what it felt like to come home on a show night high. On show nights I could never sleep, my adrenaline was always too high from performing and it was hard to wind down. I'd lie in bed till 3 or 4 a.m. just thinking. I found myself laying there tonight thinking, *oh yeah! I used to feel like this a lot before Covid canceled live events.* While I have missed performing, I have not missed *this* part of it, nor the part before the show when I'd get so anxious that I'd end up crying face down in the back seat of my friend's car.

On one show night I remember my friend driving me to the venue, her date was in the front passenger seat, and I was in the back having some sort of meltdown. I just remember crying and profusely apologizing for it.

"I'm about to get onstage and act happy in front of a bunch of people, but I am *not* happy and I'm so sorry you have to see it!"

They both told me it was okay, but that didn't change the fact that later, after killing it onstage and floating on cloud nine when the show was over (a stark contrast to my pre-show mood), I was incredibly embarrassed by my meltdown. I used to think I was bi-polar, turns out I'm just a comedian.

Though I didn't have a show tonight, I *did* help Josh out with a dinner and a stylized photoshoot earlier today. Josh has been a wedding photographer for the last eighteen years, that is, until Covid wiped *his* schedule clean. No more live events, no more big weddings. We were both at ground zero for a while, until Josh realized businesses still needed to sell products online, and thus began his venture into commercial photography. As he started picking up more and more jobs, he needed more and more help, and so me with all my free time… that's mostly what I've become in this "off season" for live performers: an assistant. Truth be told, I quite enjoy assisting Josh on his photo jobs, especially where food and drinks are involved. It's another form of art, really. On top of which, I happen to really enjoy my husband, so working with him feels more like a treat than a job. Yeah, yeah, mushy gushy, whatever, but it's true.

For this particular shoot, Josh was shooting for a wine company and he had to capture multiple meals being served with each of the different types of wine. As the assistant, I had to get the multiple meals prepared in time for the shoot, none of which I had time to make, at least not from scratch—I mean, who actually has time to make one meal made from scratch in a given day, much less multiple meals? Probably Martha Stewart does. But for this shoot, the company wasn't paying a Martha-Stewart amount of money. They were paying a freezer-section-at-Trader-Joe's amount of money. Since the meals were each going to be paired with a wine, using pre-made meals would cut my prep time in half and allow me to create a wider variety of pairings.

I should also add that when the day started, I was under the impression that all I needed to make was a charcuterie board, easy enough. But three hours before the shoot began, Josh informed me that we needed *five entrees* to be paired with the wine. *Five entrees?* And this is why working with my husband is a treat, because when he swings something like this on me last minute, I actually get to verbally express "ARE YOU CRAZY?" instead of keeping my frustration all pent up inside (as with previous bosses) so as not to lose my job and break out in hives from all the stored stress in my body. It's beautiful, really, and I do think I have much clearer skin since learning to speak up… cast another vote for marriage.

Perhaps this is where tonight's replays began in my efforts to sleep: at Trader Joe's. I started replaying over and over again if I picked out the right things, if they paired well with the wine, and if I actually pulled off the look of homemade meals... or at least if the meals looked like they belonged at the dinner party of a twenty-three-year-old who's impressed by her ability to afford Trader Joe's groceries, and maybe one day if she works hard enough, Whole Foods.

Something people don't realize about food in commercials, be it photo or video, is just how fake the whole presentation is (at least as far as taste goes). In commercials, pancake companies like IHOP use motor oil to pour over their pancakes to make it look like amazingly gooey syrup slowly flowing over those buttery breakfast pillows. It works too—the motor oil looks delicious, but think about it, have you ever seen pancake syrup that thick? Syrup literally disappears into the pancake as soon as you pour it on, but that is not photogenic. Not motor oil though, motor oil lays it on thick, kinda like a car salesman. I feel like there's more of a joke in there somewhere, what with motor oil and a car salesman, but at nearly 3 a.m., I can't get there fast enough.

For TV commercials, food just needs to be visually pleasing—the taste doesn't matter. As I started picking out freezer meals at Trader Joe's, I figured I could spruce and shift and volumize where needed without much concern for how it might change the flavor. *After all, it's not like it was for an actual dinner party.* Well, at least not really, because as I found out closer to shoot time, it wasn't just a *product* shoot, it was also a *lifestyle* shoot, which meant there would be shots of people enjoying the wine with their two charcuterie boards and five different meal options for their dinner guests... totally real life.

Since there would be people in the shoot, it meant there would be people *eating the food*, which is to say, no motor oil stunts. And I wasn't so stressed by the fact that people would be eating the food, so much as *who* would be eating it.

The couple who agreed to do the shoot were people we have hung out with before on multiple occasions, but I would often leave their presence feeling tired. Spending time with them always reminds me to make sure anytime I spend time with someone, to ask them how *they* are doing and what is going on in *their* life. At the risk of sounding like a whiner (and also becoming more unfiltered as this late night turns into early morning), all this couple talks about is themselves, their business, or whatever new toy or car they bought that week. They have "new money," which means they *spend* a lot of it. I always forget how exhausting it is to listen to people like this until I'm right in the middle of our time together and it's too late to back out and cancel plans. Not to mention, merely walking into their house makes you feel like you've just walked into a store you can't afford. While you may be curious to look around, you certainly don't want to stay there long, let alone touch anything.

"Please don't sit on that, it was $9,000!" *It's a chair.*

Maybe the "ew" feeling I get around them is because they don't see me as having money (which is fair, I don't exactly dress to kill), but it also seems like they genuinely don't care to get to know me unless I have expensive things to talk about. I can't remember the last time either of them asked me about *me*, so technically, they don't even know if I do have money or not. Perhaps we can partly blame it on social media—they may think they know me because they know *about* me given what I post publicly, but they don't actually *know* me... like, at all. Which then makes it feel more awkward for me when one of them, usually the wife, says stuff like, "I want us to hang out more" or "Love you, girl!" *But do you, though?* That's what I always want to say, and of course, I don't. I hear myself say, "Love you, too," and I can feel the hives begin to surface.

I knew it was going to be work—not just to get meals plated, but also to get meals plated that *they* found worthy of eating. After all, only the finest things in life for them, or so they say... *All. The. Time.*

I immediately regretted my decision to follow the Trader Joe's freezer food route because I knew whatever was served for this shoot would be associated with me and give them another tick in their favor for how amazingly they do everything and just how much of a simpleton everyone else is. Which reminds me of another life lesson I have learned from knowing them: it's not so much about the exact words you use but rather how you make other people feel, at least in your presence, that matters. While this couple has never directly said to me that they see me as "less than", it couldn't *feel* more obvious. Once upon a time I would have blamed my own insecurity for making me feel this way, but when you've done enough therapy and harnessed enough tools, sometimes you get healthy enough to realize not everything is you, sometimes it really is them.

The evening was off to a classic start.

"Is this cheese from Whole Foods?" The wife asked in response to a dish I was prepping.

"Uhhh, no, Trader Joe's. They're my favorite," I replied with a smile, before she had a chance to turn her nose up to it. She then examined the cheese with a slight look of disgust, as if I had found it on the bathroom floor at Walmart and brought it home to share.

"Interesting," she said (which I know is neither a compliment nor a complaint, just a subtle way to be snobby). "You know, I never drive out there," she added.

"Oh, really?" I was genuinely surprised. "Because you know it's right next to Whole Foods." We both laughed our little fake laughs, and I rolled my eyes in my mind.

When I take the time to break it down, perhaps it's their own insecurity that makes them act this way. Perhaps they feel "less than" in life sometimes and maybe bragging about all their shiny new things makes them feel important and validated. Perhaps they haven't yet learned that some people just don't care about all the stuff, and in fact, it's the stuff that often gets in the way of authentic relationships (at least it will if you don't shut up about it once in a while so you can talk about things that actually matter).

As I've had time to process and snack (yes, I caved! Chicken salad may be insane at 2 a.m., but it's delightful when you hit the 4 a.m. mark), I realized tonight felt like a sleepless show night because it technically *was* a show night—a performance on my part to present five photo-worthy meals from Trader Joe's, as if they were homemade, to a couple who brags *out loud* about being the alphas in all their friend groups because they can afford the "best style" (assuming you like their style, it's too muted for me), and the "best food" ("best" according to whom!?) because they only shop at Whole Foods. Seriously, *what do you say to that?*

And again tonight, as with each time before, I had to remind myself that I had nothing to prove to these people, that I honestly didn't even need their validation, though I admit, sometimes I want it, in part for myself and my own ego, and in part because I'm curious if it's possible for them to actually see past their own reflections.

And so, while I did perform earlier this evening, acting impressed by all of this couple's abundance, remaining calm while cooking, and keeping my panic attacks stuffed deep down inside,

I told myself that soon enough it would all be over and I would be back home in my own $5,000 bed, lying awake, unimpressed by all the comforts money can buy.

# 23

# DISHWASHER SKILLS

**LONG STORY SHORT,** we moved to Tennessee! Short story a little longer, we bought a house, a much more feasible act to do in Chattanooga, Tennessee than in Santa Barbara, California, so we took a chance and thus far are glad we did. There's no ocean and there's a lot of feelings for me around that, but we have hills and rivers, the Chattanooga Choo Choo, and not too far off in the Smokey Mountains, Dollywood.

So yes, I left Hollywood for Dollywood! I already got my season pass and have felt more at home here in the hidden hills of Tennessee than I ever felt trying so hard to make California feel like home. It's not that it wasn't home, California was very much home for a large chunk of my life, and one I will always be grateful for, but somewhere deep down I knew it didn't *feel* like home. Since I made California my home without it ever feeling like home, I'm sure you can imagine the constant tension I felt while living in a non-home home.

We moved to Tennessee during the holidays, which I've decided is a great time to move because no matter where you are, if it's

Christmas, it's magical. As soon as we moved into the house, I had the Christmas decorations up before I did anything else. It's been fun to decorate our own space and play music as loud as we want, little luxuries we did not have while living in a shared space in California.

We've gotten into two arguments so far in our new house, mostly because just like with the freedom to play music at whatever volume we want, we also have the freedom to talk at whatever volume we want, and I've come to realize that I enjoy the freedom to escalate things just a little too much. To be honest, I can't remember what one of the arguments was about, I just know when we retell "moving-in stories," there are two arguments that stand out, and both were due to learning new things about each other—now that we function freely in our own space.

So, the first argument, I can't really remember. But the other argument I remember vividly. It was about the dishwasher. In our previous house we didn't have a functioning dishwasher, so we hand-washed all of our dishes. But in our new house, we have our own dishwasher, and we love to load that thing up and run it while we watch a movie. It's kinda funny that you don't realize how many little things have crept into your psyche over the years, and you don't realize how much you still function out of them until something brings it to the surface.

For example, I grew up with an understanding that running the dishwasher costs money. We had one, but we used it more often as a drying rack for hand-washed dishes. We only ran it after big meals when we had company, so it was not an everyday luxury... along with the occasional toilet flush. My mom used to say, "When it's yellow, let it mellow. When it's brown, flush it down." Always aware that every little thing costs money, I sometimes still hesitate to flush the toilet. Josh still has to remind me that we can afford it.

Josh and I had never shared a dishwasher before so there has never been a conversation about the dishwasher, like about how often we should use it. One night before bed, Josh was loading the dishwasher and asked if I wanted him to start it. I said I didn't, that I wanted to wait until the morning. I thought that was enough of an answer (because it is, ahem), but Josh asked *why* I wanted to wait until morning, and although all he was doing was asking, I have to admit, I felt a little annoyed that he asked *why* instead of just saying, "okay." If he had said, "okay," the conversation would have been done.

I replied that I simply wanted to wait, that's all, which again seemed like enough of an answer. Again, he asked why. Irritation level officially up.

Now, I should be honest that there were two reasons I wanted to wait until the morning to run the dishwasher—one was because I didn't want to be running the dishwasher every day because "it costs money" and it seems inefficient if two people have to run the dishwasher *every day*. The other reason was that I didn't 100% trust how he loaded the dishwasher. Again, we had never had one together, so I wasn't sure what his dishwasher skills were like. I needed to see for myself, but I was already in bed and didn't feel like getting up to check, so I figured I could check in the morning, just to make sure it was efficiently filled, maximizing the most amount of space.

Perhaps that's a little on me to have such a strong preference for how the dishwasher is loaded, or perhaps it's on Josh for repeatedly asking, "Why?" As if "because I said so" wasn't answer enough.

I told Josh I just wanted to make sure it was adequately filled, to which Josh said it was because he was looking right at it.

"I just want to make sure. In the morning," I said. "Could we please wait until then to run it?"

Josh caught on to my first reason. "OHHHH, you don't think I can fill the dishwasher right, huh?" I laughed a little bit and said that wasn't totally it.

"It is!" he said, "you want to check to make sure I did it right, don't you?" He was laughing too so it seemed the tension had eased.

"Yes, okay, that's part of it!" I admitted.

"What's the other part?" he asked. "What else could there be? I did a good job loading it, I promise."

I told him I was sure he had done a good job and could we please just wait until tomorrow. I thought the conversation would end there. But Josh, the ever so curious one, very kindly continued.

"I promise I'm not trying to be rude or question you, I'm just trying to understand you or maybe the way this all works, but can you just explain to me why you want to wait until the morning to run it?"

And with his third "why," instead of trying to explain my childhood-ingrained, penny-pinching tactics and how I so often insecurely function out of them without even realizing it, I snapped.

(Begin JJ's all-caps yelling sequence, fueled in part by the realization that we've never been able to yell in our own home before because we would have disturbed our housemates, but now we can be as loud as we want and the freedom for ALL CAPS yelling really just unleashed).

"BECAUSE!!!! JUST BECAUSE!!!! WHY IS THAT NOT ENOUGH OF AN ANSWER FOR YOU? *BECAUSE* IT IS MY PREFERENCE TO DO IT IN THE MORNING, THAT SHOULD BE ALL THERE IS TO THE CONVERSATION, NOT TWENTY QUESTIONS AS TO WHY!"

To which Josh, who was annoyingly *not* yelling yet, responded, "I'm sorry, I just think I did a really good job loading it and I just don't understand why you wouldn't want to wake up to clean dishes in the morning!"

"MY GOD! JUST BECAUSE, OKAY!? WHY CAN'T YOU JUST LET IT GO?"

At this point Josh's volume did pick up but was still not all-caps worthy.

"I don't see why you're getting so mad about it! It just doesn't make sense! I'm trying to help you and understand how I'm not being helpful and you're just getting mad! I know how to load a dishwasher, so it seems pretty crazy to have a fully loaded dishwasher and not run it!"

My blood was boiling. I was trying to retain some of my sanity by reminding myself that this was just a stupid dishwasher, but if your insecurities are poked long enough, they come oozing out of you.

"BECAUSE I DON'T WANT TO USE THE DISHWASHER EVERY DAY, OKAY!? IT COSTS MONEY AND IT'S WASTEFUL... AND I DON'T WANT TO RUN IT, OOOOOKAY!!? IT'S EXPENSIVE!"

Josh looked like a mix of enlightened with this newfound knowledge and yet still confused.

"You know we can afford to run the dishwasher?" Josh asked, "and I don't think it costs *that* much money, plus we didn't even run it yesterday." Mix insecurities with exhaustion from unnecessarily defending the insecurity and that's when I started crying.

In retrospect, I can see it from his point of view... Josh was just proud of how he loaded the dishwasher in his attempt to be helpful. Instead, I saw his questions as criticisms—as someone picking on my financial insecurities, even though he didn't even know he was doing it, he had no idea what sleeping monster he was going to nudge awake. On the surface it was about the dishwasher, but underneath it was about much more.

I cried for what felt like multiple reasons because I'm the type of person who once one thing makes me sad, EVERYTHING makes me sad, and life becomes too overwhelming. But in the off chance I can remain focused on pinpointing the emotion, I was crying for two reasons. One was wondering if the childhood psyche ever grows up, or if it always stays the same—stuck in the body of an adult, secretly worried about what everyone else thinks, wondering if we can afford to keep our house, or if Hanson will ever be taken seriously as a really good band. No matter how old my body gets, there's still that scared little kid inside of me, constantly tagging along, always asking, "What about me!?"

The other reason I cried was due to a more recent life event that only fed more fear to the scared little kid who worried she might lose her house—COVID. Covid changed things for everyone, so I am not special in that way. It fed fear and took life and completely changed history, many of us are still trying to figure out how to rearrange all the pieces.

While there are many things Covid did to our world as a whole, I am but one person who can't name *all* the life-altering events so many people experienced. And like many others, life was already hard before Covid even hit. In the last two years, I have lost friends to Covid, cancer, addiction, and old age. Life has changed and yet it has also gone on as normal and we're all left feeling *without*, wondering if we can keep our houses, our jobs, our sanity.

So, there's the overwhelming global issues of Covid and its effects on everyone, and then there's the more personalized issues, which for me has meant a loss of career. And for a feeler like me, that has also meant a loss of meaning, purpose, and oftentimes, livelihood. Don't get me wrong, I am "fine," in the Christian F-word sense. I have my health and my family, and now I have my own home that I'm scared to run the dishwasher in. By all means, I am fine.

AND. I am sad. I am sad that just as it was all getting started, it was all suddenly gone. I signed a five-year contract with a manager for my comedy career in March of 2020 and two days later the world shut down, taking every live stage performance with it.

Nearly two years have gone by since then. I waited year after year as venue spaces and tour dates postponed spring shows for fall, then fall shows for the next spring, then those spring shows for the next fall again, and two years went by without any shows. I recently heard the touring company I had been waiting to work with for the last two years finally shut down entirely. No more postponing, it's just over. They held on as long as they could, but they couldn't keep up. I understand. But with that, the last thing I was holding onto for a career move once all this Covid stuff was "over" was gone. I haven't totally given up on comedy, but a comedian who can't get booked for a show feels more like a joke than a comedian. Ironic.

And while I love performing, it's deeper than that too. The sense of not contributing, not only to the world in general, but also to my own household, hangs on me. *Did I really just waste the last two years of my life waiting for something to happen that was never going to happen? How dare I have the luxury of running the dishwasher in my new home when I haven't done anything to deserve it?* And yes, I know, we have a new home, but even that was a very carefully thought-out financial decision that has us living in the hills of Tennessee, not on the beaches of California.

My own lack of income has poked at the scared little kid who doesn't want to lose her house and is back to making every little decision based on how much it costs.

I cried because I felt spoiled and broken at the same time and I didn't know how I was *supposed* to feel both at the same time. Spoiled to live in my own home with a good man and a functioning dishwasher, and broken because not even a new home and a good man and a running dishwasher fill the purpose-shaped void that Covid left in my life.

There's so much my therapist could dig into here: "Are you telling me you don't want to run the dishwasher because of a poverty mindset from your childhood or because you don't feel like you have the right to run your dishwasher because you essentially haven't worked in the last two years?"

Yes.

Josh came over and said he was sorry for asking "why" so many times and told me that I didn't have to be nervous to run the dishwasher, nor did I have to earn the right or the paycheck to do so. I told him it was less about the paycheck (although a paycheck obviously helps), and more about the lack of purpose.

"How can I still not know what I'm doing at thirty-eight!? I've been optimistic for as long as I can, waiting out the whole Covid thing, but the truth is, this sucks!" He held me while I cried. No resolving anything, just letting it suck.

He kissed me on the top of my head.

"And," he said, "if you want to wait until the morning to check my dishwasher skills and apologize to me cause you realize I'm right, that's okay too."

We laughed and went to bed shortly after—without starting the dishwasher. I got up the next morning and before getting my coffee, I peeked into the dishwasher... sure enough, it was full and pretty well-stacked. I felt the need to defend my argument, so I rearranged some things just so I could feel justified for wanting to wait to run it. Then I thought about Josh comforting me after I yelled at him, not for something he did, but because of something I was insecure about, and I realized I didn't need to be justified. I just needed to apologize to him because he was right... his dishwasher skills were really impressive.

## 24

# GOD-FORSAKEN TAMALES

**I REMEMBERED WHAT** our second "moving in" fight was about! Buckle up because this is a good one.

It was fake Christmas Eve, meaning Josh and I were having our own Christmas Eve celebration before leaving to go to Alaska to spend actual Christmas Eve with his family. During Covid when we couldn't travel during the holidays, we decided it was a good time to start our own family traditions at Christmas. Since we were living in California at the time, both with a love for Mexican food and a desire for something different from what we both grew up with, we decided to have a "Christmas Eve Fiesta." Mainly, I decided—because I wanted to try my hand at making homemade tamales, and Josh, never one to shy away from the prospect of getting delish food that he doesn't have to make, totally agreed.

In Josh's mind, "Christmas Eve Fiesta" meant that we were going to eat tamales on Christmas Eve and that was the extent of it. But this was our first Christmas all by ourselves (and perhaps our last—unless we do end up having kids and become empty nesters one day). While at first it was sad to think that we wouldn't be with either of our families at Christmas, it slowly became incredibly fun to think about all the things we wanted to do without having to check in with anyone else or make sure no one felt left out or hungry that season.

I set up a table in the backyard under our large oak tree. I hung strings of lights and decorated the table in bright colors and added candles. While the tamales were cooking, I made chips and every kind of dip under the sun. Once I had everything set up, I made "White Christmas Margaritas," which are basically margaritas made with coconut milk to make them look like snow, with bonus points because they are actually delicious! When everything was ready, I handed Josh his marg, hit play on my phone for the mariachi band to begin, and walked him to the backyard where our first ever Christmas Eve Fiesta was ready to take place.

We both agree that while we love spending Christmas with family, the first Christmas Eve Fiesta was a holiday highlight we will never forget, and one we will continue to make happen no matter where we spend Christmas.

That said, as Christmas 2021 approached, with only one fiesta under my belt (mildly uncertain as to how much of a fiesta I would be able to make happen in Alaska), Josh and I decided to celebrate our Christmas tradition ahead of time so it wouldn't get lost in the shuffle or feel like something was missing if family time consumed all of our time in Alaska. After all, it's most important to keep a tradition alive when it's new and easy to toss out.

Thus, our fake Christmas Eve was set to take place a week before actual Christmas Eve in our new home in Tennessee. I got my Instant Pot, which I knooooow is not the traditional way to make tamales, but I'm still a beginner and sometimes time is of the essence, which is why I opted for a kitchen appliance with the word "Instant" in the name, except that they don't tell you it needs about 30 minutes to heat up or pressurize first before it can do anything instant. I digress.

Since the kitchen is still new to us, I'm still trying to figure out where my stations will be. You know, where I'll chop, where I'll plug in the mixer or the pancake griddle, or in this case, the Instant Pot. In our old house in California, we had an island in the kitchen that had no cabinets above it. In our new house, we also have an island in the kitchen that has no cabinets above it, except there are also no plugs for appliances on said island. I know in the grand scheme of first world problems, a lack of outlets is no big deal, but in the grand scheme of optimizing kitchen efficiency, excuse my inner Valley girl... it's like the dumbest thing ever! Who builds a kitchen island, literally the designated work center for all the kitchen's creations, with no outlets to plug in the appliances necessary to the creating!? It's absurd. That said, I have no other complaints about our house, save our guest bathroom having no fan. WHO DOESN'T PUT A FAN IN A BATHROOM? Don't architects or contractors or whoever is designing these things know that we need white noise to go to the bathroom? Especially in someone else's house!

Anyway, I stress all this about the island to say when using the Instant Pot, steam is released from it, escaping up into the air like a cartoon soul that has just passed on but still lingering in the sky above. This is where the island *without* cabinets above it becomes important because *that* is where you would want your Instant Pot to be while it's unleashing cartoon souls into the air, NOT on the counter space *with* cabinets above it. No one wants their cabinets stained by cartoon souls; it's not good for the cabinets.

I realized right away that it wasn't good for the cabinets to have the Instant Pot underneath them, but I had nowhere else to plug in the Instant Pot because all the outlets were against the wall under the cabinets! Since I was already in go-mode for dinner, I didn't have time to reassess, I just figured I would do it this one time and figure out a long-term solution later.

I loaded up my tamales, set the pressure cook option, and let the Instant Pot do its thing. About ten minutes into the pressurizing phase, I watched the steam shoot out much quicker than I remembered, less like a soul wafting up into the air and more like a vaporized Geyser just shooting straight up… straight up into the cabinets. I told myself it's just this once and it will be fine; I'm well aware that consistently steaming your cabinets will warp the wood and ruin them over time, *but it's just this once and I gotta make the tamales.*

I was sitting at the counter of our outlet-deficient island when Josh walked into the kitchen and noticed the Instant Pot dousing our cabinets.

"Oh no," he said, "I don't think that's good for the cabinets."

I told him I knew it wasn't, but I didn't have anywhere else to plug in the Instant Pot and it was just this once and I would do it differently next time.

"Can I just move it over on top of the stove and maybe turn the fan on?" he asked.

Perhaps that didn't seem like such a big deal, but I didn't want the Instant Pot moved as it can be "sensitive" to movement. I've moved it before and never actually figured out what I did wrong in the moving process, but I had to start the cooking process all over again. I was getting flashbacks to that when I begged Josh,

"Please, no, don't move it, I don't want to have to start over!"

"I won't unplug it," he said, "I'm just going to move it over."

"I know and I really don't want you to, *please*. I know it's not good for the cabinets, I won't do it again, it's just twenty more minutes and it'll be done."

Josh was already in moving position, slowly sliding it as he said, "I'm just going to slooooooowly move it on the stove and... there!" He moved it. He turned the stove fan on and proudly smiled. "See that's much better."

Even if he was being helpful, I was incredibly annoyed that he didn't listen to me, especially that he chose to actively ignore me and move it anyway!

A few minutes later the Instant Pot started beeping. I knew it was much too soon for it to be done so I was already ready to blame Josh for whatever happened. Sure enough, the front was flashing "BURN" in bright red letters and having never seen this message before in my life, I knew it was Josh's fault.

"You see!" I said. "You moved it and now it's burning!"

"I'm pretty sure moving it didn't make the food burn," Josh said.

"Well, I guess we don't know that for sure since you didn't listen to me in the first place, and you went ahead and moved it and only *then* did it start burning!" If I'm really honest with myself, I was just the tiniest bit glad to have something wrong to point to so I could say, *SEE! I TOLD YOU!*

I had to Google what the "BURN" message meant because I had never seen it before, and I didn't know what I was supposed to do. Apparently, it meant that food had gotten to the bottom of the pot and without enough moisture, it was burning. When making tamales, you don't want the tamales sitting directly on the bottom of the pot, so they were sitting on a little trivet with some water underneath them, but apparently something had fallen off the trivet and was burning on the bottom of the pot. Everything was okay, it just meant the Instant Pot would stop cooking to prevent further burn, and if you wanted the message to go away, you had to clean out the pot and then put the food back in... which meant you had to start over with the whole pressurizing process. Everything was getting less and less instant.

Before even taking the lid off, I decided I knew exactly what had happened. I had time to create the whole story since you have to release the steam manually before you can just open the lid, and that whole process takes like ten minutes (seriously, it's the longest instant process ever).

The story goes like this... Once upon a time, Josh moved the Instant Pot like I asked him not to. In the moving process, some of the tamales got shuffled around and some of them slipped off the trivet and were burning on the bottom of the pot. (I had not yet checked the tamales to see if they were burning, but I knew) I was right. The end.

By the time I got to the end of my story, I was furious.

I locked in on one thought: *He didn't listen to me.*

The trouble with locking in on a thought like that is it's not satisfying enough to merely say it, receive an apology, and move on. It needs to be understood, it needs to never happen again, it needs to justify my anger! Which is why *He didn't listen to me* turned into *He never listens to me!* I went from creating a story about Josh accidentally (but intentionally—by way of not listening) burning my tamales to looking for stories in the memory bank of other instances when he didn't listen to me.

"Why don't you just listen to me?" I said, just slightly under a yell. "I told you *not to move it*, I asked you more than once not to move it. I said I knew it wasn't good for the cabinets and I didn't mean to do it and I wouldn't do it again, but *no*, you still had to move it!"

"Babe, I really don't think moving it is what caused it to burn!" He said, clearly irritated he was being accused yet trying to remain calm.

"Well, I guess we'll never know since you *never* listen!" I snapped.

"I *never* listen?" he asked rhetorically. "I think that's a bit dramatic!"

My eyes widened; I hate it when I get called dramatic in a serious way.

"It's not dramatic because you literally didn't listen to me, and this isn't an isolated event. There have been plenty of times I have voiced myself and you just didn't listen. You just slowly moooooove the pot over while I'm still talking and say 'See, that's better' and it's clearly *not* better because it's burning the food!"

"JJ, I didn't do it on purpose! I was trying to help, not trying to burn the food..."

I cut him off before he could finish.

"But your 'trying to help' isn't helping if I'm asking you not to! It's not helpful to help when someone says, 'I don't need help'. I didn't need you to *fix* anything, I just needed you to listen!"

Back and forth we went, Josh defending his action and stating the fact that he didn't burn the food, me saying it wasn't about the food, it was about him not listening.

"Maybe it still would have burnt if you hadn't moved it," I argued "but I guess that's the risk you took when you decided not to listen to me and moved it anyway, by *de*fault it is now *your* fault!"

With one final exhausted breath Josh yelled out, "I was trying to protect our house!"

I couldn't help but laugh a little bit, but not in a disarming way, in a mean way.

"Well, excuse me," I retorted. "Talk about dramatic. Sorry I didn't realize I was ruining our house!"

I think we both had started to feel a little ridiculous about where the argument had gone, but we were so far into it by now that it was hard to find the humor in how dramatic we both were being, at least in that moment.

When I was finally able to pull the lid off the Instant Pot, the tamales were still pretty well positioned. I noticed that cheese had come out of the top of a couple of the tamales, and one or two had cheese coming out the bottom due to the corn husk that was either too small or too thin to hold it all in. I knew this meant that the BURN warning had more to do with my preparation of the tamales than it did the movement of the pot, but again, I was cemented to my innocence because I needed it to justify my argument. I still don't even know if I know why, but I needed that to be the issue... Josh not listening to me. That's why this happened, not because I don't fully understand Instant Pots and can't be bothered to read the manual, or because I over-stuffed the tamales because I have only made them once before and that was over a year ago and I should know what I'm doing by now!

I was staring at the burnt cheese at the bottom of the pot when I heard Josh's voice.

"So, what happened?" he asked. Maybe he was just curious, but it felt more like he was asking, "Since I didn't do it, what exactly happened?"

I death-gripped my argument and fudged the truth ever so slightly.

"Well, *since you moved it*, some of the tamales got moved around and it knocked some cheese out and the cheese is what's burning on the bottom. Now, I have to take them all out and probably even re-wrap some of them!"

I could hear myself being a brat and I felt sorry for Josh but still annoyed at the same time. I cleaned out the pot, re-wrapped a few of the tamales and plugged the pot back in. As it started steaming again, Josh asked why I plugged it back in the same area.

"I thought you said you were going to do it differently next time... you just put it in the same spot?" Suddenly I no longer felt sorry for him, just pure annoyance.

"WHY ARE YOU EVEN IN THE KITCHEN!?" I yelled. "I'M MAKING DINNER, I DON'T NEED YOU IN HERE, I'M JUST GOING TO FINISH, you know what, *no...*"

I went from yelling to quick and quiet movements, which are the early signs of someone about to lose their shit. That's the only adequate way to explain what was about to happen. I yanked the plug out of the wall, picked up the Instant Pot and carried it over to a plug by the floor. I sat the pot down on the ground and continued my business.

"You don't need to put it on the ground," Josh said, and with that I had no idea where to put it because all the counters had cabinets over them, the island had no outlets, the floor seemed the only option, and now Josh was saying I didn't need to resort to the floor, but I DID NOT KNOW WHERE ELSE TO MAKE THE GOD-FORSAKEN TAMALES!

"Stop," I said, "I don't want to hear it. Just get out of the kitchen before I absolutely lose my mind. *Get. Out.*"

Josh saw the crazy in my eyes, said nothing, turned, and walked out of the kitchen into his office. After about twenty minutes of cooling down, I approached him. I usually pout and wait for him to approach me, but as I had the space to collect myself and replay the scenario, I knew I was kind of, mostly, or at least more so, in the wrong... at least when it came to the yelling part. He had taken a risk by walking into the mine field that is a kitchen when a woman (or at least me) is trying to cook.

Josh said he was only trying to help, and I said more calmly this time that I understood...

"You were just trying to protect our house!" I said in a joking yelling tone. Josh laughed at himself, and we both apologized.

I have yet to tell him the tamales didn't really get shuffled around when he moved the Instant Pot, that in fact they exploded cheese because of how I prepared them. He'll find out when he reads this.

By the time we made up, the Instant Pot was ready to have the steam manually released before opening the lid to the finally finished tamales. I turned the knob that lets the steam out and it shot straight up into the air... underneath a hanging plant we have in the window.

"Do you think that's okay for the plant?" Josh asked. I shot him a look and jokingly told him to shut up. We both agreed that this fake Christmas Eve Fiesta was our tamale trial run before I tried to do them again in Alaska for actual Christmas Eve.

When actual Christmas Eve did arrive, I was hustling and bustling in the kitchen, loading up the Instant Pot with double the number of tamales for triple the amount of people. I filled it to the brim and set it.

"No one move it!" Josh said, jokingly. Only he and I got the joke. We looked at each other and laughed.

About ten minutes in, the Instant Pot started beeping and there was that word, taunting me by flashing over and over, "BURN, BURN, BURN." It was the cheese.... again! In a rush, I had once again over-stuffed the tamales and cheese oozed to the bottom of the Instant Pot where it sizzled and burned.

Knowing the Instant Pot hadn't been touched, Josh shot me a look that said, *I KNEW I DIDN'T BURN THEM!* But instead of saying anything, he smiled and asked if I needed help.

I think he knew that I knew that he knew, but I just said, "No thanks, I got it."

And with that he grabbed a carrot, took a chomp, and strode victoriously out of the kitchen.

## 25

## LOST LUGGAGE

**GROWING UP,** we always had to buy our own clothes. Not as little kids, that'd be cruel, but once we hit the teenage working age, if we wanted the latest jacket or pair of shoes, it had to come from our own piggy banks. I loved clothes when I was younger. I'm not sure if I can call it fashion, but I loved expressing myself through what I wore—bright colors, puffy jackets, and clunky shoes. I went through a '70s phase with flowered headbands and purple John Lennon sunglasses, a redneck phase with too much plaid and John Deere apparel (yes, they have apparel), a gangsta rap phase complete with FUBU jackets and Lugz boots—a wardrobe I modeled after The Wu-Tang Clan whose lyrics I had no business singing as a fourteen-year-old.

My longest running fashion phase was probably my preppy phase, also known as the Lily Pulitzer phase. For those who don't know, Lily Pulitzer is a clothing brand, most notably in the South, especially in Florida—Palm Beach to be exact, from where Lily herself hailed. The brand is known for its bright colors and fun animal prints, not like a dress with a cheetah-spot print, but a bright pink dress with entire cheetah characters, probably green ones, sleeping in blue palm trees, printed all over it. Lily Pulitzer is basically a more sophisticated Lisa Frank; there are less rainbows, but just as much color. If you don't know who Lisa Frank is then you probably aren't my target audience, but that's okay, there is always Google.

From high school to college, I wandered in and out of my Lily phase. Growing up by the beach, I jumped back and forth between a preppy-oyster-roast girl and a wannabe-beach-bum-surfer girl. I could never fully pull off either look as neither felt genuinely like me. I did not come from "old money" with hobbies like sailing or croquet to pull off the preppy look. Nor did I live in a beach shack with no other life ambition than to surf a long wave and hit a joint at the end of each day to pull off the surfer girl look. I was somewhere in the odd middle of wanting parts of both lifestyles, but not knowing how that could work since it seemed like there were only boxes for those life descriptions.

As soon as I joined a sorority in college, beach-bum-surfer girl completely disappeared, and it was a full-on Lily Pulitzer affair. Rush Day looked like someone had vomited Pepto Bismol after eating fruity pebbles all over the place. Sorority Row was littered with squealing girls in their Lily dresses. The colors were obscene, an eyesore to anyone passing by the blockaded street filled with the newly recruited as they hunted for the house that had picked them. But the one color that shone the brightest that day was pink… So. Much. Pink. Don't get me wrong, I've gone through my pink phases—loving pink, hating pink, kinda liking pink, loving pink again, hating anyone who wears pink, hating myself for hating anyone who wears pink, and finally accepting pink as the perfect color to make any painting pop. Pink is a *great* color, even if it's the easiest color to overdo and induces nausea at the sight of too much of it.

While there were other fashion stages post-college in between living in both Chicago and Portland (Oregon), and yes, tattoos were involved, once I hit San Diego, California, beach-bum-surfer-girl was officially back—this time she was actually aspiring for the beach shack and the life ambition of surfing the longest wave. The only thing missing was the joint at the end of the day, but after a few stabs at getting high in high school, as well testing out a dosed smoothie (THC mixed into the smoothie, like an edible, but drinkable) later in life when I thought maybe it was just the smoke that I didn't like, I accepted the fact that I didn't like pot in general. It made me hungry and sleepy. As a depressive struggling to be an optimist, that was not a feeling I needed more of in my life. To each their own—pot did nothing for me. I'm not sure if we still call it pot, but in case the Lisa Frank reference didn't give it away, I grew up in the '90s and in the 90s we called it pot, thanks to the '70s.

The beach-bum life was fun for a while, but I got restless. Working at a coffee shop wasn't what I wanted for my life, but that's how San Diego tricks you—you find yourself in the most beautiful place in the country, who cares what you're doing for work? You settle on what you want out of life for the sake of living in paradise. I'm not sure why, but I woke up one day and realized paradise wasn't worth wasting away in any longer… at least not at thirty-something. My beach bum phase looked like tank tops, cut off shorts, and long-sleeved plaid shirts (for the occasional ocean breeze). I made an attempt at having dreads, but I could only get one going and even then, my hair wasn't long enough to make an actual dread, so it ended up looking like a little nub, or perhaps more accurately, a little turd.

For someone who is not in the fashion world, I have associated a lot of who I am with what I wear. I guess I always thought your

269

clothes were supposed to depict that: to show where you're at in life. At this point in my life, I am a conglomeration of all of it … I am still the '90s kid, listening to music her mother would cringe at, wanting to wear a hip-hop t-shirt without feeling like a poser (another '90s word reference). I'm also the surfer girl who eats mostly vegan for no animal-rights related reasons, so I just keep my vegan preferences to myself. I would wear a leather jacket before I wore a t-shirt that said VEGAN on it. And while I genuinely would like to spend the rest of my life surfing before or after work, I am also a mediocre businesswoman with the slightest bit of preppy sorority girl still in there, and a twinge of redneck that I don't think I'll ever be able to shake off; and not the CNN version of a redneck, but the simple life redneck who just wants to live in the woods and occasionally invite you over for iced tea, letting you decide how sweet you want your tea because I'm a little more cultured than to preemptively ruin a whole pitcher of tea with three cups of sugar.

I say things like, "Hey y'all, whatchya'll doin'?" And I have the decency to clarify my sarcasm when I say, "Well, bless their hearts."

I don't really fit in a box anymore and for the most part, I think I stopped trying to, minus the nagging feeling of my forties approaching and a deep-down fear that one day I'll have to let go of my Lisa Frank collection. People often wonder, *at what point does one grow up?* But I've aways wondered, *what does it actually look like to grow up? What does one wear to reflect that they have grown up? Can I be grown up and take life seriously and still wear pink sweaters with red hearts all over them (as I do now at thirty-eight)?*

Josh and I took a trip to California recently, and when we arrived in L.A. my luggage did not. It was apparently stuck in Seattle somewhere, likely getting rained on. The man behind the counter at "luggage assistance" asked me how much money I would need in the form of a voucher to buy what I needed to get me through the night—until they could get my luggage to me the next day. I wanted to exploit the situation, especially since we were in L.A. where everything is three times the price.

"At least $5,000?" I said, adopting an accent that implied I came from money. But little redneck JJ, who always creeps up for a peek when money is involved, as if money is some sort of holy grail she's not allowed to touch but loves to admire from far away, had to add, "That's prolly good, don'tcha think?"

I turned to Josh who was laughing at me, not only to make sure the man knew I was kidding, but also to spare me any embarrassment for thinking he'd actually approve that amount.

"How about $100?" the man asked, and out came the truth about how much money I actually come from.

"OH MY GOD, THAT'S AMAZING!"

I was afraid I had revealed that $100 was way more than what I needed "for the night," so I quickly followed up.

"I mean, yeah, I have to work tomorrow and all I have is this gross travel outfit." (Ahem, it was literally my favorite shirt and pair of pants.)

The man said he understood. I'm not sure if he meant he understood in a poor-you-I-understand kind of way, or an oh-you're-lying-I-understand kind of way. For some reason I was holding my breath until the voucher went through. I told Josh we needed to get out of there fast before they changed their minds.

"You know it doesn't work like that, right?" Josh asked as we walked out the door.

"Shut up!" I said lovingly, "Let's just go!"

We got into our rental car and as soon as we drove away from the airport, I cheered in a WE DONE IT kind of way, as if we'd gotten away with a bank heist or we'd gotten an extra-large fry mistakenly put in our bag from Chick-Fil-A. I admit, the accidental free fries did happen to me once, and I did not correct their mistake. I just chalked it up as their pleasure. Bless their hearts.

Josh, having never seen this side of me, didn't quite understand what I was so excited about.

"I'm sorry you didn't get your luggage, babe."

"Are you kidding me?" I squealed, not unlike a newly recruited sorority girl. "I have always wanted this to happen to me! It's like free money, to get whatever I want. The question is, do I buy something I could never buy but now I can because I have the money to do it, or do I buy something I would always buy but now it's like I'm getting it for free?"

I was drunk with the power of a $100 airline voucher.

"I think you just get what you need," Josh said, but I barely heard him as I rolodexed through my mind for which store we should go to. Seeing as it was already 9 p.m., most shopping mall stores were closed. I settled on Target as their 10 p.m. closing time gave us an hour to peruse the aisles. When we got to the store, I whipped out a shopping cart and bolted for the women's section as if I were in a grocery sweepstakes and the timer had started.

Josh grabbed some food while I tried to decide if now was the time for me to change up my entire style.

I had flashbacks to my senior year of high school when my step-grandmother came to visit and offered to buy me a dress as a graduation gift. I knew I wanted the dress to be Lily Pulitzer because it was hard enough to afford Lily prices on my own. I often bought Lily on eBay, it was a form of dopamine when you placed a bid, waited a few days, upped your bid if necessary, and then got the congratulatory email that you won! YOU WON THE PRODUCT YOU PAID FOR! It might as well have been cocaine.

For this graduation gift, I skipped eBay and the discount stores and went directly to "The Lily Store," the sacred motherland of the iconic hot pink and vivid green combination that was so bright even Elton John would have to squint upon walking in. Elton can suit up in as many pink feathered boas and rose-colored glasses as he likes, but those are still no match for the pink sun flare that is The Joggling Board, the only licensed Lily Pulitzer store in my hometown of Pawleys Island, SC.

Knowing that someone else was paying for the dress, I remember frantically going through the maze of multi-colored patterns and styles wondering, *do I pick a print I would buy myself or do I pick a print I wouldn't buy myself, but "since I can afford it" I might as well have an extra print.* I'm still not sure if the logic made since, but I figured, why use free money on something I would buy anyway... even though I couldn't typically afford it (I seemed to always forget that part)?

There were so many dresses I loved, and I can't quite explain it, but I panicked. I couldn't choose a favorite and I was so worried I was spending too long trying to decide that I was afraid I'd miss my chance to get my free dress, so I just grabbed one, one I didn't originally look at, try on, or even like.

I have been known to panic-order at restaurants when the waitress is patiently waiting for me to decide. I just shout something out not because I want it but because I don't want to be "that person" who induces an eyeroll from the charming waitress. But I inevitably do become "that person" when I receive my basil pizza with black olives and banana peppers and I "simply can't eat it." I am no stranger to this form of panic, but panic-ordering food is different from panic-buying clothes because there is more at stake with the clothing... a $12 pizza versus a $142 dress (that was a pretty penny in the late '90s).

I wore the dress a few times, if for no other reason than it was Lily Pulitzer and I was bound to get compliments, on top of the guilt I would have felt had I never worn the dress my step-grandmother bought me as a high school graduation gift. Aside from that, I really didn't like the dress. It wasn't even the typical shade of Lily pink, it was more of a light orange with puce cocktail drinks printed all over it. Even the umbrellas in the print were more of a sea foam green than the classic vibrant bright green. The dress was just 'meh'.

So, there I was that night, luggage-less in L.A., scouring through Target, bound and determined not to make the same mistake as the 'meh' Lily dress, but curious as to what styles I should try with this free money that, unlike my step-grandmother's patience, actually did have an expiration if I didn't make a decision. Oh, the pressure.

Since the dressing rooms were closed for the night, I tried on sweaters and sweatshirts while still pushing my shopping cart through the store. I held pants up against my hips to see if they might fit. I'd occasionally ask Josh for his opinion. He leaned against a post scrolling his phone while occasionally glancing up to watch my insanity. I went back and forth between the junior's section and the women's section... asking myself, *do I go with "this-is-me" inner child? Or do I finally accept my age and go with a more classic, boring look?* I held up everything from black leggings to mom jeans to tie-dye bootcut... I'm still not sure what those were, I think they were pants, but the flare started at the knee and I'm pretty sure the only person who could have pulled them off was Janis Joplin, and well, rest in peace, dear Janis.

Speaking of pulling it off, the two outfits I did end up deciding between were solely meant for two people on earth... one being JoJo Siwa (a more modern rainbow-y version of Lisa Frank, enhanced by bows the size of Texas), and the other being Joanna

Gaines (who, don't get me wrong, is as classy as they come, but also about as white walls and khaki as you can get).

Once again, I was stuck... I found myself somewhere between an explosion of rainbows and a subdued seat at Magnolia Table.

Do I go with the rainbow tie-dye outfit that looks like it was designed for an overgrown six-year-old, or do I go with the denim-on-denim outfit that announces to the world that I'm old enough to be your mom, but I'm still kinda cool? Right at that crucial decision-making moment, I heard the announcement that the store was closing soon and would all customers "please bring your purchases to the register."

"Don't you need contact solution?" Josh asked.

I panicked but tried to act casual.

"Oh my gosh, yes, don't let me forget before we leave."

And then I carried on as if I had longer than ten minutes to make my decision. Josh picked up on the fact that the contact solution was not nearly as important to me as the clothing decision I was facing, so he sauntered off to find the solution himself. He is, without a doubt, the absolute best.

I also remembered I would need a clean t-shirt to sleep in, *and what about underwear?* Oh God, suddenly there were all kinds of clothes I needed that I hadn't even thought of, and *the clock was ticking.* I ran to the t-shirt section, and it was all so... cliché... Def Leopard? Pink Floyd? Does anyone who shops at Target actually listen to these bands or do they just like the colors on the shirts?

I eventually found a t-shirt that was the *one thing* I knew for sure I wanted. Since the t-shirt fed my '90s kid nostalgia, I decided to go with the grown-up outfit. I checked out just in time for the store to close—they literally locked the doors behind Josh and me and not without a few eye-rolls thanks to my explosion through the clothing department. I was officially "that person" at Target.

I took a deep breath when we got in the car and remarked to Josh about how stressful the whole situation was.

"I've never seen that side of you," Josh said.

"The panicked what-do-I-do-with-free-money side?" I asked.

Josh laughed.

"Yeah, like, you even forgot contact solution."

I threw my hands up in the air, but before I could shame myself, Josh pulled the solution out. I was relieved but still a little wired from the whole experience, not even sure if the mom outfit I got would fit me. As we drove away, it dawned on me.

"I needed a toothbrush and toothpaste and deodorant and a razor…" I kept listing things. "Babe! Did you get anything you needed?" Josh blurted out.

I honestly couldn't believe the degree to which I kinda blacked out and completely forgot what exactly one needed for a night without their suitcase. Toiletries would have been a good start. As I rummaged through my Target bag, I laughed.

"No, I didn't… but I did get this sweet T.L.C. t-shirt!"

"Wow, babe!" Josh laughed with slight disbelief. "A toothbrush or a T.L.C. t-shirt? I see you got the most important one."

It was the only purchase I was proud of.

We went to our hotel, and I tried on my mom outfit. It was horrible. Everything about it was horrible… the fit, the color, the size. It was the 'meh' Lily dress all over again, except it was denim upon denim.

"Fortunately," I said as I took off the 'meh', "I think this means I'm too young to go full on mom outfit."

"You can return it tomorrow," Josh laughed, "and maybe get what you *need!*"

I put on my new T.L.C. shirt that said "No Scrubs" across the top and asked Josh if I could borrow his toothbrush.

The next day I returned to Target, a little more levelheaded after a good night's sleep. I took the denim outfit up to the returns counter. The guy working couldn't have been older than sixteen or seventeen. He was monotone, showing no emotion whatsoever as he asked me if anything was wrong with the items.

"No," I said, "the dressing room was just closed last night so I couldn't try anything on while I was here. When I got home, I tried it on, and it didn't fit."

The guy didn't blink, move, or change the tone of his voice, he just looked at me deadpan.

"Tragic," he said.

I laughed at what I thought was his sarcasm. I wanted him to know I was much cooler than the denim-on-denim outfit I had picked out but was now returning "because it didn't fit."

"Not that tragic," I smirked. "I got a T.L.C. shirt that fit perfectly."

Without moving his head, the guy rolled his eyes up to look at me.

"What's T.L.C.?" he asked.

And that's when I realized... I *am* officially old enough for the mom outfit.

## 26

# i GET iT FROM MY MOMMA!

**I'M WRITING IN MY ROOM** this morning because my mom is in town visiting and apparently in need of an office in addition to the guest bedroom where she is sleeping. To be fair, I have an office in addition to my bedroom, so I certainly understand the need for a separate space to work, but last night after she arrived, I was caught off guard while having dinner when she asked, "Now, where shall I set up my computer?"

"Your laptop?" I asked, trying to hint that its very name suggested the location for its set up, literally anywhere, the true beauty of the laptop.

She affirmed yes, her laptop, and I tried to think of places to suggest where she might be able to sit with her laptop.

"Well, you could use the living room and sit on the couch."

"But where would I put my computer?"

"On your lap?"

"Well, I like having a desk to sit at."

I knew I needed my own space for writing, hence my office, and

I knew it wouldn't be fair to offer up Josh's office. The beauty of having a four-bedroom house and no kids is that we each get an office of our own and still have one room left for a guest room. We apparently didn't think through the necessity of having a *guest office*.

I was trying not to be irritated that my mom didn't want to use her laptop on her lap. I reminded myself she was older, and I think her computer was even older than her. It no longer stays on without being plugged into the wall, for some unknown reason the side of it is taped together with *scotch tape*, and its roughly the size of a VCR (if that acronym doesn't age me, I don't know what will). It's basically a desktop that looks like a laptop. It makes sense that she likes "having a desk to sit at" when using her non-lap laptop.

"Well, you can use the kitchen counter," I suggested, tapping the island countertop and ignoring the large empty space in our kitchen where a table would fit nicely. If we had a kitchen table it would be the perfect place for my mom to sit with her laptop, but despite the fact that we moved into this house three months ago, we haven't yet purchased a kitchen table because Josh insists he can make one. His deadline appears to be Thanksgiving, which at this point is eight months away, so I have rapidly lost patience and have begun secretly window shopping for tables behind his back.

"Well, I don't want to be in your space," Mom said, and I thought how the kitchen counter was the only place in the house that literally *wasn't* in our space because it was in neither Josh's office nor mine, but then I remembered there was no outlet at that spot. (Again, who builds an island in a kitchen with not even one outlet?!) Whoever designed our kitchen clearly wasn't a baker or a pancake maker—whipping out eight pancakes at once on an old-school electric griddle. I knew that spot wouldn't work with her computer cord stretching across the kitchen.

"I have a breakfast tray table! You could use that and sit in your room," I suggested, clearly wracking my brain for a solution that involved *anything* other than my office.

Mom curled up her nose as if she were considering my suggestion, but it was clear she did not like that idea.

"Well, I don't want to be sitting in bed for the webinar," she responded.

My mom hosts a monthly webinar centered mostly around all aspects of health: mental, physical, spiritual, and emotional health. She provides a wealth of information. Most of the webinar participants seem to be women round about her age, a few younger, a few older. I've attended a number of the webinars and I'm always so struck by how eager these women are to learn and grow. Perhaps it's my own cynicism, but I guess I've always thought when you got to a certain age, you just gave up. I was actually looking forward to the day when I got to stop trying so hard and sit in my recliner eating Little Debbies while watching Wheel of Fortune until the good Lord called me home.

I think that was my view of "the good life" ever since childhood, when we'd go over to my Grandma Ruth's house—the only place we were allowed to eat Little Debbies and white bread—and no, she did not make us eat the crust. She was a boss of a grandmother (that's a good thing). She'd have Wheel of Fortune on while she worked on needlepoint and we learned what vowels were, trying to decide if we liked the Star Crunch or the Swiss Rolls the most. *One day, this will be my whole life,* I used to think, excited to grow old and waste away.

Maybe that is what old(er) people did back in the day, after a lifetime of work and struggles—they just sat back until it was time to go; but in more recent generations, the whole self-help field no longer applies only to the young. Older and older people are still working on themselves as they try to stay physically fit and mentally sharp. While I know (and genuinely think) it's a good thing to offer such resources to old(er) people, I almost had a panic attack the day I realized I may not finally reach that point where I've worked on myself long enough that I get to stop and reward myself with the never-ending comfort of junk food, a comfy chair, and Pat Sajack.

I'm proud of my mom for all she does with hosting webinars, and despite my cracks at her aging quirks, she is incredibly sharp, as well as really good at teaching people how to make the best out of an often-hard life. She's had plenty of reasons in her life to give up and resort to a recliner and Little Debbies, and it would be justified, a reward for hard work. But she keeps showing up, day after day, with her hot lemon water first thing in the morning, and she tries to live well, contributing where she can to those who desire a little guidance in their own lives. She is a remarkable woman.

That said, I didn't want to give her my office.

"Okay," I resolved, "that makes sense not to lead a webinar about living your best life from your bed."

"Yeah, what message does that send?" She laughed.

"Well, for the webinar you can definitely use my office…"

"Oh, great!" she interjected, a little too eagerly.

"But as far as working the rest of the day, every day, we'll have to think of something."

I honestly debated going to Goodwill first thing in the morning to find a desk to put in the guest bedroom. My office is *my space*. It's where I go to reset, to think, to create, to write. My office not only has a desk for writing, but it's also packed full of every glitter product available from Hobby Lobby should I be in the mood for arts and crafts. Josh *hates* glitter, it's not allowed anywhere in our house, except my office. Often when I come tromping downstairs from "Glitter Bomb Central," as Josh has deemed my office, he follows behind me with the vacuum cleaner to suck up every flake I've tracked out. I'm fine with no glitter in the rest of the house, I'm even fine with having company in our house all day long, but I need my space to retreat to, to hide in, or if need be, to escape to so I can make a glitter crown out of pipe cleaners and pompoms.

"Yeah, we can figure it out later," Mom said.

I internally battled myself for the rest of the night about whether or not I was being a good daughter. *Am I protecting my own mental health and space, or am I being selfish and careless toward my aging mother?*

After dinner, Mom went upstairs to put her pajamas on before we started a movie. When she came down, she let me know that she had gone ahead and set up her computer in my office, since, you know, she'd be using it for the webinar the following night. Right away, I knew this meant she would also be in there the next morning, working on her material for the webinar. *Do I cave or do I hold my ground? And was that even what was happening here? Had I not voiced how sacred of a space my office was to me? Had I not expressed how much I needed the solitude of that space to write anything worth reading?* (Oh, the things we convince ourselves of when we dig our heels in, even if only internally). My mother was not trying to *take my space;* she simply wanted to know which space she could use that would be functional to her needs. Suggesting every other room in the house for her to work in, save the bathroom, was not the way to successfully communicate my needs. I was avoiding addressing the fact that I had needs because my needs didn't feel legitimate, given that at thirty-eight, with a high functioning MacBook Pro, which *is* a laptop, I, too, could easily sit anywhere in the house and work.

I wanted a desk for my laptop, but I didn't want to *want* a desk for my laptop because it was the very thing I was suggesting was ridiculous about my mom's needs. I was literally telling her it was called a laptop for a reason, because it doesn't need a desk to function, all it needs is a lap! Mentally though, for some reason, I am never convinced I'm truly working as a writer unless I am writing *at a desk*, preferably *my desk*, but any desk will do as long as there is a lamp, a candle, and a window nearby (I clearly don't have ridiculous requests). If there's anything I have learned from my mom, it is the importance of communicating, especially communicating your needs. And so, like a true grown-up, who's learned these tools from a loving mother, I said nothing. I diverted to trying to come up with a space for her to work in without voicing how I needed *my* space to work in as well.

By the time I got up the next morning, Mom had already been awake for two and a half hours. She wakes up at 5 a.m. every morning and I suppose she reads, writes, and tries not to eat breakfast too early so as to give her body time to digest her meal from the night before. I had already set the coffeemaker to ensure there would be some coffee ready for her when she got up. When I awoke, I stumbled out to the kitchen to pour myself a cup (of ambition) before climbing back into bed with it. I like to wake up slowly. As an introvert, I prefer minimal to no interaction first thing in the morning. My mom, who had already been awake for three hours, was sitting on the couch with her coffee, ready to engage.

"How'd you sleep?" she asked.

"Great," I mumbled as I walked straight to the coffee pot.

I had set the coffeemaker to brew five cups the night before. When I held up the pot, the coffee was nearly gone. I swirled the muddy sludge at the bottom of the carafe. I think my mother heard my eyebrows raise in disbelief.

"I drank a lot of coffee," she laughed.

"Yeah, apparently," I said, as I dripped the last of it into a coffee cup, filling it less than halfway.

"I drank it black," she added. "I wasn't sure if I could use the cream in the fridge."

I looked down at the note I had left for her on the counter last night that said: "Newly opened cream in the fridge. Help yourself!"

"Yeah, I just opened it last night—for you," I said, trying to make sure my tone didn't imply anything other than I hadn't fully woken up yet.

"I'm gonna go lay back down for a while and wake up slowly," I told her. "Do you need anything?"

She replied that she was trying to avoid the coffee cake. After spending a week at home in Pawleys Island, I had brought my mom back with me to Chattanooga so she could see our house and stay with us for a while. On the drive from South Carolina to Tennessee we stopped to see friends and they made us gluten-free coffee cake for the road. My mom tries to avoid sugar, sometimes annoyingly so, but I know it's good that she does. Since Josh and I had both been gone from home for a while, there were no groceries in the house except for the coffee cake.

"So, I tried to avoid it all morning," she continued, "but I looked all over and couldn't find anything else to eat, so I ate some of the coffee cake." She laughed.

In retrospect I think she was laughing at herself for avoiding something only to cave into it, a funny predicament many humans find themselves in every so often. In the moment, without caffeine in my veins or enough alone time to charge up, I associated her laughter with there being no food in our house (it's odd how we can personalize everything).

"There's no food because we've been gone," I said, again checking my tone while also wondering, *why am I taking this so personally?*

"Oh, I know," she said.

I told her we could go to the grocery store later.

I went back to my room. Josh was out of town for work, so I could easily get my alone time in from the comfort of my own bed. I laid there and drank the little bit of muddy coffee from the bottom of the pot. I was too tired to analyze my thoughts about mother-daughter relationships, how terribly, beautifully odd they can be. As a daughter, you want to be your own person, separate from the child your mother will aways see you as; you want to be your own person in much need of space, but at the same time you want your mom to be there as soon as life gets hard or feels scary. It's even odder the older you get, realizing the roles start to flip a little—your mom becomes less the protector and more the one who needs to be protected. What a beautiful, yet heartbreaking, reversal of roles.

I have spent time with elderly women, some still mentally sharp, others whose memories have faded long ago, and the one thing they all have in common is how much they remember their moms; some of them even believe they have just seen their moms the previous week—even though their moms may have died years or even decades ago. Other women tell stories from their childhood about what their mom used to be like, a figure that disappeared from their lives long after they aged and continued to live so much of life without their mothers.

It's odd to think that one day my mother will be gone. I won't have the ability to call her up on the phone, I won't be able to drag my friends over to meet her and, as a result, have them totally understand where I come from. I thought about this as I laid in bed with my half cup of muddy coffee and my mom sat in the living room on her fourth and a half cup of the fresh stuff. I knew she would only be at my house for three days, and the truth is, I didn't need my office *that badly* to write something worth reading. My aging mother needed the desk for her laptop much more than I did.

I read some David Sedaris for a little while, in part because he makes me feel sane and less like a horrible person. *And I thought I was self-absorbed*, I gleefully think when I read his work, and I internally praise Mr. Sedaris for his honesty while sitting on my much higher horse.

I got out of bed and went to tell my mom she could use my office to work in, but she was already upstairs working there. Though I had already decided it was fine, I noticed I felt a little annoyed. I wanted it to be known that I was acting in a selfless manner—I was *letting* her use my office. I didn't get to say, "Okay, Mom, you can use my office." She was just already using it.

Although it clearly didn't need to be said, I said it anyway.

"You can use my office today, Mom."

"Oh, thank you, honey!" she said surprised, as if she wasn't already doing so.

I laughed at her, I laughed at myself, and I laughed at how the things that annoy me most are perhaps the things that I am myself most guilty of.

Later in the day, Mom and I went to the grocery store to pick up a few items.

"We need cream," she said as she grabbed the brand she knows. I reminded her that I had fresh cream and that I had opened it just for her.

"Oh really?" she said, "I wasn't sure. I didn't recognize the brand."

There it was, the *real* reason she didn't use the cream—she didn't recognize it as one of her "trusted" brands, which is to say, a brand that she was familiar with, one that is most likely organic and grass-fed, because God forbid we drink cream from corn-fed cows. So, the cream at my house was going to sit in the fridge, newly opened and unused, while we spent five more dollars on the brand she trusted.

When she put the cream into the shopping cart, I wanted to give her a hard time about it, but I guess I am no different when I go over to a friend's house, and they don't have organic food, or they want me to use their Keurig... *What is this crap?* I'll ask myself while smiling and pretending like it doesn't bother me to get my coffee from a plastic pod. Immediately upon leaving their house, I will go to a grocery store or coffee shop and buy my needs without ever having to voice them to anyone. A true grown-up, really.

I hope to be as openly ridiculous as my mother when I reach her age, if for no other reason than it's not actually ridiculous to voice your needs and preferences—it just seems ridiculous to me because I am not used to doing it. But as I mature more each year, I am learning to do just that—voice my needs and preferences, which is why I wrote this story...

Just so my mother can read it before the next time she visits.

Man, it feels good to be a grown-up.

# 27

# JOLENE— A LOVESEAT STORY

**I'M TRYING A NEW SPOT FOR WRITING.** So far, I'm not sure about it. The loveseat isn't nearly as comfortable as I thought it'd be, or as I remember it being in my sister's apartment.

"Her name is Jolene," my sister said when she called me to see if Josh and I wanted to take the loveseat off her hands before her upcoming move, she had no room for it in her new place.

"The fact that you named it," I said, "and refer to it as 'her' makes me question if you're ready to get rid of her."

Betsy laughed and explained that Jolene was the model name of the loveseat, and was, perhaps, even why she eventually bought it.

"It is a good name," I said, "and a *great* song… it would be kinda fun to sit on Jolene…" As if Dolly Parton had really written a song about being wronged by a conniving loveseat.

On the second floor of our home, Josh and I have a sitting area that has one armchair and a lamp. I had been wanting to fix this area up for a while so that more than one person could sit in it and not feel like they were the only patient in a doctor's office waiting room (left waiting an hour past their scheduled appointment time before the doctor was finally ready to see them).

I told Betsy we had the perfect place for Jolene and would be happy to open our home to her.

"But I don't want any of those dirty tricks she plays."

I got a sympathy laugh out of Betsy and then we focused on figuring out how to get Jolene from Betsy's apartment in Arlington, Virginia all the way to Tennessee.

My dad had already planned to drive up from South Carolina to help Betsy with her move. As an empty nester who lives on his own and has the only truck in the family, he jumped at the opportunity to help. Side note: for some reason, both of my parents hate flying. They hate it to the point that they would rather drive eight hours than fly for one and a half.

"I don't like taking off my shoes," my mom always says, as if the two minutes you stand in your socks while you wait for your shoes to go through security is an inconvenient enough reason *not* to book a flight for the sake of actual convenience.

Now that my parents are divorced, if we have family functions outside of South Carolina, say at Betsy's in Virginia or at mine in Tennessee, we kids have to figure out how to get both parents there without using the same car. While they are completely amicable and fine to be around each other at family functions, they aren't quite to the point of riding together in the same car for eight hours.

The plan was for my dad to drive up to Virginia, help Betsy move, pack up Jolene in his truck and take her back to South Carolina where she would wait for us in my mom's garage until Josh and I could come get her.

"Be careful," I joked to my dad. "Jolene's a home-wrecker." He laughed slightly more than a sympathy laugh.

"Honey, I don't think we need to worry about our home life getting wrecked anymore," he said, and I felt the sting of my own joke.

So, last October, Josh and I flew into Myrtle Beach, hung out for a week, and then my dad, who would be going to a retreat just outside of the Chattanooga area, offered to drive us back to Tennessee—along with Jolene. This is when I can see driving eight hours as a benefit over flying—when you need to transport a loveseat. Since you can't check a loveseat as oversized, despite it being a miniature version of a couch, you must bite the bullet and drive long distance. And so, once again, instead of a two-hour flight, we packed up dad's truck, and headed to Tennessee with Jolene in tow.

I thought it would be perfect timing to get Jolene to our house just before the holidays. I was going to be hosting Christmas for the first time that year, and with both my parents coming, as well as my two younger siblings and a dog, I thought an extra sitting area would provide room for everyone to spread out and feel comfortable. I decorated the upstairs sitting area "so cute." Every time I hung a picture, tossed in a new throw pillow, or added a potted plant I'd hear myself say out loud: "So cute." I envisioned my family walking up the stairs and saying the same thing as they fought over who would cozy up and hang out with Jolene.

Except... that Christmas, *not one person* used the upstairs sitting area. Not one. Instead, everyone crowded into the living room with its limited seating options. Apparently, no one cared about cute decor—all they wanted was to be together, squished into the same room. *Was that really it? Togetherness?* As soon as someone got up from the couch, someone else would swoop in as if it was a game of musical chairs. People started waiting as long as they could before getting up to go to the bathroom for fear of losing their seat; they waited until they thought they would burst forth like a champagne cork being popped.

"I can't hold it anymore!" *Swoop*. Bobby would steal Betsy's seat.

"Thanks for keeping it warm, sis!"

I'd remind people that we had space upstairs, where Jolene sat all alone, surrounded by Christmas trees that I assumed people would gaze upon as they lounged. I even lit candles up there to lure people into Jolene's comforting arms, but instead, my mom would come downstairs, her voice filled with mild concern.

"You know you left candles lit up there?"

I imagine the fireplace was the main reason everyone wanted to crowd into the living room together, or perhaps it really was the spirit of the holidays, and everyone wanted to be around each other. When my siblings and I visit our parents, we're often split between two different homes, but here, with our parents visiting us, we were all together in one house, even if just for a few days. It was like we wanted to be as close as possible so we could soak it all in.

I didn't go sit upstairs with Jolene simply because I didn't have time. This sitting area that I had daydreamed about lounging in was finally fully lounge-able, but when was I thinking *I* would be lounging? The holidays were much too busy. And even if it's not the holidays, most of the time Josh and I are traveling or I'm working in my office or rehearsing a stand-up set. When we host, I'm busy cooking, cleaning, and lighting candles upstairs to tempt people to stay up there. It really is the cutest little area, and I can't for the life of me imagine why no one would want to linger up there. From the rugs and lamps to the pillows and paintings, Jolene's little area belongs in a magazine (in my biased opinion), maybe not *Magnolia Journal*, as my taste is much too colorful to be showcased by Chip and Joanna, but surely a mention in *Better Homes & Gardens* or *Southern Living*.

When Josh is out of town, I have my morning coffee in the bedroom while I write. But this morning I had to decide where I would write because Josh is home and still sleeping. Five months after welcoming Jolene into our home, I finally decided to take advantage of my beautifully curated sitting area (that I want other people to love) and opted for a morning with Jolene.

I came upstairs and lit a candle.

"Good morning, Jolene, I'm here," I whispered, as I approached her welcoming arms. The colorful blanket I had thrown on her back and the decorative pillow I used to give her denim color a little more pop made her look all the more inviting. I sat down to take it all in, repositioning myself a few times before realizing that despite her good looks and welcoming appeal, Jolene was not fit for a home. She was too stiff to enjoy lounging. She was all show, no comfort whatsoever. Maybe she would be good for half an hour, but that's about as much of Jolene as you can handle.

For about ten minutes, I tried to convince myself I loved my sitting area, until finally, I stood up.

"This is not comfortable at all," I said, out loud.

The side arms were so short you couldn't even stretch your legs out on the cushions and lean up against the opposite side without your head wanting to fall back and snap your neck. I tried using the decorative pillow as a bolster, but that only revealed why the pillow is called "decorative" and not "comfortable." I eventually sat up in a position that I could handle for a few minutes, if for no other reason than to try to finish writing, but almost immediately my back was aching, my legs were cramped, and I seriously couldn't wait to get away from Jolene.

I feel bad talking bad about her right in front of her, but the truth is out ... Jolene looks good, but I don't think we have to worry about her taking anybody's man.

Perhaps this is why no one gathered in the sitting area over Christmas.

Perhaps this is why Betsy got rid of her in the first place—she fell for the name, same as I did, and same as Dolly Parton's man did, but in the end, I think we all realized ... Jolene's the worst.

# 28

# SOUTHERN CHARM AND SAVASANA

**IT WAS EARLY 2022.** In the hills of Tennessee, far removed from the surfers and yogis I used to be one of, I went to a yoga class for the first time since the summer of 2018. When I lived in Ocean Beach, California, I did yoga almost every day. Occasionally, I'd burn out and take a few days off, but I was always back in class after a long mental battle that'd result in me deciding maybe it was a good thing to get out of my head… and bed.

I had been living in Ocean Beach for two years when I first found the yoga studio because they were running a special. The studio was only a few blocks from my house, and while the location was a draw, it was the word "discount" that really pulled me in. How much power does the word "discount" have on me? Well, I was thirty-two years old and had never practiced, nor taken an interest in yoga before—I basically decided to take up a new hobby since it was discounted, so I'd say pretty powerful.

My roommate, Jena, and I signed up for our *discounted* introductory packages and went together to see what this woo-woo chakra business was all about. Both of us were raised in the Southern church and had our own misunderstandings that practicing yoga was the equivalent of stretching for Satan. I had seen my first yoga studio when I moved to Portland, Oregon at the age of twenty-seven, which made sense to me that it was in Portland, because before I moved there, I had been warned.

"Be careful, Portland is dark, and it's not just the weather!"

Fortunately, I had experienced the city life of Chicago, Illinois as a buffer in between moving from South Carolina to Portland, so the "dark" city was less of a culture shock. While Chicago is also completely different from Portland, had I moved to the Pacific Northwest cold turkey, I might have been more disturbed by "progressive" city living, as Portland likes to call themselves.

To be clear, I loved living in Portland, but it was vastly different from my small Carolina hometown— for example, the first weekend I moved to Portland was the annual "Naked Bike Ride" through all of downtown. I got caught at a red light when I suddenly saw a bunch of body parts whizzing past my car. I seemed to be the only person surprised by it all, everyone else cheered as the riders went by. *Where am I?* I thought after seeing a bunch of "plumber's cracks" out for a joy ride. Portland's slogan is "Keep Portland Weird," but since everyone strives to be weird, weird is no longer weird, but actually quite normal, at least in Portland. If you want to stand out in Portland, wear an Ann Taylor pantsuit and walk down the sidewalk.

I lived in Portland for four years and though I was aware of yoga the whole time I lived there, no one I ran in circles with did yoga, so I was neither curious about it nor was I ever invited to try it. My friends made art or wrote stories or played guitar, usually sitting in a coffee shop doing one or all three of those things simultaneously.

If they weren't sitting in a coffee shop, they were working in a coffee shop, myself included. We were all going to be the next Basquiat or Hemingway or Joni Mitchell, and something about Portland made us believe it to be true. Woo-woo has many shapes and forms.

It wasn't until I moved to the sunny beaches of San Diego, California that I discovered the "spiritually dark" practice of yoga and made it my own. The first day of class, Jena and I were slightly intimidated by all the women in spandex pants and low-cut tank tops. Jena at least looked the part; she has the body for a yoga outfit. I looked like a twig in need of a sprout.

Melanie, the owner of the studio, was teaching our class that day. Jena and I used the mats provided by the studio and set them up next to each other in the back. I noticed all the other women stretching while they waited for class to start. *Are we supposed to stretch before we stretch?* I wondered. At that point in my life, I had a total range of three stretches; I opted for the one of least resistance, the butterfly position. Occasionally I'd lean forward as if to stretch my nose to my toes, knowing my nose wasn't actually going to make it anywhere near my toes.

I waited for chimes or chants or some form of Eastern music to begin. Melanie came in the studio, hit play on the stereo, and there it was… except it wasn't, it was Ed Sheeran. Even I was like, *what kind of white people stuff is this? Are we allowed to do yoga to Ed Sheeran!?* Melanie led us through sun salutations, explaining their meaning, explaining our gratitude for Mother Earth and the sun, all of which I was on board with. As we continued, Melanie led the class through a flow in which she had to really break things down into layman's terms for Jena and me. Meanwhile, the jams kept flowing, the most memorable of them was Mumford and Sons. Call me white, but I'll admit it, I was stoked.

Towards the end of the class Melanie posed a question.

"Do you know what would happen to you if you *didn't* do a chaturanga every day for the rest of your life?"

I looked at Jena and mouthed, "What's a chaturanga?"

Knowing she couldn't answer, Jena tried not to laugh. I had heard the word used during class, but I just dismissed it, figuring I'd Google it later, I didn't know there was going to be a pop quiz on Sanskrit.

Apparently, everyone else understood that the question was rhetorical because the room remained silent. I was prepared for Melanie to say something along the lines of, "You wouldn't be as strong, you'd lack discipline, you'd never challenge yourself."

I felt like I had joined this journey to self-enlightenment a little late in the game, yet maybe I had gotten in by the skin of my teeth while there was still time left to grow into a better human being.

After a long pause, Melanie began to answer her own question. *Here we go*, I thought. *What's going to happen to me if I don't do at least one chaturanga every single day?*

"Absolutely nothing," she said. "It's just yoga—don't take yourself so seriously."

*Was that really the right answer? Did I take advantage of the discount only to find out yoga didn't really matter all that much?* My mind was blown. Perhaps in some weird way, that was the enlightenment of it all. Yoga mattered because it didn't. It was not the ultimate end-all, be-all for a better life, but for that day, perhaps even just that moment, when you practiced yoga and were present in gratitude, aware of yourself and others, life was better.

After class I told Melanie how much I enjoyed it.

"I feel physically better, emotionally healthier, and spiritually conflicted."

"Sounds like you just did your first yoga class," Melanie laughed.

I learned that Melanie had also been raised in the church, and while she still held out hope in God, she left a lot of the church culture behind. Fair enough. Melanie let us know that the studio also held classes that were more "seeker-friendly," a term the church uses for people who are curious about church (apparently the same term can be applied to yoga culture), as well as more traditional classes with less Mumford and Ed Sheeran.

On the walk home, Jena and I debriefed, deciding we liked how laid back and welcoming the studio was.

"Not at all as snobby as I thought it'd be," I told Jena. "Especially given how many yogis I serve coffee to. They may be zen in class, but out in the real world they can be real a-holes."

Jena laughed. "That's probably why they need the class!"

Good point.

When we returned home, we told our other housemates about it.

"And then," I said excitedly, "she played Mumford and Sons!" As if I was a kid who just heard their youth pastor swear for the first time—totally not allowed, but totally cool.

After our discount ran out, Jena and I went all in, investing in a full membership until we could no longer afford rent. We ended up befriending Melanie who wasn't just a yoga teacher/studio owner, but a real active presence in the Ocean Beach community, taking care of it, cleaning it, and providing for it. She let us barter our talents for yoga classes. Jena's talent was photography, so she helped with marketing, and my talent was painting, so I helped spruce up the studio. I ended up painting the inside of the studio, as well as a mural on the outside.

I got so involved in the yoga community that two years later, when Melanie decided it was time for her to head to Mexico to pursue her dream of big wave surfing, I stepped in to manage the studio in her absence. I tried my best to fill her shoes, but she was always barefoot, so it was nearly impossible. Eventually Melanie moved to Mexico full-time and then later to Hawaii, slowly but surely mastering the big wave scene. With her newfound passion and pursuit, she decided to sell her little studio in Ocean Beach, California.

By then, I knew that season of my life was coming to a close, not just with yoga, but with Ocean Beach. I had met Josh earlier that year and was already contemplating a move to Santa Barbara to be closer to him. After the studio sold, I helped for a brief period of time with the transition to the new owner before I made my own transition and left Ocean Beach. Once I was in Santa Barbara, I knew I could find a new studio, but it wasn't the same. It wasn't so much the practice of yoga that I had been attached to; it was *that* studio, Tri-Power Yoga. It was Melanie. I had become the parishioner who only likes to attend church when a certain pastor is speaking, and Melanie was my pastor of choice. While I'll be the first to criticize this style of church attendance, I am also the first to own up to it.

When Jena and I joined the studio, Melanie told us she saw two girls in her own shoes years prior (when she used to wear them).

"I see bits of myself in both of you," she often said.

She helped us lighten up a bit, teaching us that we didn't have to take ourselves, or life, or even God, so seriously. Melanie was one of the first people who taught me that God is also a fun God.

I knew God meant business when I lived in the South. I knew God was self-sacrificing when I lived in Chicago. I knew God was a God of suffering when I lived in Portland. But lighthearted? Fun? Dare I say, funny? Maybe I had glimpses of that side of Him over the course of my life, using phrases like "God has a sense of humor" when I made sarcastic comments about unlikely friendships or the limited options of presidential candidates, but I had no awareness that God's humor might run deeper than that.

One day during class, Melanie had us write one affirmation on a sticky note—something that we had a hard time saying or accepting about ourselves, but something that we hoped was true about who we were. This was before I got involved in comedy, so I don't know why I wrote it, other than deep down, I guess I *hoped* it was true: "I am funny." If we were created in the image of God, I wanted to reflect that side of God, the funny side, the side that took chaturangas very seriously and yet not seriously at all. We put the sticky notes in front of our mats so we could look at them throughout class, claiming our affirmation to be true for ourselves and letting it sink in.

"You don't have to *make it* be true," Melanie said, "just let it *be* true... because it already is."

I still sometimes get confused by the woo-woo-ness of yoga, but I suppose that's the beauty of it, I can show up and engage and learn and grow, opting to leave some of it behind and take some of it with me. Between yoga and church, I never did find a place where I felt I fit in Santa Barbara, if for no other reason than Josh and I traveled all the time, and to be honest, I didn't make the biggest effort to take part. Then Covid happened. I did a few free yoga classes from home, but the more time that got between me and my practice, the harder it was to keep up with it until eventually I just stopped.

Right or wrong, sometimes you decide to keep going, and sometimes you decide to take a break. So instead of beating myself up day in and day out for not doing yoga, I decided yoga and I were on a break, and that was okay, because after all, it was not going to kill me if I didn't do another chaturanga for the rest of my life.

If we're not counting my brief dabbling in online classes during the COVID-19 shutdown, my break from yoga lasted about four years. Some might say four years is not a break so much as it is quitting, and maybe for a time, it was quitting, but honestly who cares? I might be tighter than I used to be, and I might get sore more easily, and my mental strength is sometimes lackluster, but for the most part, I remain intact as a mildly normal, healthy human being.

That said, in more recent years I began to physically feel the need to lengthen and stretch and be more careful to take care of my posture, mainly so I wouldn't develop my grandmother's hunchback. She literally shrank about three inches in her old age. I could also feel my need to pause more, breathe deeper, and be more careful about responding too quickly out of irritability (just ask Josh). So, after my long hiatus, and this move to Tennessee, I found a studio down the street with an *amazing discount* on an intro package and I signed up.

I went to my first class yesterday. I sat in my car in the parking lot before going in, pep-talking my reflection in the rear-view mirror.

"You don't have to perform at the level you used to, you don't have to perform at all. It's just yoga, don't take yourself so seriously!"

Just as I finished telling myself to have fun, I noticed a car blitzing through a stop sign into the yoga studio parking lot. *I really hope that's not my teacher*, I thought to myself. *I know we're all human, but I don't think I want a yoga teacher who runs stop signs.*

It wasn't my teacher, but it *was* another student in the class who entered a few minutes behind me, clearly flustered and desperately in need of a moment to simply breathe.

As soon as class started, I wanted it to end, which honestly has been a frequent feeling of mine no matter how long I've done yoga. It's like with anything else in life: just because you know it's good for you doesn't mean you feel like doing it. I was rusty, but I was okay with it. I noticed my tendency to hold my breath or to hurry into the next position. I was aware this was how I'd been living the last few years—waiting with bated breath while simultaneously rushing through life.

I tried not to, but I definitely looked at my watch, fully aware that I should have removed it, but concerned Apple wouldn't be able to track my workout if I had. After all, it doesn't count if technology doesn't record it. My first time back in a yoga class in four years, and all I wanted was to get to savasana. *I live for savasana.* It's probably the reason I do yoga, the final pose in which you just lay there, face up, soaking in everything you've done for the last hour. I think life needs more savasana in general, more moments in which we just lay there, grateful for all we have, all we have done, and how far we've come, without any pressure to have, do, or be more. Perhaps 2020 was one big savasana, a worldwide pause in the pressure to keep up. Then again, between toilet paper and hand soap, I think the panic levels were too high for a collective savasana.

When class ended, I noticed the instructor had been using a "yoga voice" the entire time. I had suspected she was trying a little too hard to sound soft and sultry, exaggerating her words: "And noooow with conscious breathhhhh, mooooove to the front of the maaaaat." Once class was dismissed, she returned to her Tennessee twang, which I preferred but I didn't feel I had known her long enough to share that with her. She was young and I suspect her time will come when she finds her voice (or maybe she already has and I'm just judging her. Whoops!). Naturally though, I thought of Melanie, how she always seemed to be herself and how comforting it was to feel like you could be yourself in her presence.

In addition to the practice, I enjoyed the people in class as well, all of whom mingled and introduced themselves after class was over, something that *never* happened in a yoga class in California. I had gone so long without this Southern charm, this simple "howdy, neighbor," that I had forgotten about it. I decided this was going to be my yoga studio. I was finally going to get back in touch with my body, mind, and spirit. I had finally come home—back to the south and back to yoga.

When I got home, I told Josh all about the class, feeling as alive as I had the first time I had done yoga. I looked up the membership packages online, and upon realizing it cost $150 month, I officially decided... I don't like yoga that much after all.

A little too woo-woo if you ask me.

# 29

# '90$ CHRI$TiAN$

**WHAT A WHIRLWIND** the last two years have been. I think
many of us thought the whole Covid thing was going to last two
weeks, and now here we are nearly four years later, and we're still
affected by the toll it took on us as a society. It seems pointless to
even pose the question: "Where did the time go?"

I think we all know the answer... COVID.

I go back and forth between being bummed over all that the
pandemic took away, and trying to suck it up because it took away
a lot—from *everyone*—and in the grand scheme of things, I really
came out okay. I suppose both can exist at the same time—the sense
of loss and sadness as well as gratitude and fullness. I'm learning
to function less in extremes and more in the middle ground of life
being hard and beautiful, oftentimes simultaneously. One year, my
grandmother died on my husband's birthday, and I mourned *and*
celebrated. I hopped between the two emotions as if it were a game
of hopscotch, alternating which box I stepped into at any given
point. While that day was a condensed version, to me it reflected all
that life contains—beauty, pain, loss, gain, sweetness, and sorrow.

As I've worked on this book over the years, sometimes unaware a book was even forming, I've gone through so many seasons and changes of perspective. I find it hard to put out a book based on one perspective, because the more we allow ourselves to grow up, the more we become comfortable being ourselves, yet also the more we evolve into someone better than who we were. I stand by the young surfer girl who so desperately wanted to be accepted into that culture, as well as the budding comedian who wanted to be taken seriously. I stand by the awkward single girl, the newlywed, the introvert in need of friends. I stand by the world traveler and the homebody, the girl who speaks up and the girl who takes time to listen. I have been all these people, I remain all these people, and yet I am no longer like any of these people.

I recognize my growth while also wondering where I went. As I look back on my thirties (which aren't yet entirely behind me), I can't help but ask, *how did I become more myself and yet more insecure at the same time?* I am still trying to figure out how to articulate the answer, but I think it has a lot to do with my spiritual life; it's easy to neglect and easy to blame everything on my spiritual life when things don't go the way I think they should. I don't publicly talk about my spiritual life very often, unless asked in a podcast interview or over coffee. In part because I don't want to push my spiritual life onto other people, and (many) Christians have a way of doing just that. In other part, I don't bring it up because I'm still navigating it.

I find it hard to form sentences around these thoughts, because what is spirituality if not something that is *not human?* In other words, no human words will suffice. Nonetheless, since I am attempting to not only understand my own spirituality but also to share it, I will try to harness the words.

If you've read this far you know by now, I grew up in the church. I have evangelists in my background and Bible verses in my blood. They're hard to shake. I've jumped in and out of church life more frequently than dentist visits, settling on the fact that I trust dentists more than pastors, and I don't exactly trust dentists. 2015 was the last time I was an active member of a church. I dipped my toes in a few services at a local church upon moving to a new town, but by 2017 I had stopped going to church altogether. By the end of 2021, save Christmas and Easter, I hadn't attended a single Sunday service since.

I'll admit, upon realizing church was no longer a regular part of my Sunday morning ritual, I felt free. In many ways, I still do. Once I left the church, I finally felt like myself, unshackled by the expectations of church and untethered from a word that has often caused a lot of hurt and pain—Christian. I grew up in the '90s when a lot of Christian authors and musicians grew their platforms based on their extreme "Christian" views. After reading *I Kissed Dating Goodbye* in college, a book that taught Christians how to "break up" with dating so your life works for God, I promptly ended things with the guy I was in love with, thinking surely he'd see how much he needed me in his life and instead of allowing me to end it, he would ask me to marry him. After all, as Christians we didn't need to date, we needed to marry… as soon as possible, even if that led to a miserable marriage, because love is hard and Jesus loves us even when we're difficult, and if Jesus can love me like that then certainly I can love someone completely unsuited for me and endure the toxic relationship for as long as the Lord calls me to.

That was essentially the dating advice for Christian young adults in the late '90s/early '00s: get married, figure it out later. Spoiler alert, the guy I ended things with never asked me to marry him. I held out hope for years that one day he would knock down my door and fight for me as we were told men were supposed to do. At the same time, I wasn't supposed to let on that I loved him, I was supposed to be won, so I carried this dream in secret.

The next relationship I entered after that, I decided I would make sure there was no way it could fail. To be honest, it failed as soon as it started because I knew deep down that I didn't love him (half the time I didn't even like him), but he was a worship leader and *everyone* loved him, and as I was told, I was "*so lucky* to be picked by him." Another trend of Christian culture in that decade was an obsession with charismatic male leaders in the church, blinded by their humanity, and considering ourselves (especially women) lucky if they would but look in our direction. I am guilty of not only giving in to this behavior but also promoting it.

Whether I was trying to walk the moral high ground as eloquently as this worship leader appeared to be in public, or I genuinely believed it would benefit our relationship, I told this man that I was not going to kiss any man (including him) until I was married (another piece of advice from *I Kissed Dating Goodbye*). At first, he was impressed, but it soon became apparent that while he boasted about his intact virginity, he definitely wanted the side dishes. Our form of "kissing-but-not-kissing" involved weird mouth mashes with no tongue. Essentially, we rubbed up against each other with our pants on and our mouths closed. Jean Jammin'... it was as awkward as it sounds.

On Sunday mornings, this guy stood in front of his church and sang about surrendering all to Jesus, and by Sunday nights he was trying to take my pants off and get off without going in. It was, if nothing else, confusing. To be honest, I think I would have preferred just having sex with the guy and feeling guilty about it after like all the other premaritally sexually active Christians. Instead, I ended up tangled up in these weird mind games about what God was "okay" with me taking off, resulting in half-assed attempts at intimacy, further increasing my distaste for the worship leader and wondering who exactly I was supposed to look to for authentic spiritual guidance. After all, as a woman, I needed a leader, or so I thought.

From where I sit now, I can see that guy was probably (hopefully?) just as confused as I was about his role in the church, about his own humanity, and about what it looked like to love God—was it a choice, a feeling, an action? Maybe it was all of those or none of those; maybe it was just accepting that we were loved, and we didn't need to keep proving we were moral while keeping quiet that we weren't at all.

When I ended the relationship with the worship leader, he was shocked—how could I end it with him? He was the one all the girls wanted. Instead of appearing upset over the breakup, he told me he hoped I didn't get too jealous over how many moms were going to want to set him up with their daughters. I wanted to ask their names so I could warn them, but I was also terribly insecure, never trusting my own intuition (hence getting into the relationship in the first place). I knew no one would listen to a girl complain about a worship leader making her feel uncomfortable, especially when he didn't actually have sex with her.

Another eleven years went by as I struggled with church life, trying to feel like I fit in and trying *not* to nitpick. *No church is perfect*, I would tell myself, and I would dismiss any discomfort I felt theologically, or in my role as a woman. I dated an "edgy" youth pastor for a while, but I was promptly told that I wasn't radical enough for him, this from a church that at the time didn't let women speak up front.

Shortly after him, I dated a Jesus-loving alcoholic who had "accepted" Jesus but hadn't yet dealt with the pain from his past.

"I'm a new creation in Christ," he'd say as he slurped his whiskey neat. "The past is in the past."

I have no problem with whiskey neat, but when you drink it to the point of blacking out, then wake up in bed with someone else, and excuse it all as "forgiven" by God, I take issue. I forgave him *and* I left the relationship. It took a while for me to realize those two actions are not mutually exclusive.

You can forgive *and* you can leave.

I later took a job as a youth leader in an affluent area. The affluent church wanted full-time hours without full-time pay (not uncommon among churches). When I approached the leadership for help—it was hard enough trying to find an affordable place to live in the area—they said they would "pray about it." Meanwhile, the parents who wanted to keep me in the position offered financial support. The lead pastor said their financial support of me would take away from the church tithes.

"It's not personal, it's just business," he said.

He thanked me for my time and let the parents know it was my decision to leave.

I understand there's a lot of business that goes into running a church, but if there's one thing I understand about the gospel, the very word that the church is attempting to represent, is that it's personal. And since it seemed I was no *personal* matter to the church, I was just a business transaction that didn't work out, I was tired of defending the men I'd either dated or worked for who saw me as secondary, and I tapped out. It wasn't business, just personal.

Unlike the radical Christian authors and musicians of the '90s who have since abandoned their toxic faith and denounced God altogether, I simply walked away from the church, not from God. I learned to separate the two and that, in fact, one did not need the other. The church needs God, to be sure. But I honestly don't think God *needs* the church. I think God *loves* the church, but *needs*? That would imply that God is without something, and I don't feel comfortable making that argument. I'm no theologian, so take it or leave it, but God is God—with or without the church. I made no big dramatic exit from the church, I didn't post about it on Facebook or "deconstruct" it in an Instagram post, I simply stopped attending and took a sigh of relief as I set about to reset.

For all intents and purposes, I know the church is meant for good, but because it is made up of human people, it will inevitably get something wrong. There's no perfect church and it would be a disservice to myself to think otherwise. Because the church cannot be perfect, I can forgive the church for the ways it has failed... because I, myself, have failed in so many ways and I am no better. I'm not against church, I'm just not currently in it. I don't want to deconstruct, defund, or denounce the systems that are meant for good, especially when they have admitted along the way that they've actually done a lot wrong. Change begins with admitting, not with throwing away. And while I don't want to throw the baby out with the bathwater, at the same time, I don't feel compelled to *defend* the church either. I'm in some weird middle ground of wanting to champion good, while struggling to see it clearly, taking a beat before jumping to one side or the other.

I admit I have spent time truly hating the church, but at some point, I recognized that the answer to the problems in church cannot come from an extreme backlash of hate. Hating someone for their hatred is becoming just like them, full of hatred. While I hate some experiences and interactions I have had in the church, while I hate what I understood to be "Christian" living, while I hate that so many churches are still so focused on the rules that they are missing opportunities to love, I do not hate the church itself or the people in it. And while I hate that I relied so heavily on man's view of God for so long, I do not hate the God I have come to know personally, without the middleman, without the pastor, and without the confused worship leader.

In 2018, the author of *I Kissed Dating Goodbye* apologized for writing his book and I remember feeling oddly validated in my hurt, while also feeling a bit angry, still blaming him for the reason I ended things with the guy I had been in love with. *And* blaming him for why I spent years awkwardly *not* dating, curious about guys, but waiting until I was ready for "courtship" before I even accepted an invitation to coffee.

I could easily say "it all turned out for the better anyway," and I'll be honest, I'm beyond glad and grateful for the man I'm married to, so yes, it did turn out for the better, but prior to all that was a toxic mindset that rarely got addressed, and we often brush over toxicity and trauma for the sake of everything being better in the long run.

"It's all part of God's plan," some people say.

Sometimes when I hear this phrase in regard to trauma, I want to throw up in my mouth. Much like pain and beauty coexisting in life at the same time, there can be both the truth that we turned out okay AND the truth that a lot of damage was done, damage that we still need to work through. I do not think it is part of God's plan for us to go through trauma. I think humans are human and as a result, there is trauma. God's plan is that we find healing and love and comfort *despite* all we have done or been through.

I think you can abandon a toxic faith or belief system without abandoning God; whether or not you want to is up to you.

Abandoning all of it is freeing, sure—faith, God, all of it. I won't disagree that it feels amazing to have no pressure and no expectations, nothing and no one to answer to, but over time I started to realize how much I longed for something bigger than myself... it didn't have to be the church, but there had to be something bigger than humanity out there. When I realized God was God with or without the church, I told God I was interested in hanging out again.

"Not at church," I said, "but how about at the ocean?"

The ocean was my safe place then, and I experienced more of God's power out there than I ever had sitting in a church pew. I still do.

And that's where I found God again, on the beaches of San Diego: surfing, wave after wave washing over me, cleansing me of every faulty belief I've ever had about religion, church, God, and myself. I discovered strength in my heart, body, and mind. I learned to have grit and not depend on the opinions of others to determine my worth or tell me how much I belonged. I belong... if I never step foot in another church again, I still belong to God.

It's been almost five years since I have stepped foot in a church (for reasons other than doing a comedy show), and I'm still very much at peace with God.

I truly believe everyone's life process is different. God is much too big for this not to be the case. I'm still in process, be it spiritually, emotionally, or mentally—feeling more like myself yet still insecure about using my own voice, only because it's unfamiliar.

I haven't navigated a spiritual life outside of the church perfectly, but I suppose there's no expectation from anyone other than myself for it to be perfect. I acknowledge the ways my heart has hardened toward Christians in my time outside of the church walls, I have moments when I feel it thawing, and I know my work is not done.

I am a part of this group I dislike and yet not at all at the same time. I entrust myself to God alone, who is patiently teaching me to love even the most difficult of people, myself included.

## EPILOGUE

**I DON'T KNOW HOW TO WRAP UP** a book of stories collected over a nearly six-year period of my life, if for no other reason than my story remains unwrapped. More often than not, there is no resolve in life until, maybe, our dying breath. This is why I find it particularly hard to publish a book in my style of writing—publishers, editors, and perhaps even readers all crave resolve. They want all the juicy details of failures and triumphs, and then a mildly happy but not too unrealistic ending. I leave too many things open-ended and unanswered. Most authors wait until they have an answer or a take-away before they publish a book, giving people a clear reason to buy the book in the first place. I had a hard time trying to sell this notion of stories for the sake of stories to publishers.

"But what's the take-away?" they'd ask. "And who even are you?"

What a great question.

As I look back on these stories, I see a girl who started out so unsure of who she was that she packed a bag full of three glass water bottles for a first date simply because she felt like she needed to carry a handbag but had no idea what to put in it. She eventually found love and realized that not even the most amazing man in the world would make her feel complete... it's quite simply not someone else's job to make you feel whole (I still remind myself). I look back and see an insecure comedian, a girl who clearly has a natural talent but has been so afraid to live into it for fear of what others might think, say, or comment online. I see a girl whose parents are aging and who is trying to navigate the role reversal that comes along with that. I see a girl who's been spiritually confused, even spiritually homeless in terms of a church building, and who, quite simply, has no answers for how to navigate a faith without walls.

Unlike the opinions of publishers, editors, and authors (most typically in the self-help field), I don't think we always need answers. After all, in the last story of this book I dove into my spiritual life, without a ton of backstory or detail, and pretty much left it at, "I love God and I don't know." It's abrupt, I know, but what is life if not abrupt? One day we're kids playing outside, the next we're trying to figure out how to pay rent. No one really warns us about the abruptness of life, that there really are no guarantees, certainly not for happiness.

*And why is a comedian talking about her spiritual life?* One might ask. Well, I'm not just a comedian. None of us are just our job descriptions. We're layered, like onions and ogres. People need to feel the freedom *not* to confine themselves to a box just because they'll get more likes on Instagram if they narrow their content. I fell into comedy by accident and I'm sometimes still trying to convince myself to stay in the scene. I love making people laugh, mostly because I know how good laughter feels and I want to offer that feeling to people, especially when they are hurting or lonely or feeling like life is meaningless. I like using comedy not just as a means to make people laugh, but more so as a means to make people feel. I like saying something worth saying, I like reminding people of their worth, their meaning, and their importance in this world. I so often forget that for myself, so I know how good it feels to hear it. If a comedy show is the only space I'm given a chance to slip in that reminder, so be it.

By the time this book is published it'll be 2024. As I come close to wrapping up 2023, I'm grateful where the year has taken me, it's been a mix of career highs and life lows. I performed at a Women of Joy conference in Pigeon Forge, Tennessee for 10,000 women. 10,000 people in one audience. Talk about a high—I'll never forget the feeling of hearing that much laughter in one room. I had to slow my pace just to let the sound travel to the back of the room and come back up to me. I got smacked in the face with their laughter and it will always be a career highlight for me. As I took on bigger and bigger gigs, seemingly "going places" in the eyes of the onlookers online, I also struggled in my personal life.

In 2023, Josh and I reached the point in our relationship where we decided to have kids, not just *decided* as if it were a business transaction, but knew it was something *we* wanted. Josh has wanted kids from day one, if anything it was me who was so unsure. But whether it's age or the realization that not even performing in front of 10,000 people will be what completes me, something in my heart drastically changed and out of nowhere, I wanted to be a mom. I know that I know that I know that. It's unfamiliar territory and it still feels weird to say it out loud.

To be clear, I am *not* saying I think being a mom will complete me. I have a mom and I know better than to think that having a child fixes everything, after all, I did not make life easy on her. But I suppose it was because of this awareness that kids are not a guarantee to make your life better, that I had no desire to bring kids into the world, as if *they* would finally give *me* a sense of purpose. I did not want them to feel that pressure. I always thought I needed to have myself more figured out before I could be responsible for someone else's upbringing, and while maybe a degree of that is healthy thinking, the reality is, none of us will ever be "figured out" enough to be fully equipped and ready to be parents. Even some of the best parents have kids in therapy, and that is okay.

Unlike what I was taught growing up, that sex instantly leads to pregnancy, at nearly forty I began to realize that it's not so simple. Josh and I haven't had success right away and all of our struggle has made me wonder, *how in the world do people get pregnant by accident!?* Between trying to figure out the right window of time and the perfect time of day to increase our odds, it all seems quite calculated, and when I'm most honest with myself, it also seems unfair that pregnancy happens so quickly for some people, especially when some of them don't even want it.

But! Against my nearly forty-year-old (geriatric) odds and excitedly enough, Josh and I were eventually able to get pregnant. We were both beyond excited. We had already started creating the story of our life with this baby—daydreaming, planning, and thinking of names. I was quick to enjoy the perks of pregnancy by constantly asking Josh for favors.

"Don't you think it's a little early to be asking so many favors?" Josh curiously joked.

"I only get nine months of this and I'm gonna milk every second!" I laughed. "Now bring me some olives and orange juice!"

We were careful not to announce it too soon, but we wanted to have a few safe people in the process with us, so we shared the news with our parents who were over the moon about it.

And then, I lost the baby.

I miscarried on August 8th, 2023, just ten days before my fortieth birthday.

It was an abrupt ending to an exciting beginning. Like I said, no one really tells you about the abruptness of life. It felt cruel and I was angry. It was the first loss Josh and I had gone through as a couple, and he held me each night as I cried. I have no resolve for this part of our story, at least not yet. We want to try again, we remain hopeful and optimistic, and yet, we don't know.

I'm learning to be okay in the "I don't knows" of life. After all, ever since Covid we've all had to navigate not knowing what in the world is going on. I look back at my writing in "Aunt Flo" about not being impressed by kids, and I think about my current desire to have one, and I laugh at myself. Proof that while we may always be ourselves, we also change drastically, even abruptly, during our lifetimes. I need to remind myself that people are not always who they used to be.

I'm not sure where I'll be or what my life will look like by the time this book is published. I'm not sure what will have changed; I'm not sure if these stories will feel close or distant from who I'll continue to become. And I'm okay with that, letting myself grow into the kinda funny, kinda deep, kinda spiritual person that I am.

May you feel the freedom to explore all those sides of yourself. Whether or not you find the answers to life's questions, keep asking the questions. It matters that you're here, figuring things out as you go, sharing your stories, and accepting yourself as you are. All while evolving into the kinda person you want to be.

Peace for now,

JJ

# ABOUT THE AUTHOR

**JJ BARROWS** is a Comedian, Author, and Mixed Media Artist who's performed in comedy clubs, churches and awkward dinner parties all over America. However, don't assume colorful and comedic means a lack of honesty. JJ has also traversed the difficulties of eating disorders, family dysfunctions, and an on-and-off struggle with depression. With a refreshing story-teller style, she reveals the freedom a quippy sense of humor can reveal in all of us by giving breath to those gritty moments.

She released a Dry Bar Comedy Special, "Doodle All Day," published her first book, "it's called a spade," and wrote, produced and starred in her own comedy special, "The DIY Comedy Special," filmed on location at home... thanks to COVID clearing her schedule for nearly two years and freeing up all her time. Her favorite career highlight was meeting Rob Lowe in a parking lot, until most recently when Dolly Parton waved to her and she momentarily forgot to keep breathing.

When she's not performing, painting, or trying to find her way back to the ocean, she's either at Dollywood or introverting at home in Tennessee with her husband, Josh Newton. While JJ has dabbled on all the social media platforms, you can find her most frequently on Instagram @jjbarrows, as well as watch her videos, shop her art, and sign up for her email list at jjbarrows.com. If you message her on Facebook, she won't get it, life is too short to constantly check social media.

Made in the USA
Monee, IL
02 April 2024

56228442R00177